EVALUATING NEIGHBOURHOOD WATCH

To Cassandra . . .
who is always listened to

CAMBRIDGE STUDIES IN CRIMINOLOGY

Evaluating Neighbourhood Watch

Trevor Bennett
University of Cambridge
Institute of Criminology

Series Editor: A.E. Bottoms

Gower

Aldershot · Brookfield USA · Hong Kong · Singapore · Sydney

© Trevor Bennett, 1990

Published by
Gower Publishing Company Limited
Gower House
Croft Road
Aldershot
Hants GU11 3HR
England

Gower Publishing Company
Old Post Road
Brookfield
Vermont 05036
USA

This work contains Crown copyright material which is published with the
permission of the Controller of Her Majesty's Stationery Office.

British Library Cataloguing-in-Publication Data

Bennett, Trevor
      Evaluating neighbourhood watch – (Cambridge studies
      in criminology No 61).
      1. Great Britain. Crime. Prevention. Crime Prevention.
      Neighbourhood Watch schemes.
      I Title. II. Series.
      364.4'0458

Printed in Great Britain by
Billing & Sons Ltd, Worcester

ISBN 0 566 05648 8

Contents

Foreword

Over the last two decades there has been an important expansion in the social sciences in the use of systematic evaluations of social interventions. A similar expansion has occurred during this period in the application of evaluative research techniques to the study of crime and the criminal justice system.

Evaluative research designs have been used particularly widely within criminology in the assessment of new policing programmes. It is now common practice to measure the impact of new policing initiatives by experimental or quasi-experimental research designs. Evaluative research conducted by the American Police Foundation, for example, has been influential in revising common assumptions about the effectiveness of foot patrols. It is in part because of this kind of research that there has been an almost world-wide reappraisal of policing strategies during the 1980s.

The methods of systematic evaluation have been used less frequently in the assessment of crime prevention programmes. Studies such as the Seattle evaluation of a community crime prevention programme, and the Hartford evaluation of a neighbourhood crime prevention programme stand out in part as a result of their rarity. There have been very few systematic evaluations of community crime prevention programmes in Britain. Until the study on which this book is based was conducted there was no independent, survey-based evaluation of neighbourhood watch schemes in this country.

Trevor Bennett's book explains clearly and concisely the ways in which police and independent researchers have tackled the problem of assessing the effectiveness of community-oriented crime prevention programmes. It also explains in greater than usual detail the practice of constructing and implementing a research evaluation, using his own study of neighbourhood watch schemes as an example. This does not mean that the contents will be of interest only to those with a professional interest in evaluation. The book provides considerable detail and insight into the design and operation of neighbourhood watch schemes in Britain and the United States, and presents the findings of his own and other research which addresses the issue of whether these programmes work. It is a major contribution to the debate on neighbourhood watch schemes.

A.E. Bottoms

Acknowledgements

It is right that attention is drawn to the many people who helped in the administration of the research on which this book is based. Before so doing, however, I am sure that they would prefer me to say that the contents of the book are my own responsibility, and do not necessarily reflect the views of any of the individuals or groups acknowledged below.

I would like to thank the following individuals and organizations: the Home Office Research and Planning Unit; the Metropolitan Police; the senior police officers at Acton and Wimbledon; the crime prevention officers, home beat officers, home beat sergeants and Neighbourhood Watch co-ordinators at Acton and Wimbledon; the staff of the Police Intelligence Unit at Wimbledon; the senior officers and liaison sergeant at Redbridge; the Directorate of Management Services; the Metropolitan Police Crime Prevention Department; the Metropolitan Police Statistics Department; the area co-ordinators and street co-ordinators in Acton and Wimbledon; the directors of National Opinion Polls; the residents who took part in the crime surveys; the statistical advisers and computer advisers at the University of Cambridge; the Director, Librarian and Assistant Librarians at the Institute of Criminology, together with the teaching staff and assistant staff; the secretary to the project; and finally, Gail Bennett, who is worth mentioning twice.

1 Introduction

In 1985 the Institute of Criminology received a grant from the Home Office Research and Planning Unit to conduct an evaluation of the recently created Neighbourhood Watch (NW) schemes in London. The decision to fund the evaluation arose out of discussions between the Home Office Research and Planning Unit and the Metropolitan Police, who saw a need for an independent assessment of NW. At the time, the Metropolitan Police were conducting their own global evaluation, using police recorded crime as a data source. It was hoped that the funded evaluation would be able to compliment this research by providing a more detailed investigation of a small number of schemes. The results of this evaluation are contained in this book.

Background
The decision by the then Commissioner of the Metropolis, Sir Kenneth Newman, to launch NW throughout the Metropolitan Police District within a year of taking office was both courageous and unexpected: NW schemes had had a relatively short history in the USA, and virtually none in Britain. The earliest versions of NW in North America appeared in the late 1960s (Washnis,1976), while NW schemes in Britain had a history of only a few years (Anderton,1985). Until 1983 no force in the country had committed itself to launching NW on a force-wide basis.

The background of the decision of the Commissioner to implement NW schemes in London can be found, in part, in worldwide developments in 'community-oriented policing', and in part, in innovations over the last half-century in the USA in community crime prevention.

Developments in community-oriented policing are a result of a radical reassessment of the nature of the police role (Murphy and Muir, 1985). It is argued that traditional policing methods are based on an unrealistically narrow definition of the police role which focuses almost exclusively on the detection and prevention of crime (Ekblom,1986; Weatheritt, 1983). Community-oriented policing is based on a broader conception which takes into account the service functions of the police; it is a more open policing philosophy which is receptive to the needs of the local community (Eck and Spelman, 1987; Goldstein, 1987). One consequence of the spread of community-oriented policing is an expansion of innovations in patrol methods and community-oriented crime prevention partnerships between public and police.

Developments in community crime prevention can be traced back to the social disorganization perspective of the Chicago sociologists of the 1920s and 1930s (Shaw and McKay, 1942; Park, Burgess and McKenzie,1925). The main principle of this perspective is that crime is a product of disrupted informal social control mechanisms brought about by industrialization and

1

urbanization. The view that informal social control is the key to understanding and controlling crime rates dominated the theory and design of community crime prevention programmes for almost thirty years. During the 1960s and 1970s, however, a second theoretical perspective began to influence community crime prevention programmes, and this became known as the 'situational' (Clarke, 1980) or 'victimization' (Lewis and Salem, 1981) perspective. Crime prevention strategies based on this perspective aimed to reduce crime by reducing the opportunities for its commission. They were based on the view that crimes could be prevented by changing the cues emitted by potential victims and the perceptions and decision-making of potential offenders. These two perspectives served jointly to shape recent developments in community crime prevention programmes in the USA and generated the environment in which NW schemes were spawned.

The background to the research design used in the evaluation of NW schemes in London can be found partly in the development of crime surveys, and partly in the development of sophisticated quasi-experimental research methods. The first crime surveys were conducted in the 1960s for the US President's Commission on Crime, in response to the growing recorded crime rate following the end of the Second World War (Biderman *et al.*, 1967; Ennis, 1967; Reiss, 1967). The Commission recommended that there should be regular national and local crime-surveys. About the same time, other countries, including Canada, Holland and West Germany, also launched their first national crime surveys.

Questions about victimization were included in the General Household Surveys conducted in Britain in 1972, 1973, 1979 and 1980 (Home Office, 1982). The surveys covered a wide range of issues and the questions on victimization comprised only a small part of the total questionnaire. The first survey to focus specifically on victimizations was a local survey of three areas of London conducted by Sparks, Genn and Dodd (1977) and the first national victimization survey was conducted for the Home Office Research and Planning Unit in 1982 (Hough and Mayhew, 1983). Since 1983 there has been one further national crime survey, conducted in 1984 (Hough and Mayhew, 1985); and a third national survey is to be conducted early in 1988.

Since the first British crime survey there has been a proliferation of local crime surveys aimed at assessing the particular crime problems of small communities. Local crime survey, have been conducted in Nottinghamshire (Farrington and Dowds, 1985); Merseyside (Kinsey, 1984); Sheffield (Bottoms, Mawby and Walker, 1987); and in London in Islington (Jones, MacLean and Young, 1986); Newham (Harris Research Centre, 1987); the Broadwater Farm estate (Lea, Jones and Young, 1986) and the Metropolitan Police District (Smith, 1983).

The relevance of crime surveys to the London evaluation of NW is primarily that they pioneered an alternative method of collecting crime data. It was well known before the first national crime surveys that police recorded crimes did not constitute *all* crimes committed and, in addition, that not all crimes committed were reported to the police and that of the crimes reported to the police not all were recorded in the Home Office returns. The debate progressed little from statements concerning the recognition of a 'dark figure' of crime and speculations, and other estimates about how large this figure was. The publication of the early national surveys provided empirical evidence of the deficit between victim-reported and police-recorded crime.

The early crime surveys also indicated the usefulness of survey methods in extracting large amounts of data on crime and the experience of crime. The first British crime surveys made full use of this facility by including questions on public attitudes and perceptions, reporting rates, reasons for non-reporting of crime and self-reported offending. Crime surveys were also important, in that they provided considerable detail on the nature of offences and the characteristics of victims. It became possible to conduct detailed analyses of differential victimization rates among social groups and to examine relationships between victimization and demographic variables. Victim surveys also made it possible to examine fear of crime and public reactions to the threat and experience of victimization.

The background of the NW evaluation also includes recent developments in the design of evaluative research. The systematic evaluation of social experiments has a short history (Rossi and Freeman, 1985); the earliest evaluations based on rigorous research design were conducted during the 1930s. Most of the expansion in the use of evaluative methods took place after the Second World War. The first evaluations of social programmes, involving the analysis of large data bases, emerged during the early 1950s. Throughout the 1960s and 1970s the number of large-scale evaluations grew alongside improvements in research design and statistical procedures, assisted by advances in computerization of data analysis.

The growth of evaluative research led to an expansion of publications on evaluative methods and research. Modern methods of evaluating crime prevention experiments, including the evaluation of NW schemes, have been influenced by a small number of important publications (Campbell and Stanley, 1966; Campbell, 1969; Cook and Campbell, 1979), which have been useful in providing detailed descriptions of and justifications for the rigorous evaluation of social experiments. The research designs outlined in these publications have been used as a basis for many evaluations of social programmes concerning the treatment of prevention of crime.

One of the most widely used evaluative research designs used in the assessment of police initiatives and community crime prevention pro-gramme is the quasi-experimental design (Cook and Campbell, 1979; Judd and Kenny, 1981). The quasi-experimental design can be used when it is not possible to control the assignment of subjects to treatment and control conditions. This method has become popular with evaluators of crime prevention programmes since often it is not possible to build random assignment into the programme design.

In the past few years there has been a proliferation of research based on quasi-experimental designs; and some of the more recent studies have combined advances in quasi-experimental design with advances in crime survey techniques. One of the earliest attempts to combine quasi-experimental design and victimization data was the evaluation of the Kansas City Preventive Patrol Experiment (Kelling *et al.*,1974): two 'treatment' groups and one 'non-treatment' group of police beats were compared before and after the implementation of the patrol experiments, using victim surveys of residents living in the study areas. Since the early studies many other patrol experiments conducted in the USA have been evaluated by use of quasi-experimental designs based on victims surveys (Pate, 1986; Pate *et al.*,1986; Trojanowicz, 1986; Skogan and Wycoff, 1986); in addition, a small number of patrol experiments in Britain have been evaluated by use of crime surveys (Butler and Tharme, 1983).

In the USA quasi-experimental designs have also been used in the evaluation of community crime prevention programmes. The first major evaluation of NW employed crime surveys to gather victimization data and a pre-test /post-test, treatment/non-treatment research design (Cirel *et al.*, 1977). Many subsequent US evaluations of NW have based their methods on less rigorous designs, using police recorded crimes as data sources (Titus, 1984). However, more recent studies have adopted sophisticated quasi-experimental design methods to investigate NW programmes (Rosenbaum, 1986).

Until recently in the UK there has been little use of either victim surveys or quasi-experimental design in the evaluation of community crime prevention programmes. One of the first evaluations of a crime prevention experiment based on victim surveys was the police study of the Kingsdown NW scheme in Bristol (Veater, 1984). The experiment was not a rigorous quasi-experimental design as the victim surveys were conducted in only the experimental areas. Since then two other evaluations of crime prevention programmes in Britain have used victim surveys and quasi-experimental designs. The first was an evaluation of a multi-agency, community development project designed to reduce vandalism and crime on a run-down council estate, based on victim surveys conducted before and after the programme was launched (Hedges, Blaber and Mostyn,1980). The second study was an evaluation of the effects of the installation of additional security devices on burglary rate and on fear of crime on a high-crime council estate. The research utilized a pre-test/post-test panel design and employed treatment and non-treatment area comparisons (Allatt, 1984a,1984b).

Apart from these studies, there are currently at least three unpublished evaluations of crime prevention measures, using victim surveys and quasi-experimental designs: one in south London, conducted by the Home Office

Research and Planning Unit; another in north London, conducted by the Centre for Criminology at Middlesex Polytechnic; and the other in south London and south Birmingham, conducted by the Institute of Criminology at the University of Cambridge.

Aims and structure

An important aim of this book is to present the findings of the Cambridge evaluation of NW schemes in London; however, it is *not* the only aim. The London evaluation was undertaken at a time both of radical reassessment of evaluative techniques and of innovation in research methods. This study represents one of the first evaluations in Britain of a crime prevention programme, using both victim surveys and a quasi-experimental research design. It is likely that in the future such techniques will be employed increasingly in the assessment of crime prevention measures. The present book provides an opportunity to describe in detail the way in which one quasi-experimental evaluation was conducted and some of the problems encountered by it. It also provides an opportunity to discuss other evaluative designs and the benefits and drawbacks associated with each of them. It is hoped that the book will be of interest not only to those who want to know about the research findings, but also those who intend to conduct their own evaluations.

The structure of this book reflects that dual aim. Part One comprises an assessment of the nature of NW schemes by looking at their structure and operation (Chapter 2) and at the underlying theory on which these pro-grammes are based (Chapter 3). The second part comprises a review of published evaluations of NW programmes in the UK and USA (Chapter 4). Detailed summaries of the most comprehensive published reports are included in the text to provide an easy-to-access reference source of evaluative designs and research results. Part Three comprises a detailed presentation of the London evaluation, including the research methods (Chapter 5); the nature of the programmes implemented (Chapter 6); the impact of the programmes on crime (Chapter 7); the impact of the pro-gramme on public attitudes and behaviour (Chapter 8); the results relating to the non-survey part of the evaluation (Chapter 9); and interpretations of the research results (Chapter 10). Part Four comprises an assessment of the problems associated with implementing and evaluating NW, and proposals for improving the design of NW programmes and the ways in which they are evaluated (Chapter 11).

PART I

WHAT IS NEIGHBOURHOOD WATCH?

2 Neighbourhood Watch: The Practice

History of Neighbourhood Watch in North America

'Neighbourhood Watch' (NW) (also known as 'Block Watch', 'Apartment Watch', 'Home Watch' and 'Community Watch') grew out of a movement which began in the USA, which promoted greater involvement of citizens in the prevention of crime (Boston, 1977; Duncan, 1980; Titus, 1984; Washnis, 1976). It emerged during the late 1960s as one of a number of collective responses to crime control. Other contemporary collective responses have included: Radio Watch, Citizen Patrols, Mobile Patrols, Police–Community Councils, Citizen Alerts and Citizen Anticrime Crusades (Duncan, 1980).

In the UK it is widely believed that the first US Neighbourhood Watch Programme was the Seattle Community Crime Prevention Project, launched in September 1973 (Turner and Barker, 1983; Delaney, 1983), whereas NW schemes in fact existed as early as 1966, and many programmes resembling contemporary versions of NW were launched both before and during the Seattle programme; a useful source of information about NW in the USA prior to the Seattle programme is a review conducted by Washnis (1976) of such programmes.

Oakland

The earliest NW programme reported by Washnis (1976) was set up in Oakland, in 1966, under the title 'Home Alert'. The programme was the product of collaboration between the local police department and the newly established Citizen Crime Prevention Committee. The Home Alert scheme was co-ordinated by a police district commander and by a civilian director. Under the civilian director were civilian co-ordinators responsible for about 30 blocks each, and group leaders responsible for one block each. Participants in the Home Alert schemes were expected to attend regular meetings, display window stickers, mark their property and to act as the 'eyes and ears' of the police.

Philadelphia

Another early scheme which predates the Seattle programme was the 'Block Association of Philadelphia', which was formed in 1971 and became operational in 1972. The Association was formed in response to an increase in the rate of robberies and burglaries which angered the community and prompted them to action. The programme was based on neighbours meeting at monthly intervals to discuss methods of watching one another's homes and to exchange information on home security.

The programme was run in collaboration with the local police who were contacted by telephone when crimes or other incidents were seen by members of the scheme. The schemes included 'Community Walks' (a version of Citizen Patrols) and the use of loud horns to alert neighbours and scare off potential offenders. Once again, the residents were encouraged to act as the 'eyes and ears' of the police.

Seattle

The most famous of the early NW programmes is the Community Crime Prevention Program in Seattle, Washington. It has became famous, in part, because a full report of the scheme was prepared and widely distributed, and in part, because it included a built-in independent evaluation which showed encouraging results.

The report of the scheme describes the way in which the programme was established (Cirel *et al.*, 1977). In 1972 the Law and Justice Planning Office conducted a public survey and found that residents in Seattle were more concerned about burglary than any other crime. It was also found that the characteristics of the burglaries committed in the area suggested that the offence was capable of being prevented by citizen actions. The Community Crime Prevention Program (in effect, a comprehensive Block Watch package) was initiated as a result of a grant from the Law Enforcement Assistance Administration to the Law and Justice Planning Office.

The Seattle programme comprised four principal tactics: (1) to encourage citizens to protect their homes against burglars by providing residential security inspection; (2) to provide assistance and equipment for marking personal property to deter burglars, discourage fencing of property and to assist in returning property to its owners; (3) to organize Block Watches to 'augment the range of vision of traditional police preventive methods'; and (4) to supply information to promote citizen awareness of their role in reducing burglary rates (*ibid.*). The Block Watch is described in the report as 'the most important feature of the Community Crime Prevention Program' (*ibid.*, p. 25).

It should be stressed that the Seattle Project differed from many other NW schemes in the USA (and from all NW schemes in the UK), in that it was initiated and administered almost wholly by local government and civilian organizers. The Law and Justice Planning Office was a division of the Office of Policy Planning in the Executive Department of the Seattle City government. Its main function was to identify problem areas in the administration of criminal justice. The role of the local police, in administering the programme, was basically collaborative and supportive.

History of NW in Britain

Some of the elements of NW can be found in England shortly after the Norman invasion in the system of 'watch-and-ward' (a watch of up to sixteen men stationed at the gate of every walled town between sunrise and sunset), 'hue-and cry' (the obligation of residents to pursue criminals) and 'frankpledge' (the principle of collective obligation among communities to prevent crlme in their areas) (Critchley, 1978). Elements can also be found in the crime prevention programme, launched in 1943 by the Metropolitan Police, under the heading of 'Good Neighbours Can Prevent Crime' which focused on the ability of neighbours to look out for and report suspicious incidents to the police (Turner and Barker, 1983). Unfortunately, there is no thread which connects these early forms of NW to contemporary examples. The most convincing explanation is that NW was transplanted in the UK– almost intact – from the USA. Evidence of this can be found in the publications associated with the implementation of the first few schemes in the country.

Cheshire
It is widely believed that the first NW scheme in the UK was the Home Watch programme implemented in July 1982 in the village of Mollington, Cheshire. The official publication of the launch explains that the reason for adopting this programme was the combined result of pressure from residents for the police to do something about burglary rates and the fact that the Chief Constable had a keen interest in North American police methods and was aware of neighbourhood crime prevention programmes (Anderton, 1985). It is also recorded that the force crime prevention officer had access to some of the North American literature on neighbourhood schemes and drew on this in advising the Mollington residents about appropriate crime prevention strategies (Cheshire Constabulary, 1985).

The Mollington scheme began as a result of the Chairman of the Lea and Mollington Residents' Association (LEMRA) visiting the local force crime prevention officer and expressing the villagers' concern over burglaries in the area (Anderton,1985; Cheshire Constabulary,1985). The burglary rate for the village was not particularly high, with just 12 burglaries in 1981 and 7 in the six months preceding the launch of the programme in 1982. The force publication explains that the concern of the villagers was not the number of offences committed, but the high value of property stolen at each offence (Anderton, 1985).

The initial request of the Chairman of LEMRA for an increase in police presence was turned down on the grounds of limited police manpower. An alternative method was sought, based on what the residents themselves could do to prevent burglaries in the area. The choice of scheme was decided upon as a result of discussion between the crime prevention officer, the detective inspector and the Chairman of LEMRA. The dependence on the examples of the North American schemes is stated explicitly in the official publication: 'At this stage no other police force in this country had done anything on these lines so we had to rely on what was printed about the American schemes as a basis for discussion' (Cheshire Constabulary, 1985, p. 12).

The design of the programme used was based on the North American examples and comprised a comprehensive package of: (1) NWC which was defined as the public keeping their 'eyes and ears open for suspicious person' and reporting 'useful information to their local representative, who would, if necessary, pass it on to the police'); (2) property marking; and (3) improvements in physical security in homes by fitting additional door and window locks. The crime prevention officer presented the proposals for a Home Watch scheme to the residents of the village at a public meeting and they were almost unanimous in favour of launching the programme.

The launch of the Mollington Home Watch in 1982 was an individual, isolated event, not part of a force-wide policy to adopt NW as a crime prevention strategy. The number of schemes in the Cheshire Force area grew slowly at first from one in July 1982 to 21 by the end of August 1983. By November 1984 there were 913 registered schemes in the force area, and in March 1985 there were 1,190 (Anderton, 1985).

Devon
The Cheshire Constabulary might be justified in claiming that the scheme in Mollington was the first fully fledged NW (or Home Watch) scheme in Britain; it is possible, however, that prototype schemes existed in the country before the Mollington initiative.

In October 1981, almost a year before the Cheshire Force implemented their programme, the Devon and Cornwall Constabulary launched a community crime programme known as 'Neighbours Against Burglary' (NAB) (Delaney, 1983). The programme contained many of the elements of the North American NW schemes. The main elements of the programme were listed in the publicity material accompanying the scheme:

1. to combat house burglaries;
2. to shift the emphasis of the campaign from a purely police motivated activity back to the community;
3. to alert the public of the possibility of burglary and to encourage the seeking of advice on protecting their property;
4. to encourage the marking of valuable items;
5. to encourage the immediate reporting of suspicious activities;
6. to encourage neighbours to take an interest in the houses in their street and neighbourhood;
7. to educate the public to be more security-minded;
8. to relate the campaigns to the smallest community unit;
9. to create a climate suitable to achieve these aims;
10. to encourage the public to act as NAB contacts. (Devon and Cornwall Constabulary, 1981)

In many ways, the campaign was similar to contemporary comprehensive NW programmes. The official press-release distributed by the crime prevention department towards the end of the campaign promoted a message which would not appear out of place in the publicity material of fully fledged NW initiatives:

> Be a good neighbour yourself and keep a lookout for anything suspicious in your locality. Never be afraid to contact the police if your suspicious are aroused. *(ibid.* p. 5)

The major difference between the Devon and Cornwall Constabulary scheme and contemporary schemes is that it was launched as a short-term crime prevention campaign which lasted just two weeks between 14 and 30 October 1981. Had the scheme lasted longer, it would almost certainly be regarded as one of the first NW schemes in Britain.

Hampshire
There is one more rival for the distinction of the first scheme in Britain which predates both the Cheshire and the Devon and Cornwall schemes. In 1978 the Hampshire Constabulary launched a burglary prevention programme called 'Home Watch'. The programme contained five main messages to the public (1) use the security devices fitted to all houses; (2) fit standard thief-resistant locks to front and rear doors and windows; (3) take steps not to advertise your absence; (4) involve your neighbours in mutual protection; and (5) be security conscious. The third and fourth messages comprise the basic elements of contemporary NW programmes. The booklet on the Home Watch scheme describes the meaning of these messages in more detail:

> Your neighbours should be encouraged to watch over your home while you are away. That includes whilst away for short periods of time as well as the more obvious ones of holidays. This friendly assistance can be most effective and your neighbours should be asked to report any suspicious happenings to the police. (Hampshire Constabulary, 1978, pp.32–3)

Once again, the programme differed from contemporary NW programmes, in that it comprised a short-term crime prevention campaign. The scheme was launched on 15 May 1978 and ran for a four-week period. The campaign was primarily directed at the individual resident and little attempt was made to involve members of the community in the organization and running of the programme.

Bristol
The Kingsdown Neighbourhood Watch Project in Bristol, launched on 28 February 1983, is an example of one of the first fully fledged NW schemes in the UK. The implementation of a NW programme in the Kingsdown area

was initiated by the police rather than the public. A crime analysis of the central division of Bristol revealed that Kingsdown, a dominantly residential area, had one of the highest rates of crime in the inner city area (Veater, 1984). The choice of NW as an appropriate crime reduction strategy is explained in the evaluation of the scheme: 'It was felt that one of the only likely solutions to the problem was to encourage an involvement of the public living in the area in preventing crime and reporting suspicious incidents to the police' *(ibid.,* p. 1)

The programme implemented was a comprehensive package comprising: (1) NW; (2) a recruiting drive for special constables; (3) increased regular foot patrols; (4) home security survey campaign; and (5) property marking.

The preparatory work in launching the scheme involved circulating a letter from the Chief Constable to every resident in Kingsdown, outlining the problem of crime and requesting their assistance either by becoming a 'contact person' (the equivalent of an area co-ordinator through which information would be channelled) or becoming a special constable (to carry out crime prevention patrols). In addition, a questionnaire was included, requesting information on victimization and public attitudes. The letters and questionnaires were delivered by community beat officers and special constables. The returned questionnaires were used as a mandate for establishing a scheme in the area and as a pre-test victimization survey which was used in evaluating the scheme.

South Wales

The South Wales Community Watch Project was launched within a month of the Kingsdown project. The first scheme is reported as being launched in March 1983. Detailed guidelines for the implementation of Community Watch in South Wales were published in February 1982 (Bowden, 1982). An important difference between the South Wales and Cheshire constabularies is that South Wales was committed from the outset to a force-wide policy to promote NW. South Wales Constabulary was one of the first forces in Britain to implement NW on a force-wide basis.

Again, the evidence points to a transplantation from the USA of NW schemes. The decision to implement Community Watch in South Wales was influenced by the detective chief inspector of the Crime Prevention Department, who had recently completed a Churchill Fellowship in the USA. The fellowship involved investigating community crime prevention methods and preparing a paper on their effectiveness *(ibid.).*

History of NW in London

The history of NW in London begins in October 1982, with the appointment of Sir Kenneth Newman as Commissioner of the Metropolitan Police. On his first day in office, Sir Kenneth declared an interest in using NW as a means of tackling burglary and other crimes. An article in *The Times* on the day of his inception reported that the new Commissioner believed that NW could be effectively applied to the densely populated areas of London (*The Times*, 2 October 1982). By September 1983, less than a year following the Commissioner's appointment, NW was officially launched in London on a force-wide basis.

The history of NW in London can be traced through the major policy documents issued by the Metropolitan Police: the first of these is the Turner–Barker Report, entitled *Study Tour of the United States of America*, published in the spring of 1983; the second document is the *Instructions: Neighbourhood Watch*, circulated to all divisional chief superintendents on 13 July 1983 (Assistant Commissioner 'A' Department, 1983); the third is Police Order 24, entitled *Crime Prevention – Neighbourhood Watch and Property Marking Schemes* (Metropolitan Police, 1983); the fourth is the first annual report by Sir Kenneth Newman, *Report of the Commissioner of Police for the Metropolis for the Year 1983* (Newman, 1984); and the fifth is the official policy document, *A Guide to Neighbourhood Watch schemes*, which outlined the principles and practices of NW in London (Russell, n.d.).

The Turner-Barker Report

There is no doubt that the main inspiration for NW in London derived from the experiences of similar programmes in the USA. The Turner–Barker Report documents in detail the connection between US schemes and those projects to be implemented in the Metropolitan Police District. The aims of the visit by the superintendent and detective inspector who wrote the report are stated on the first page:

> To study community crime prevention programmes with particular reference to neighbourhood watch projects, in order to promote and implement a pilot neighbourhood watch scheme in each area of the Metropolitan Police District. (Turner and Barker, 1983, p.l)

The study was undertaken in four cities: Washington, DC, New York, Detroit and Seattle. The report also includes a discussion on the schemes operating in Orlando. As a result of interviews with police officers, information gathered from the Police Foundation, the Police Executive Research Forum and the National Criminal Justice Reference Service, and on-site visits to active scheme areas over the two-week period of the visit, the two officers assessed their experiences and recommended a programme they felt suitable as a pilot in the Metropolitan Police District.

The report strongly favoured the programme launched in Seattle in 1973, on the grounds of effectiveness and longevity:

> The programme selected for the pilot study in London is principally but not exclusively based on the Seattle model, which continues to operate effectively

while others more recently formed have foundered. (*loc. cit.*)

The report recommended a comprehensive programme based on four main components: (1) NW (a network of members of the community who watch out and report suspicious incidents to the police); (2) property identification (of valuable property with a personalized mark); (3) home security surveys (free home surveys conducted by the police to provide advice on minimum levels of protection); and (4) community crime prevention and environmental awareness (promotion of crime prevention and community campaigns to address particular local problems).

Force Instructions
The recommendations of the Turner–Barker Report were broadly accepted and formed the basis of the *Force Instructions,* circulated along with the 'A' Department Memorandum, by the Assistant Commissioner of 'A' Department on 13 June 1983. The two documents were sent to all divisional chief superintendents with a request to make plans for the implementation of NW schemes in their areas, in preparation for the official force-wide launch later that year.

The 'A' Department Memorandum is a one-page document which draws out the main points of the accompanying *Force Instructions*. In particular, the Memorandum points out the force intention to launch NW in London earlier than planned as a result of 'mounting pressure, both from within the Force as part of divisional planning and from the public' (Assistant Commissioner A' Department, 1983). The stated aim of the Turner–Barker visit was to devise a plan for a pilot NW scheme in London which could be observed and evaluated before further commitment. The *Force Instructions* elaborated the change of plan noted in the Memorandum:

> The present level of public interest has generated a demand to introduce schemes without first operating pilot studies. While pilot schemes would in ordinary circumstances be desirable and provide some valuable lessons for the future, the urgent need to make an impact on residential burglary and at the same time take advantage of the perceived public enthusiasm is paramount. (*ibid.*, pp. 1–2)

As a result of the perceived pressure to launch NW as soon as possible, the *Force Instructions* proposed that the official force-wide launch date would be 1 September 1983, and from that date NW could be implemented in all divisions.

The speed of operation of the process is impressive. No more than six months elapsed from Sir Kenneth Newman's first day in office to the publication of the Turner–Barker Report recommending an NW pilot scheme in London. Within two months of receiving the report, the official policy had been revised and distributed to the divisions in the form of the

Force Instructions, and within the next three months NW had been launched in London on a force-wide basis.

The main contents of the Force Instructions comprise a description and guidelines for the type of NW programme to be implemented in the Metropolitan Police District, the nature of the proposed programme bearing a close resemblance to the programme recommendations of the Turner –Barker Report: NW is conceived as a comprehensive package containing the four key components described above.

Police Order 24

Police Order 24 is important to the extent only that it officially announced the launch date (and method of launch) of NW in London. The date was moved from 1 September 1983, the date reported in the *Force Instructions,* to 6 September 1983, and the launch place was to be a specially prepared conference held at New Scotland Yard, to which members of the media were invited. The programme was identified as a force-wide 'Neighbourhood Watch and Property Marking Scheme' and much of the Police Order was devoted to explaining the principles of the property marking component. The main paragraphs dealing with the NW component describe it as 'a working partnership between police and the community to reduce crime and the fear of crime' (Metropolitan Police, 1983)

The Commissioner's Report for 1983

The first major policy document following the launch of NW by the Metropolitan Police is the *Commissioner's Report for the Year 1983* (Newman, 1984). In this report, Sir Kenneth Newman outlined his 'preventive model' for policing the metropolis and the concept of a 'notional contract'; NW was seen as an important part of this new model:

> In asking for a public contribution towards reducing crime, I have offered on this occasion a clear framework for co-operation in the form of neighbourhood watch and property marking – two London-wide projects. *(ibid.* p.10)

The report outlines the way in which NW is conceived by the Commissioner: NW, he reports, seeks actively to involve the public in caring for their own community by encouraging citizens to gather into neighbourhood groups, helped and advised by the police. The purpose of these groups, Newman continues, is for neighbours to look out in order to deter thieves, to provide communal support and to give the police an early warning of likely crime.

The Guide to Neighbourhood Watch

The *Guide to Neighbourhood Watch Schemes* was published in 1985 (undated) as a means of providing an accessible and easy-to-understand description of NW in the Metropolitan Police District and as a guide to 'good practice'. The aim of the publication is stated in the Introduction as being 'to identify the principles and elements of Neighbourhood Watch, to encourage good practice and generate fresh ideas' (Russell, n.d.).

The bulk of this booklet comprises recommended methods of establishing and maintaining schemes and the role of the police and public in achieving those aims. The principal elements of NW remain unchanged from the principles outlined in the Turner–Barker Report. The main contribution of the guide is the detail in which it spells out current and recommended practice; it proposes that NW schemes should be between 300 and 500 households in size, based on existing community structures.

Elements of NW

There are at least three different ways of examining the elements of NW. First, it is possible to investigate the principal elements which guide the organization and operation of the scheme. Secondly, it is possible to consider the structural elements or the component parts which shape the scheme. Thirdly, it is possible to consider the organizational elements which determine the way in which the scheme is managed and administered. In the following section the nature of NW is examined by looking at these three kinds of element as they exist in selected examples of the scheme.

Details of less well-publicized schemes launched in the USA have been obtained from published reviews and from a custom search of NW material provided by the National Criminal Justice Reference Service (NCJRS). Details of less well-publicized schemes launched in the UK have been extracted from the periodicals *Crime Prevention News* and *Good Neighbour,* published by the Home Office in conjunction with Security Publications Limited.

Principal elements

The first theme that emerges is that NW is often implemented as part of a comprehensive package. In Britain the typical package is NW, together with property marking and home security surveys. The same conclusion applies to US schemes, where many of the programmes operate as comprehensive packages. The typical package in the USA, often referred to in the literature as the 'Big Three' (Titus, 1984), includes NW, property marking and home security; however, a comprehensive package is not always an integrated programme whereby these three (or more) crime prevention elements are launched simultaneously and adopted by residents as a package. There are a number of reports of US schemes which describe NW as one of a number of crime prevention initiatives available to residents in an area. The particular selection of programmes that the residents adopt is a matter of their individual choice. NW can also be implemented (albeit less frequently) as a discrete programme. This sometimes happens during the early stages of experimentation with the scheme (e.g. the South Wales scheme in Britain).

An interesting difference among schemes is where the third or fourth element of the package is often an idiosyncratic programme devised to fit the needs of a particular police force or area. The Kingsdown NW scheme in Bristol, for example, included in its package a recruitment drive for special constables and increased regular foot patrols (Veater,1984). The NW programme in Wilmington, Delaware, included in its package: a Senior Citizen's Educational Program; 'rap' sessions with youth groups; and the formation of an Auxiliary Police Unit to support the watch groups (Decampli, 1977). A Block Watch programme, conducted in Philadelphia, comprised two elements: Block Watch and victim services, which included providing emotional support for victims after the crime and during court proceedings (Finn, 1986).

An important difference which distinguishes British and North American schemes is that sometimes the package includes citizen patrols. The 'Neighborhood Fight Against Crime' programme in Brooklyn, New York, for example, comprised a package of NW, operation identification, home security surveys, a telephone alert chain, and car and tenant patrols (De Jong and Goolkasian, 1982). The use of citizen patrols as part of a NW package is not common in the USA (Titus, 1984). There is no police force in Britain which has formally incorporated citizen patrols as part of a NW package.

The number of titles under which NW-type programmes fall is large and growing, some of the most common include: NW, Home Watch, Community Watch, Crime Alert, Block Watch, Block Clubs, Apartment Watch, Business Watch, Marine Watch, Seafront Watch, Farm Watch, Radio Watch and Crime Watch. Perhaps the most common name in use in the USA, and the most common type of NW scheme, is the Block Watch, while the most common name in Britain is probably Neighbourhood Watch. This difference in choice of schemes between the two countries is important. Typically, Block Watches and Block Clubs cover only a small number of households i.e. 20–30, whereas Neighbourhood Watch and Community Watch cover a larger number of households (i.e. 300–3000). It is significant that the Metropolitan Police, and many other forces in the UK who looked to the USA for guidance, chose the larger rather than smaller type of NW programme; however, there are signs that this is now changing and forces are looking more at schemes comprising no more than a single street or block of apartments.

There is an almost complete consensus in the published literature that the main aim of NW is crime prevention. There are small variations among the programmes in terms of which crimes are to be prevented. The vast majority of programmes reviewed identify residential burglary as the sole or most important target crime of NW. Some programmes focus solely on residential burglary, but most list other offences which they hope NW will effectively reduce. The list of other offences is sometimes explicit (e.g. 'street robberies, auto thefts and vandalism': Assistant Commissioner 'A' Department, 1983) or general (e.g. 'street crime': Cirel *et al.*,1977; 'property crime': Anderton, 1985). Apart from the possible reduction of crime, many schemes have additional or supplementary aims such as: reduction of fear of crime, improvement in police–community relations (Russell, n.d.); improvement in crime reporting rates (Turner and Barker,1983); generating a more positive community image and improvement of the quality of life (Pilotta, n.d.).

There is an almost complete consensus in the literature about the way in which NW schemes should operate in order to achieve those desired ends. The dominant mechanism mentioned is the public watching out for suspicious incidents and behaviour and reporting these to the police. The number of references to the phrase 'the eyes and ears [of the police]' is striking. Many reports cite public reporting of suspicious events as the only role of residents in NW schemes, and as the only mechanism by which NW is effective in preventing and reducing crime. Some police departments ask the public to look out for crimes (rather than anything else suspicious) and actively discourage the public from doing more than this (Henig, 1984). Others encourage effective reporting by issuing cards which specify the precise information to record when identifying suspects (Blue Ash Police Department, n.d.). Some programmes include additional activities which the public can take to prevent crimes in their area. The Seattle programme, for example, is one of the few NW schemes to propose that residents should attempt to make neighbours' homes look occupied when they are away by mowing their lawn and filling their trash cans.

Structural elements
The sizes of the NW schemes have already been touched upon. In the USA, NW schemes are often based on small blocks of dwellings and include no more than 20–30 households. The size of the Block Watch units in the Seattle scheme varied between just 10 and 15 households. Some of the largest schemes can be found in the UK, and a scheme of 3,500 households reported in No. 1 Area in London is the largest scheme identified in this review of the literature (Trotman, *et al.*1984).

The reports are unclear on the number of schemes which are provided with window or property marking stickers or engraving pens by the police. It is also not possible to determine from this review what proportion of schemes included regular newsletters. It would appear that most programmes are supplied with some kind of information pack by the police which includes information on the creation and running of NW schemes or material on crime prevention and home security. Not all schemes have street signs as the police are seldom willing to pay for and organize their erection. It is interesting that the Metropolitan Police appear untypically generous in their willingness to pay for street signs for all bona fide NW schemes in London (when this is approved by the local borough councils).

Organizational elements

Typically, NW schemes are both public and police initiated. Schemes which are launched in the early period of a programme, however, tend to be police initiated (e.g. the Kingsdown scheme in Bristol and the early NW schemes in the Metropolitan Police District). Schemes which are launched at a time when the programmes are well developed and active are more frequently public initiated. The Metropolitan Police, for example, found no need to initiate schemes when the number of requests for NW exceeded the ability of the police to launch and manage them. Some police departments continue initiating their own schemes, even when the programme is fully developed. The programme implemented in Detroit, for example, maintained a section of police-initiated schemes in order to promote NW in areas which were unlikely to generate public-initiated requests.

The issue of the number and type of public meetings is hard to resolve from the scant information contained in much of the literature. The evidence suggests that some schemes have public meetings which involve all of the residents participating in the scheme, while others have meetings which involve only the organizers of the scheme. In Britain the evidence points dominantly to the latter method of organization. The Bristol scheme included regular meetings of contact persons, but no regular meetings of residents who were not contact persons. The London schemes also operate on this principle that only the organizing members of the schemes take part in regular meetings, while the remaining residents have no formal contact with one another apart from the launch meeting. In the USA there is more evidence of meetings involving all residents. The main reason for this difference is that a large proportion of the US schemes are Block Watches, covering a small number of households. Under this arrangement it is possible for meetings of all residents in the scheme to be held at the home of one of the block members.

Block Watches are usually run by a block captain who is, in turn, responsible to a block co-ordinator or block organizer. The block co-ordinator acts as the liaison person to the local police department (Baltimore Police Department, 1985). The organization is similar to that of the NW programme in London, which includes street co-ordinators (equivalent to block captains) and area co-ordinators (equivalent to the block organiser). Unlike the US system, the London system does not mobilize the street co-ordinator as a street watch captain responsible for a partly autonomous street watch scheme. Instead the street co-ordinator does little more than enlist the support of residents at the beginning of the scheme and post newsletters through the doors of residents once the scheme is under way.

The funding of NW schemes is nearly always a joint venture between the local police department and the scheme members through their fund-raising activities. The relative contribution of the two sources varies considerably. Some schemes in the USA are provided with no more than an information package from the local police (produced at police expense). Others are provided with police facilities for the production of newsletters and the use of police premises for meetings (Turner and Barker, 1983). The NW programme in London is one of the schemes most heavily subsidized by a police force. The Metropolitan Police are willing to pay for the hire of local halls for the launch meeting, stationery and equipment, the production of the regular newsletter, all publicity material and the erection of street signs. Apart from police funding, the majority of schemes are encouraged to raise some funds from other sources such as voluntary contributions, local businesses and the proceeds of fêtes, raffles, etc. It is estimated, however, that the majority of schemes in London rely wholly on police resources and do not hold an independent NW account.

3 Neighbourhood Watch: The Theory

Introduction

The conceptual and theoretical background of NW can be found, in part, in the thinking behind recent innovations in urban policing which have sought to establish a closer relationship between the police and the local communities they serve) and in part, in the thinking behind experiments in the USA over the past half-century which have sought to prevent crime by drawing on community resources. The former can be referred to as developments in 'community policing' or 'community-oriented policing' and the latter can be referred to as developments in 'community crime prevention'.

Commmunity-oriented policing

The police role

The development of the idea of community-oriented policing arose out of a recent and radical reassessment of the police role. The debate is based on a comparison and appraisal of two dominant models of policing: the 'crime control model' and the 'community policing', or 'community-oriented policing', model.

Crime control perspective

The crime control perspective of policing is sometimes referred to as emphasizing the 'crime-fighting' or 'crime-busting' role of the police (Eck and Spelman,1987; Murphy and Muir, 1985). The perspective is based on the premiss that the most important objective of policing is the suppression and control of illegal activity. The focus of police activities is on the apprehension of criminals and the detection of crime. The control of crime is seen as the exclusive responsibility of the police; the community is seen as important only to the extent that it is supportive of police functions) (Murphy and Muir, 1985).

The organization and management of a police department based on the crime fighting model would be shaped by its perspective. The organization would tend to evaluate its performance, and the performance of its officers, through an assessment of crime rates, clear-up rates, arrest rates and number of convictions. Less importance would be attached to non-crime-oriented police work, the individual police officers serving in the department seeing themselves primarily as law enforcers or crime fighters. They would regard their primary role as crime related and believe that other police activities were peripheral or less important. Encounters between the officers and the community would be regarded primarily as opportunities to gather information to detect crime or to enforce the law.

Community-oriented policing perspective
In essence, the phrases 'community-oriented policing' and 'community policing' describe the same thing. There appears to be a slight preference among British commentators to use the term 'community policing' and a slight preference among North American writers to use the term community-oriented policing'. Because the term 'community policing' is well recognized and associated with a particular style of policing in Britain, it might be helpful to detach the concept from the current conceptions by referring, in the following discussion, to the less well-known phrase 'community-oriented policing'.

Community-oriented policing is based on the principle that it is justifiable and desirable to involve the community in the delivery of police services. It regards the crime-fighting model as unrealistically narrow and unable to match the reality of day-to-day police work. The approach acknowledges that the broad range of activities that the police perform is a legitimate and necessary part of the police role. Community-oriented policing is also based on the principle that the police cannot succeed in fulfilling their aims without the support and co-operation of the public they serve. At its broadest level the community-based philosophy of policing supports the view that the community has a legitimate and important part to play in determining the way in which the community is policed (Murphy and Muir, 1985).

Reactions to traditional policing
The development of community-oriented policing over the past twenty years is a product of a growing disenchantment with traditional policing methods. Critics of the system have pointed to increasing crime rates, high levels of fear of crime and low clear-up rates as evidence that the traditional crime control approach is no longer appropriate for policing urban environments.

Weatheritt (1987) identifies the shift from foot to vehicular patrols as an important catalyst which prompted discussions about community-oriented policing. She argues that the introduction of policing technologies in the late 1960s and early 1970s, particularly cars and personal radios, fundamentally altered policing methods and policing styles and upset relations between police and public. Motor vehicle patrols created a physical barrier between the police and public and reduced opportunities for informal interaction. Policing technology also encouraged the growth of a more distant, more abrasive policing style.

Paul Ekblom (1986) identifies four more shortcomings of conventional unformed policing which, he reports, provided the context for the debates about community-oriented policing. One shortcoming is the problem of 'fire-brigade policing', which he defines as the confinement of police response to crises. With this form of 'reactive' policing, he argues, little attention is paid by the police to prevention (before the crisis starts) or follow-up (after the crisis has passed). This approach obstructs the development of a more strategic and planned response to community problems. The second shortcoming identified by Ekblom, is the growing awareness both among academics and the police of the limited effectiveness of conventional policing methods in the control of crime. The awareness of police limitations has grown within a period of just over a decade. The third shortcoming mentioned is the reduction in contact between police and public, brought about by the move from foot to vehicle patrols, and by a trend towards management centralization. The increasing isolation of the police, Ekblom believes, has led to increased fear of crime and a reduction in trust between the police and public. The fourth shortcoming noted is the belief that conventional policing methods exacerbate hostilities between the police and young people. It is felt that these hostilities are most likely, and most evident, in the case of street encounters between members of ethnic minorities and inexperienced officers who are unfamiliar with the locality and the customs of the inhabitants.

The 'new' community policing
The concept of community-oriented policing has undergone some expansion and change during the course of its development. A great deal of this expansion and change has occurred in the USA. The different ways in which the concept is viewed in the USA and UK is reflected in the current level of interest shown in community-oriented policing. In recent years British commentators have tended to be critical and pessimistic about the future of community-oriented policing (Short, 1983; Manning, 1984). Many police officers in the UK are dismissive of community-oriented policing efforts and believe that, at best, they are no more than a public relations exercise. During the same period, however, writers in the USA have been more optimistic about the future of a community-oriented policing; in a recent publication two leading academics of policing issues wrote, '[we] conclude that community-oriented policing is the way of the future' (Skolnick and Bayley, 1986, p.212), while a leading commentator has written: 'I would argue that a fully developed concept of what we now allude to by "community policing" could prove the umbrella under which a more integrated strategy for improving the quality of policing could be constructed' (Goldstein, 1987, p.8)

The difference between British and North American commentaries is partly a result of differences in the growth of the concept of community-oriented policing in the two countries. In many respects, the 'new' community-oriented policing philosophy of US writers is different from the 'old' community policing philosophy expounded by influential British writers (Alderson, 1978, 1979, 1981). Here the first theme which emerges from US writings is an acknowledgement that the police deal with a wide range of problems that are defined by and relate to the communities they serve. This acknowledgement leads to an acceptance that the police role should be broadened to integrate that function more fully into policing philosophy. Goldstein (1987) argues, for example, that the general objective of community-based policing should be community problem-solving, where the police become the problem-solving agency. Problem-solving has also been entered into the equation by Eck and Spelman (1987), who compare the traditional police role of 'crime-busting' with the new police role of 'problem-busting'. A second broad theme is that the police cannot achieve any of this without the assistance and co- operation of the community.

Community-oriented policing in practice
The adoption of community-oriented policing strategies in both Britain and the USA is manifested most visibly in recent experiments with police patrols.

Directed patrol   One example of attempts to improve the quality of police service to the public are the recent experiments with 'directed patrol' (DP), where it is intended to free officers from dealing with calls for service in order to conduct specific assignments. A recent review of DP programmes in the USA notes that directed patrols are usually based on one-to- three-hour assignments usually involving one officer who is freed from 'calls-for-service duty' in order to complete a pre-planned activity (Crowe, 1985). The kinds of activity pursued on an assignment might be crime-control oriented (e.g. stake-outs, bar checks, surveillance of known offenders and saturation patrols) or community-oriented (e.g. family disturbance follow-up, neighbourhood dispute resolution meetings and child neglect case filed visits). The aim of directed patrol is described not only to reduce crime and improve detection rates, but also to 'expand service to the public' and to 'improve positive contact with citizens' (*ibid.* p. 14).

Team policing   Team policing is based on allocating a small team of officers and their commanders to a small neighbourhood, in order to deal with all of the problems arising from that neighbourhood. It is described as a way of decentralizing police command and of making a team of officers responsible and accountable for the quality of police service and control of crime in a specific neighbourhood (Bloch and Specht, 1973; Schwartz and Clarren, 1977).

The community-oriented aims of team policing are to strengthen the relationship between police and community, to use the 'ears and eyes' of the community in the control of crime and to obtain community support in the control of crime (Bloch and Specht, 1973).

Citizen contact patrols   Citizen contact patrols involve a high level of contact between the police and the public. They were pioneered in Houston,

Texas, in 1983 as part of a comprehensive programme of innovations in community policing strategies implemented by the Houston Police Department and evaluated by the Police Foundation (Pates *et al.*,1986). Two exploratory schemes have recently been implemented by two police forces in Britain as part of a similar evaluation (Bennett, 1989). The Houston programme involved patrol officers making contacts with local residents in their homes or on the streets. During the contact officers would introduce themselves as the person who patrolled the neighbourhood, tell the resident that the purpose of the visit was to make contact with the public in the area and to ask whether there were any problems in the area that the police might be able to do something about (Pates *et al.*, 1986).

Community crime prevention

Community crime prevention is a general heading which is used to cover any kind of citizen involvement in crime prevention; it is often subdivided into 'individual' crime prevention initiatives and 'collective' crime prevention initiates. Individual crime prevention initiatives are directed at the individual or the individual household and cover such activities as security programmes and property marking. Collective crime prevention initiatives require co-operative efforts among residents and cover such programmes as NW and citizen patrols.

Theoretical background

Over the past century or so there have been two major perspectives on the way in which communities might co-operate with the police in the control of crime. The two models are referred to as the 'victimization perspective' (Lewis and Salem, 1981) or the 'situational approach' (Clarke, 1980) and the 'social control perspective' (Lewis and Salem, 1981) or the 'social disorganization perspective' (Lewis, Grant and Rosenbaum, 1985).

The victimization perspective   Crime prevention strategies based on the victimization perspective aim to prevent crime by altering the potential victim rather than the potential offender. It is based on the view that crimes can be prevented by reducing the opportunities for their commission. These opportunities may be attached to individuals, to physical targets or to whole communities. Opportunity reduction may be achieved by altering the cost and reward balance of offending, either by increasing the constraints or by reducing the inducements to crime (Bennett and Wright, 1984; Clarke, 1980).

Opportunity reduction may be accomplished either formally or informally. Residents might take informal actions which are aimed at reducing opportunities for crime such as avoidance behaviour (not going out after dark) or home protection behaviour (locking doors and windows). They might also become involved in a formal crime prevention initiative which includes any individual or collective programme which might have an impact on the opportunity structure of buildings or neighbourhood or individuals.

The social control perspective   The social control perspective is based on the view that crime and fear of crime are indicators of social disorganization and weak informal social control.

The earliest version of the social disorganization perspective can be found in the works of the Chicago sociologists of the 1920s and 1930s (Shaw and McKay, 1942; Park, Burgess and McKenzie,1925). The main argument in their writings is that as traditional communities become urbanized and industrialized, they become socially disorganized and crime-prone. Social disorganization leads to crime partly through an erosion of community norms, and partly through an erosion of the community's ability to enforce rules. The erosion of community norms means that standards set by the community become weakened and delinquency and other forms of deviance became tolerated and even accepted as a part of community life. The erosion of the community's ability to enforce rules means that community members no longer feel responsible for social control in their areas and relegate their responsibility to formal organizations like church, school and the police.

The Chicago sociologists saw social organization as the cure for social disorganization. In 1932 the Chicago Area Project was established, one of the first (and one of the largest) community crime prevention programmes in the USA. The main aim of the project was to integrate and organize communities, by bringing together local residents and institutions (churches, unions, business groups, sports clubs, etc.) to work together in creating community programmes. It was not considered important what kinds of programme were developed, and it was not considered necessary that the programme directly concerned delinquents or delinquency prevention. The important thing was that they all, in some way, operated for the benefit of the community as a whole. The underlying aim was to generate a spirit of self-help and self-determination, and this was to be done by carrying out activities which fostered active control over the community. Such activities included the planning and operation of summer camps and community centres, health and sanitation programmes, improvements in schools, development of parent–teacher association and environmental improvement campaigns.

The social control perspective has undergone a shift of emphasis over the past few years. The more modern versions focus on the role of informal social control and the way in which community members take direct action (compared with the formation of generalized local group organizations) to alleviate crime and other problems within their community (Greenberg, Rohe and Williams, 1985).

It is believed that informal social control can affect the incidence of victimization in a neighbourhood as a result of the ability of the community to control the behaviour of its members (*ibid.*). This might be accomplished as a result of the generation of acceptable norms of behaviour among residents (including potential offenders) in the area, and as a result of direct interventions. It is believed that informal social control can affect the incidence of nuisances, incivilities and misdemeanours (e.g. vandalism, litter, abandoned cars, graffiti, public drunkenness, prostitution and the open use of drugs) as a result of attempts among residents to enforce conventional standards of public order. Finally, it is argued that informal social control can affect levels of fear of crime as a result of generating a sense of responsibility and control among residents in relation to what goes on in the neighbourhood (Skogan and Maxfield, 1981).

Community crime prevention in practice

The label 'community crime prevention' covers both 'individual' and 'collective' crime prevention initiatives. One of the most common 'collective' community crime prevention initiatives currently in the USA is the NW programme. These programmes have been described in detail in Chapter 2 and need not be repeated here. It might be helpful, however, to outline briefly details of other 'collective' community crime prevention programmes in order to highlight some of the similarities.

Citizen patrols There are many different types of citizen patrol. The authors of a large-scale evaluation of citizen patrol programmes in the USA have developed a four-category typology: community protection patrols; building patrols; neighbourhood patrols and social service patrols (Yin *et al* 1977).

Community protection patrols are organized to monitor the activities of the police, rather than criminals, and are mainly associated with the civil rights movement and urban riots of the 1960's. Community protection patrols were formed in some Southern states to protect black residents against brutality from the white community and from the police. Building patrols are organized to protect residents of specific buildings, or groups of buildings usually operating as stationary guards or foot patrols. Neighbourhood patrols may operate on foot or in vehicles and are usually co-ordinated by the police. Neighbourhood patrols vehicles may be marked or unmarked, manned by a volunteer or a private security guard, and follow either a regular or irregular schedule of activities. When the patrol observes a suspicious incident, the observation is radioed to a base station or to the police; in some cases an armed patrol might be used in order to intervene directly. Social service patrols protect an individual building or a neighbourhood and also engage in other community service functions; the patrol may operate for example, an ambulance service, perform civil defence functions (e.g. giving assistance during a tornado) or be involved in community projects (e.g. a clean-up campaign) (*ibid*.).

Crime reporting   There are many different kinds of campaign which aim to encourage the public to report crimes or suspicious incidents to the police. 'WhistleStop', for example, was a US programme whereby citizens carried whistles and were encouraged to use them when they were victimized, when they observed a crime or anything of a suspicious nature or when they heard another whistle blown. On hearing the whistles, the citizen was instructed to telephone the local police and then sound the alarm in an effort to disrupt the commission of crime (Duncan, 1980).

'Radio Watch' projects involve the participation of citizens who have access to two-way citizen band (CB) radios. This usually limits the programmes to taxi drivers and other employees working within the community in vehicles with CB radios. Participants are urged to report suspicious activities through their dispatchers or directly to the police departments which monitor emergency frequencies. Recent estimates indicated that more than 46 CB radio patrols were in operation in Chicago (*ibid*.).

'Secret Witness' projects are based on special telephone lines located within a neighbourhood to facilitate anonymous reporting of suspicious or criminal activity. Some of the projects offer monetary rewards for information leading to conviction; the amount of the reward is often determined by citizen committees (*ibid*.).

The theory of Neighbourhood Watch
In order to understand the nature of NW, it is necessary to examine its underlying philosophy and the general and specific assumptions on which the programmes are based. The philosophy underlying NW is a composite formulation built upon the foundations of both the 'victimization' and the 'social control' perspectives.

The primary aim of nearly all NW schemes is that residents watch out for and report suspicious incidents to the police (often nothing more). The main purpose of watching and reporting is to reduce the opportunities for offending by altering the cost–rewards balance as perceived by potential offenders. To this extent, NW programmes fall within the framework of the 'victimization perspective'.

It is also argued that NW is based on the assumption that programmes generate or strengthen informal social control. The simple fact of residents joining with the police to tackle a local problem might be conceived as evidence in itself of informal social control, regardless of the level of interaction among local residents. It is also argued that interaction among residents resulting from scheme membership increases social integration and cohesion, which indirectly promotes a degree of informal social control

(Rosenbaum, 1987). To this extent, NW programmes fall within the framework of the 'social control perspective'.

The theoretical background of the approach can be more fully revealed by examining the process or mechanism by which the programme elements are supposed to achieve the programme ends. The process by which NW is supposed to reduce crime can be investigated by examining evaluative reports, programme summaries, policing documents and publicity material relating to specific NW programmes. The prime mechanism which emerges from this literature is that NW aims to reduce crime by a process of 'opportunity reduction'. The most frequently recorded mechanism by which NW is supposed to reduce opportunities for crime is as a result of residents observing suspicious activities and reporting them to the police. The link between crime reduction and reporting is not usually elaborated in the literature; however, it has been argued that visible surveillance might reduce crime as a result of its effect on the decision-making and perceptions of potential offenders (Rosenbaum, 1987). It is possible that watching behaviour among residents, and the knowledge that residents are willing to report suspicious behaviour to the police, might alter the perceptions of potential offenders. Watching and reporting might deter offenders if they are aware of the propensity of local residents to report suspicious behaviour, and if they perceive this as increasing the risks of getting caught. to an unacceptable level.

It is also possible that NW schemes might reduce crime as a result of an increase in the flow of useful information from the public to the police. An increase in information concerning crimes in progress, and suspicious persons and events, might lead to a greater number of arrests and convictions and result (when a custodial sentence is passed) in a reduction in crime through the incapacitation of local offenders.

NW might also lead to a reduction in crime by another mechanism, mentioned less frequently in the literature. An important element of the Seattle programme was the creation of signs of occupancy. This element might be implicit in other schemes, but it is rarely mentioned in the policy or publicity material. Some of the methods by which members of NW schemes might create signs of occupancy are discussed in the Seattle scheme report (Cirel *et al.*, 1977) – and in the Home Office guidelines in the UK (Smith, 1984) – and include removing newspapers and milk from outside neighbours' homes when they are away, mowing the lawn and filling up trash cans. The way in which signs of occupancy might reduce crime would be through the effect that they have on the perceptions and assessments of potential offenders.

NW might also reduce crime through the other components of the programme package. Property marking, security surveys and greater security awareness might lead to crime reduction through opportunity reduction. It has been argued that property marking might lead to a reduction in crime as a result of making the disposal of marked property more difficult, (Assistant Commissioner 'A' Department, 1983). Presumably, this would reduce offending rates if potential offenders perceived marked property as increasing the risks of offending (which might deter them) or making offending more difficult and troublesome (which might prevent them). Other methods by which property marking might reduce crime include the belief that offenders will perceive the theft of marked property as too risky and the belief that more offenders will be caught (Duncan, 1980).

Home security surveys and greater security awareness might lead to crime reduction as a result of actual increases in home protection. This is a direct result of the independent programme package or an indirect result of the NW scheme heightening security awareness (Rosenbaum, 1987). An improvement in the level of security might reduce crime if potential offenders are physically unable to enter a property that had been properly secured (they are prevented) or if they perceived the time required to enter the property as an unacceptable risk (they are deterred) (Bennett and Wright, 1984).

The way in which NW might lead to a reduction in the fear of crime among citizens is described differently by proponents of the 'victimization' and 'social control' perspectives. The victimization perspective is based on the assumption that fear of crime is a product of actual or vicarious victimization (Conklin, 1975). The appropriate response to fear of crime consistent with the victimization perspective is some kind of individual or collective action aimed at reducing opportunities for crime. The social control perspective is based on the assumption that fear of crime is a response to signs of disorganization and lack of informal social control. The appropriate response to fear of crime consistent with the social control perspective is the strengthening of social integration (DuBow and Emmons, 1981; Lewis and Salem, 1981).

Conclusion

The theoretical formulation of NW derives both from the 'victimization' or 'situational'' and the 'social control' or 'social disorganization' perspectives. Some writers have stressed the importance of NW in terms of 'opportunity reduction' (i.e. derivative of the 'victimization perspective'); others have stressed the importance of NW in terms of developing or strengthening informal social control (i.e. derivative of the 'social control perspective').

The combination of elements of the two perspectives makes it unclear exactly how NW is supposed to work. The dominant conceptualization is that NW reduces opportunities for crime as a result of residents watching out for anything suspicious and reporting what they see to the police. Such acts do not in themselves constitute informal social control because residents take no direct action in the control of behaviour. Watching cannot be considered as social control if no behaviour is controlled by it; reporting what has been seen to the police cannot be considered as informal social control if the behaviour is controlled by a formal agency.

There are further problems which concern the extent to which holding formal meetings may constitute informal social control. It has been argued that evidence from research into group dynamics does not support the view that such meetings will lead to greater informal social control (Rosenbaum, 1986). Rosenbaum argues that it is probably unsound to believe that social interaction at NW meetings can reassure citizens that something can be done to affect crime. His study found that such meetings can heighten anxiety, reduce efficacy and feelings of social cohesion (Rosenbaum, 1987).

PART II

PUBLISHED
EVALUATIONS

4 Evaluations of NW Programmes

Introduction

Evaluations of NW typically concern the effectiveness of programmes in achieving their objectives – i.e. whether they are effective in preventing crime. Some evaluations have more limited aims, and seek to determine whether the programme is reaching its intended target or whether the programme elements are effectively implemented. The following review includes both kinds of research and is divided into two main parts: the first dealing with evaluations of programme effectiveness, and the second with programme operation.

Evaluations of programme effectiveness: Published reports

The review of published reports includes a detailed summary of those evaluations which are published in full. The reports have been divided into police and independent research conducted in the UK and police and independent research conducted in the USA. Research reports are included in the following review if they are available as published documents, and if they include at least a 'before' and 'after' comparison of crime rates or public attitudes. The label 'police research' refers to studies conducted and published by the police; the label 'independent research' refers to studies conducted by non-police researchers and published independently. However, there were no studies available from the UK which fell under the heading of 'independent research' which comprised at least a 'before' and 'after' comparisons of crime or public attitudes (apart from the current study). There were also no reports available from the USA of research which fell under the heading of 'police research'.

The UK

Kingsdown, Bristol (Veater, 1984)   The study was based on pre-test and post-test victim and public attitude surveys conducted in the scheme area. A comparison was also made of crime rates in an adjacent area to the NW site using police-recorded crimes. The experimental survey area comprised just over 2,000 households. The first-round questionnaires were delivered to each household by community beat officers and special constables in February 1983 and covered crimes committed between March 1982 and February 1983.

The second round of questionnaires were delivered in March 1984 and covered crimes committed between March 1983 and February 1984.

The results of the victimization surveys showed that the offence rate fell from a total of 247 reported offences from 979 households (a rate of 25 offences per 100 households) in the first round to 174 reported offences from 1,060 households (a rate of 16 offences per 100 households) in the second round. The reporting rate of victimizations increased from the pre-test to the post-test periods from 71.7 to 74.2 per cent. The study also found small reductions in the fear of crime. Fifty-seven per cent of respondents in the first survey compared with 50 per cent of respondents in the second survey reported that they were worried about leaving their homes unoccupied. Seventy-eight per cent of respondents in the first survey and 77 per cent of respondents in the second survey said that they were worried about theft from cars. During the experimental period the number of police-recorded crimes committed in the control area increased.

The report concludes that crime rates fell during the course of the NW experiment and reporting rates increased and that the main objectives of the scheme had been achieved. The author was concerned about the apparent increase in crime in the adjacent control area but concluded that it was unclear whether this could be attributed to the existence of the NW scheme.

No tests of statistical significance were applied to the recorded changes from the pre-test to the post-test surveys. Some of the reductions in fear of crime were unlikely to be significant. No victimization surveys were conducted in the displacement area, referred to as the 'control area', or in any control area away from the experimental site (i.e. an area which would be unaffected by any displacement of crime from the experimental area). The response rate for both surveys was quite low (just over 50 per cent).

Cheshire (Anderton, 1985).   The evaluation of the Mollington scheme was based on police-recorded crimes measured for a period 18 months before the launch of the programme and a 30-month period following the launch. A further evaluation comprised a comparison of the rates of particular crimes recorded in all areas in Cheshire covered by Home Watch scheme, and in all areas not covered by the schemes for a 3-month period between January and March 1985.

The results of the evaluation of the Mollington NW scheme showed that there was a reduction from 19 house burglaries during the pre-test period to 2 house burglaries during the post-test period. The results of the comparison of crimes committed within Home Watch areas and non Home Watch areas over a 3-month period showed that the rates for all crimes were lower in the Home Watch areas than in the non Home Watch areas.

The author writes in the conclusion of the evaluation report: 'It appears from the experience in Cheshire so far that Home Watch is one of the most effective, efficient and successful crime prevention initiatives ever undertaken' (Anderton, 1985, p.53).

The Mollington evaluation is based solely on a 'before' and 'after' comparison of residential burglaries with no control area comparison. The trends over the same period in crime rates in similar areas without Home

Watch schemes is unknown. The force-wide comparison is based solely on a Home Watch and non Home Watch comparison, with no comparison over time. The extent to which there were pre-existing differences in the crime rates of these areas is unknown. Both evaluations are based on police-recorded crimes, with the associated problems of unknown variations in public reporting and police recording practices.

Merseyside (Jenkins and Latimer, 1987) The study was based on a comparison of police-recorded crime rates for a period 12 months before and 12 months after the launch of the HomeWatch scheme in four areas of Merseyside. The four schemes were implemented in areas covering between 43 and 97 households. A public attitudes survey was conducted among residents living in areas which were about to launch a HomeWatch scheme and another public attitudes survey was conducted among residents living in (different) areas which had an existing HomeWatch scheme.

In three out of the four areas the number of residential burglaries was lower during the post-test period than in the pre-test period. The changes in rates per 100 households from the pre-test to the post-test periods for the three areas experiencing a reduction were: 13 to 10 in the first area; 19.5 to 5 in the second area; and 9 to 'nearly zero' in the third area. The technique of converting the number of burglaries to a rate per 100 houses hides the small numbers of crimes involved. Recalculating the rates show that the three reductions mentioned comprised a fall from 7 to 6 in the first area; 19 to 5 in the second area; and 4 to 'nearly zero' in the third area. The fourth area experienced a 'substantial increase' in burglary following the launch of the HomeWatch scheme. Burglary rates in the subdivisions of two of the three areas also fell during the same period but by smaller amounts. The comparison of the results of the 'before' and 'after' public attitudes surveys (conducted in different areas using different respondents) suggested a number of favourable changes in public attitudes.

The authors acknowledge that the number of crimes is small. They conclude, however, that the research suggests that HomeWatch is having an effect in reducing burglaries. They believe that the failure of the fourth scheme area to show evidence of a crime reduction effect indicates that HomeWatch is unlikely to be successful in all areas in which it is implemented.

The evaluation suffers from a number of serious drawbacks. The number of burglaries recorded in the pre-test and post-test period are too small to be used to claim that the changes are meaningful, or that they can be attributed to the experimental programme. The method of comparing the results of a pre-test public attitudes survey conducted in one scheme area with the results of a post-test public attitudes survey conducted in another area is almost impossible to interpret. The study does not include crime data on comparison areas (apart from crime rates in the subdivision) and relies on police-recorded crimes as the main measure of victimization.

Stafford (O'Leary and Wood, 1984)   The study is based on a comparison of police-recorded crimes over a 7-month period before the launch and the same 7-month period following the launch.

The results showed that only 207 out of 5,500 residents took an active part in the scheme. They also showed that the number of police-recorded crimes fell by 74 per cent during the first seven months of the scheme. The report concludes that the scheme was an over-riding success in terms of reduction in recorded crime. It was noted, however, that the participation rate was disappointingly low.

A 7-month period is a fairly short period of time in which to compare changes in recorded crimes. The total number of crimes recorded on the estate over this period was uncomfortably low. There was no control group comparison, which makes it difficult to know whether crime levels were increasing or decreasing in similar areas. The reliance on police-recorded crimes is problematic. The authors' conclusions that the recorded reduction in crime was the result of the activities of participants is not wholly convincing, considering that only 4 per cent of residents took part in the scheme. There was no attempt to consider alternative explanations for the reduction in crime.

Northampton (Northamptonshire Police, 1985)   The main part of the evaluation was a comparison of police-recorded crimes over a 12-month period before the launch of the schemes, and the same 12-month period following the launch. The total numbers of crimes committed fell slightly in the two NW areas (541 to 521 in one scheme, and 204 to 202 in the other). The number of burglaries in a dwelling, however, increased from 93 to 108 in the former, and from 14 to 30 in the latter. Crime in the subdivisions in which the schemes were located, and in the force area as a whole, increased over the same period. The report estimated that only 9 per cent of the community were actively involved in the NW schemes.

The report concludes that it is uncertain whether the small reductions in crime in the two experimental areas could be attributed to the NW schemes. The low participation rate was attributed to the low levels of crime in the experimental areas.

The low participation rate and the small percentage difference in the number of crimes reported in the post-test compared with the pre-test period is not indicative of a NW success, and the author is correct in being cautious in the conclusions. The reliance on police-recorded data is problematic, as discussed earlier, and the absence of a proper control area makes it difficult to determine whether the change in crime levels is better or worse than might have been expected.

US research

Seattle, Washington: (Cirel et al., *1977)* The study was based on telephone and door-to-door surveys of residents, covering both scheme participants and non- participants. The surveys were conducted in five census tracts in Seattle. The research design was based on pre-programme and post-programme measurements. The first round of surveys was conducted in mid-1975 and covered victimizations during 1974. The second round of surveys was conducted in mid-1976 and covered victimizations during 1975. The pre-test surveys covered an area of 1,474 residences and the post-test surveys covered an area of 1,216 residences. The data was collected by independent researchers trained by the programme organizers. Adjacent non-scheme census tracts were used to provide a comparison group to assess possible displacement effects.

Within experimental tracts pre-treatment burglary rates of scheme participants and non-participants were almost identical (6.18 compared to 6.45 per cent. A comparison of the post-treatment data for participants and non-participants within the experimental tracts showed a statistically significant lower burglary rates for participants (2.43 compared to 5.65 percent). The reduction in burglary among participants represented a reduction of 61 per cent (from 6.18 to 2.43 per cent). Burglary rates in the control tracts were not significantly different between 1974 and 1975 (10.43 compared 9.95 per cent).

Reporting rates did not differ significantly between experimental and control tracts in the pre-treatment period. Reporting rates increased from the pre-test to the post-test surveys for the experimental tracts (50.9 compared to 76.5 per cent), but not for the control tracts. Within experimental tracts pre-treatment reporting rates differed significantly between participants and non-participants (68 compared to 40 per cent). Due to the small number of burglaries no comparison was made of the post-treatment differences.

The percentage of both participants and non-participants burgled over the experimental period declined. The authors note that this result alone does not provide evidence of non- displacement.

A telephone survey conducted in August and September 1976 and covering the preceding 6-month period found that participants continued to record lower levels of burglaries than non-participants (5 compared to 6.1 per cent over the 6-month period), but this difference was not statistically significant.

The authors concluded that the programme was successful in reducing the number of burglary victimizations for participants. The results of the telephone survey suggested that the project effects lasted from 12 to 18 months, and after this time, scheme participants began to become burglary-prone.

The major finding that the number of burglaries among participants fell by 61 per cent over the experimental period was based on uncomfortably small numbers (a reduction from 22 to 6 burglaries from the pre-treatment to the post-treatment periods). The failure to replicate the successful result 6 months later, using the telephone survey, is also troubling and weakens the impact of the first survey results.

Washington, DC: (Henig, 1984)   The study was based on an analysis of the activities of 193 neighbourhood block watches in one police district in Washington, DC. The study was conducted by students at George Washington University in a single semester without outside funding. The author notes that the research represented a limited pilot study. The aim of the study was to investigate the organization and administration of block watches in Washington and to assess their impact on crime reduction. The organization and administration of the schemes was assessed by randomly selecting 25 watches from the sample and conducting telephone interviews with residents. The characteristics of the block areas were determined by examining census data. The impact of block watches on crime was assessed by comparing the levels of police-recorded crime in the study police district for 1980 (the year before NW was launched in this police district) with levels of crime for 1983 (a year after NW had been launched in the police district).

The activity of the block watches was determined by generating an activity score ranging from +4 (very active) to –4 (very inactive). One out of three watch schemes scored below zero on the activity scales. The results of the crime analysis showed that there was an increase in the number of crimes among participants during the first 6-month period following the launch of the scheme, and a decrease in the number of crimes during the second 6-month period. There was no evidence that crime fell more sharply in the second 6-month period in active compared with inactive schemes.

The author concludes that the research finds little support for the proposition that the drop in crime in the study police district was the result of the NW programme. He concludes that much of the difference in crime rates between scheme and non-scheme areas can be attributed to differences in social and economic variables.

The study does not use matched or randomly selected control areas. The use of the police district as a control is problematic as it contains block watch and non-block watch members. The use of the city as a whole is problematic because it is unknown what other crime prevention initiatives were operating. It is also unknown to what extent the sample areas were similar to the city population as a whole in terms of social, economic and other characteristics. There are problems associated with relying on police-recorded crime as the only data source.

Chicago (Rosenbaum et al., *1985)* The research method was based on a quasi-experimental, untreated control group design with pre-test and post-test surveys. Crime and public attitude surveys were conducted in programme and non-programme areas before the launch of the schemes and again one year after the launch. The first wave of surveys was conducted early in 1983, and the second wave surveys in 1984. The survey method included independent cross-sectional sampling (a representative sample of respondents interviewed in each round) and panel sampling (the same respondents interviewed in each round). The main research methods were telephone surveys of residents, participant observation and interviews with community organization leaders and staff. The sampling frame was published telephone numbers in relation to the target areas, and a random digit dial telephone survey of the whole city in relation to the control areas. In the first round of surveys a total of 3,357 interviews were completed, and in the second round a total of 2,824 surveys were completed. The analysis strategy was based on an assessment of differential change over the one-year research period between programme and non-programme areas. Four of the community organizations were chosen for inclusion in the evaluation.

Programme neighbourhoods showed significant gains relative to non-programme neighbourhoods over the one-year period in terms of having 'heard or read about' and having had the 'opportunity to attend' at a 'neighbourhood crime prevention meeting' or a 'block watch programme'. Feelings among residents that 'people on their blocks can make a difference to the neighbourhood' were weaker after the implementation of the programme in two of the programme areas and stronger in another two. There was no difference between programme and non-programme areas in terms of home protection behaviour, watching out for suspicious behaviour or crime reporting behaviour. There was no overall improvement in levels of social integration as measured by 'chatting to neighbours' and 'knowing neighbours by name'. Two programme areas showed a significant increase in the number of victimizations per respondent over the study period. One area showed a decrease in victimizations, which was 'marginally significant'. The other areas showed no change in victimization. Overall, there was an increase in youth disorder and incivilities in the programme areas. There were significant increases in fear of personal crime in three of the neighbourhoods, and a significant increase in fear of property crime in one of the neighbourhoods. Optimism about the neighbourhood declined in three programme areas, and residents in two areas were more likely to report an intention to move out of the neighbourhood.

The authors conclude that the evaluation had generated little empirical support for the hypotheses embodied in the block watch programmes. Most of the findings were either non-significant, or significant in a direction opposite to the hypotheses.

This is one of the most sophisticated evaluations of NW programmes. The research design implemented matches closely the model of quasi-experimental designs using untreated control groups and pre-test/post-test surveys. The major problems with the method are largely those which are associated with all quasi-experimental designs. Multivariate analysis is limited in its ability to control for sample difference between experimental and control groups. There may be important variations between the groups which cannot be measured by the research instrument. There is also a problem of interpreting the research findings and deciding whether the changes recorded – both negative and positive – can be justly attributed to the experimental programme.

Evaluations of programme effectiveness: secondary analyses

Many evaluations of NW programmes have been conducted which are either not widely published (e.g. the results are reported in an internal police report or in a local newspaper) or are difficult to obtain in this country (e.g. when the report is out of print). It is possible to learn something about the results of these evaluations from the published reviews of the literature.

One of the most comprehensive of these reviews has been conducted by Titus (1984), who summarized the results of nearly 40 community crime prevention programmes. Most of the programmes included NW elements. Many of the studies were conducted by police departments, or were based on data provided by police departments. Titus divided the studies into two groups: 'simple before/after studies' and 'studies with treated/untreated area comparisons'.

The review of research which falls under the heading of simple before/after studies provides results on the effectiveness of 14 NW-type schemes (excluding one result based on residents' perceptions of changes in crime rate). Twelve of the schemes reported reductions in the number of burglaries committed following the implementation of the programme (the follow-up period ranged from 6 months to 20 months). One scheme reported an increase in burglary and another reported no change. The author argued that these were the weaker of the two sets of studies, and acknowledged that they may be methodologically flawed.

The review also presented results on the effectiveness of 20 NW-type schemes which fall under the heading of studies with treated/untreated area comparisons (excluding one result based on residents' perceptions of changes in crime rate). The review showed that all of these studies reported favourable comparisons between NW and non-NW areas in terms of burglary rates. Nearly all of these studies, however, were based only on post-test comparisons; the absence of pre-test data makes it difficult (if not impossible) to interpret the meaning of post-test differences.

The overwhelming finding from this selection of US research conducted by police departments or from data supplied by police departments is that

NW programmes are effective in reducing burglary. The majority of studies, however, are based on research methods which are seriously flawed. The major problem with before/after studies is that it is unknown whether the burglary rates were reducing in similar areas at the same time. If so, it would be expected that burglary rates would have reduced in the experimental areas in the absence of the NW programme. The major problem with treated/untreated post-test-only comparisons is that it is unknown whether post-test differences between the areas could be explained by pre-test differences; and if so, it would again be expected that post-test burglary rates would be lower in the treatment than non-treatment areas in the absence of the programme.

Evaluations of programme effectiveness: NCJRS summaries
Another source of information about US evaluations of NW schemes is the abstracts of research obtainable through the National Criminal Justice Reference Service (NCJRS). A custom search of all documents on NW in the NCJRS library produced 206 abstracts of studies. Most of the abstracts comprised references to the administration and operation of the programmes without any reference to their effectiveness. Twenty-one of the abstracts reported findings relating to the impact on crime of the schemes. The results showed that 16 studies reported a reduction in burglary or in total crimes, and 5 studies reported an increase in burglary or in total crimes.

The abstracts are usually short and do not reveal the methods used in sufficient detail to be able to comment on their methodological adequacy. It would appear, however, that many of the studies were conducted by police departments or from data prepared by police departments and experienced many of the problems noted in the review by Titus (1984). The major problem revealed in these abstracts is an almost equal tendency to compare crime data in an experimental area before and after treatment with no reference to a control area, and to compare crime data after treatment in an experimental and a control area with no reference to crime rates before treatment.

Discussion
The review of evaluations of NW effectiveness reveals that the vast majority of studies conclude that NW is effective in preventing crime in general, or burglary in particular. Most evaluations have been conducted by the police. The results of research conducted by the police tends to conclude that NW is successful in achieving its objectives. The results of research conducted by independent researchers tends to conclude that NW is partly or wholly unsuccessful.

With few exceptions, the bulk of this research suffers from serious methodological weaknesses. As a result, it is almost impossible to arrive at an overall conclusion about the effectiveness of NW in preventing crime. In order to identify the problems in more detail, it might be helpful to comment on some of the more frequently recurring research weaknesses of these studies. As most of this research has been conducted by the police, it is inevitable that the main thrust of these criticisms will be directed at police research. It is not intended to be disparaging of police evaluations, which are most welcome and should be encouraged; it is hoped that the following critique will be taken in the constructive way that is intended, both by the police and independent researchers.

Police studies are (with a few notable exceptions) based on police-recorded crimes as their primary data source. It is now widely recognized, especially since the publication of the first British Crime Survey (Hough and Mayhew, 1983), that police recorded crimes exclude a large number of offences and are strongly affected by changes in public reporting and police recording practices. This is a particularly important problem in relation to NW evaluations as increased public reporting of crime is one of the stated functions of NW.

There is also the problem of small numbers. Police evaluations are often based on programmes operating in small areas which have lower than average crime rates. A short post-test period of one year (or three months in the case of one evaluation) will result in a small number of crimes. The dramatic 90 per cent reduction in burglaries reported in the Cheshire Constabulary evaluation report, for example, was a result of a change in crime from 19 to 2 offences. The Merseyside Constabulary evaluation reported a NW success on the bases of a fall from 7 to 6 burglaries in one area and a reduction from 4 to 'nearly zero' in another.

Many of the evaluations are based on 'before/after' comparisons, with no adequate control area comparison. It is not obvious from 'before' and 'after' comparisons whether a measured reduction in crime is a result of the programme. It could as easily be assumed that the reduction was a result of broader changes in the crime levels and would have happened in the experimental area in the absence of the programme. The most effective way of determining what might have happened to the area in the absence of the programme is to used a matched or randomly selected control area.

Another common method of evaluation is the post-test-only, 'treatment/non-treatment' comparison. The crime rates among participants in the scheme are compared with the crime rates of non-participants. Unless pre-existing differences in crime rates between participants and non-participants are known, it is not possible to interpret the post-test differences. This is a real problem in relation to NW scheme, which are more likely to be implemented in areas with lower than average crime rates.

Other methodological problems associated with NW evaluations can be found equally among police and independent research. Few of these studies pay any attention to the problem of 'construct validity' (Cook and Campbell, 1979), which concerns the nature of the programme implemented and the extent to which it matches the theoretical formulation of NW. The issue is not so much that these studies fail to engage in a detailed theoretical discussion, but fail to provide an adequate description of the kind of programme being evaluated. The problem is exacerbated when the evaluation relates to a comprehensive programme comprising NW and additional crime prevention measures. It is often uncertain to what extent the studies are evaluations of one programme, or many types of programme. The problem can only be resolved by fuller explication and description of the nature of the treatment being investigated.

Few of these studies attempt to deal with the problem of 'internal validity' (*ibid.*) which refers to the extent to which the measured outcome – e.g. crime reduction – can be justifiably attributed to the NW programme. This can be done only by providing evidence of a causal link, between the treatment and outcome, and by providing evidence of an attempt to refute alternative explanations (Rosenbaum, 1986).

Evaluative research rarely includes statements about the 'external validity' (*ibid.*), which refers to the extent to which the findings can be generalized across times, targets, settings and programmes. The main problem is not that the research design is insufficiently sophisticated to be able to make these assumptions, but that researchers evade the issue and leave it up to the reader to work out the implication of the findings for other programmes.

Evaluations of programme operation: participation

In order for NW to be effective, it is not only necessary that it is capable of achieving its aims, but also that it is accepted by residents and widely implemented. Over the past few years, a number of studies have been published, mainly in the USA, on the willingness of communities and individuals to adopt neighbourhood crime prevention programmes. As NW schemes are often included within the neighbourhood crime prevention package, the findings of the research are relevant to this review.

One of the major findings of this research is that there are important differences among participants and non-participants. In particular, participants are more likely than non-participants to be involved in other community organizations (Skogan and Maxfield, 1981; Lavrakas, 1980). One of the few independent studies of NW in Britain, conducted by students at the University of Surrey, showed that over 90 per cent of participants in the NW scheme in one of the areas investigated were members of other community organizations, usually residents' or tenants' associations (Bennion *et al.*, 1985).

A related finding which emerges from this research is that participants are also more heavily integrated within their communities than non-participants. A study by DuBow and Podolefsky (1982) found significant differences between participants and non-participants in terms of a number of measures of social integration, including: attachment to neighbourhood ('feel a part of the neighbourhood'; 'expect to live in neighbourhood in two years');

neighbourhood social knowledge ('ease of identifying strangers in the neighbourhood'; 'proportion of neighbourhood children known'); neighbourhood crime knowledge ('number of local crime victims known'); and neighbourhood social interaction ('frequency of visiting in neighbour's home') (*ibid.* pp. 310-12).

The research also provides some evidence on the relationship between participants in community crime prevention programmes and various demographic characteristics. The survey by Lavrakas showed that blacks were significantly more likely than whites to participate in block clubs and were found to be more active within the schemes. (The greater involvement of blacks in neighbourhood crime prevention programmes has also been reported in studies by Washnis, 1976, and Marx and Archer, 1971). Homeowners were significantly more likely to participate in block watch schemes than renters. More educated people were significantly more likely to belong to block watches than less educated people. Residents from high-income groups were significantly more likely than residents from low-income groups to participate in these schemes (Lavrakas, 1981). The Washington evaluation found that participating blocks had a higher number of homeowners, more expensive rental housing, fewer children and fewer elderly persons (Henig, 1984). Other studies have shown that older respondents are more likely than younger respondents to be participants (Skogan and Maxfield, 1981}. The research also shows a tendency for the age relationship to be curvilinear with participation peaking in the 50–59-year-old group and then falling off.

Studies have also found that there are important similarities among participants and non-participants. It has been shown, for example, that participants are no more likely than non-participants to take additional security precautions (DuBow and Podolefsky, 1982). It has also been shown that there is little difference between participants and non- participants in terms of perceptions of crime or beliefs about the efficacy of crime prevention measures (*ibid.*).

Reasons for joining neighbourhood crime prevention programmes vary between studies. North American studies have sometimes divided reasons for participating in these programmes into 'private-minded' and 'public-minded' motives.

These studies have shown that collective actions, such as participation in NW schemes, are often associated with 'public-minded motives' whereas individual actions, such as fitting security devices to the home, are often associated with 'private-minded' motives (Lavrakas, 1981). Other research has shown that reasons for joining neighbourhood programmes often concern the prevention of potential problems from arising in the future (e.g. higher crime rates) rather than existing problems (Lavrakas and Hertz, 1982). The main reasons reported for not joining neighbourhoods schemes have been categorized as 'no time', 'no interest' and 'no opportunity' (*ibid.*).

Other studies have reported non-participation as a result of respondents claiming that they were 'too old' or 'too sick' or generally hostile towards the police (Donnsion, Scola and Thomas, 1986).

Research into participation rates and scheme activity levels have shown considerable variations. Most of the evaluations discussed in the first part of this chapter did not comment on participation rates or activity levels. Those that did, reported surprisingly low levels of both. The NW scheme in Stafford reported a 4 per cent participation rate (O'Leary and Wood, 1984), and the Northampton schemes (Northamptonshire Police, 1985) reported a 9 per cent participation rate.

The study by Henig (1984) of block watch schemes in Washington, DC, included an assessment of the level of activity of each scheme. An activity score was devised, based on the nature of information, recruitment and sense of community. Blocks that held regular meetings, or had good attendance at meetings, were given a score of +1. Those which had no meetings, or meetings which had poor attendance, were given a score of -1. Block watch schemes which fell in the middle were given a score of zero. The information score was based on whether the block had a newsletter; whether it had other formal channels for communicating to members; and whether it had crime data disseminated to residents. The recruitment score was based on the presence or absence of methods for contacting and involving new members. The sense of community score was based on the stated interests and involvement by block residents. The analysis of the results of the investigation showed that one out of three block watches scored below zero on the activity scale.

A similar kind of activity score was constructed in an evaluation of two NW schemes in London (Bennion *et al.*, 1985). The scale related to the number of NW activities performed by residents living in the area of the NW scheme. The activities included displaying a NW window sticker, attendance at NW meetings, looking out for anything suspicious, property marking and receiving a home security survey. The analysis showed that 35 per cent of residents in one area, and 74 per cent of residents in another area, did none of these things. Conversely, 3 per cent of residents in the first area, and no residents in the second area, had engaged in all five activities.

Does it do any harm?

The evidence on possible harmful or unwanted side-effects of NW can be found in the reports of evaluative research and also in anecdotal material (e.g. conversations with police officers and residents) and in opinions expressed in newspaper or magazine articles.

Evaluative research

The main evidence on unwanted side-effects from the evaluative research concerns the possibility that the implementation of NW schemes might serve to increase crime and the fear of crime. The evaluation of block watch schemes in areas of Chicago (discussed earlier) showed that there were significant increases in fear of personal crime in three of neighbourhoods and a significant increase in fear of property crime in one of the neighbourhoods (Rosenbaum, 1986). The author offered some possible explanations for this finding.

It has been argued that meetings among residents, or among residents and the police, will reduce fear of crime as a result of increased social interaction and social support. It is also argued that interaction with others will stimulate the belief that something is being done which will, in turn, lead to a feeling of efficacy and control over the local environment. Rosenbaum (*ibid.*), believes that these meetings might also serve to heighten fear of crime and reduce feelings of efficacy and social cohesion.

One way in which NW meetings might increase fear of crime is as a result of discussions which focus on crime in the area. It is not uncommon in Britain, for example, for the police and the Home Office to attempt to motivate participation in crime prevention measures; (including NW programmes) by heightening public awareness of crime. The Chicago evaluation found that residents who attended these meetings often used them as an opportunity to describe their direct and indirect experiences of victimization and to express their personal concern to others. Rosenhaum argues that exposure to reports of local criminal activity and to other residents' concern about crime might heighten fear among group members. Support for this argument is provided in the findings of the Reactions to Crime Project, which showed that fear of crime was correlated with vicarious victimization (Skogan *et al.*, 1982). It is also possible that fear of crime might be heightened in NW meetings as a result of discussions about security, which might draw attention to the vulnerability of residents' homes.

Another way in which NW meetings might increase fear of crime is through changes in the groups' feelings of efficacy and control over their environment. The common belief is that such activities will enhance the sense of efficacy and control. Rosenhaum argues that the reverse may be true. It is possible that these meetings provide the opportunity for a more realistic assessment of the abilities of the group which lead to a feeling of less efficacy and control. The group might realize, for example, that victimization is not prevented by available crime prevention measures (home security or membership in the NW scheme), or it might realize that crime in their area is the result of factors beyond their control (residential transition or environmental design) (Rosenbaum, 1986).

Anecdotes and opinions
Anecdotal accounts and published opinions on the possible harmful effects of NW do not constitute evaluative research, nor empirical research evidence.

Nevertheless, these accounts present some of the issues that have arisen out of the NW debate and are worth discussing. No attempt has been made to assess the validity of the claims made.

A common argument cited against NW is that it is socially divisive. Proponents of this view argue that NW is run by a small, unrepresentative section of the community for the benefit of their own social group. The social divisions referred to usually concern social class and income divisions. Some critics have taken this line of argument further to suggest that NW could reinforce race differences and exacerbate racial tensions. Alternatively, it is argued that in an area of racial tension, it is unlikely that people will unite behind an NW scheme. Attempts to promote NW in such areas can cause the police to be accused of exacerbating or perpetrating social inequalities.

A second criticism, linked to the first, is the view that the organizers of NW schemes are unrepresentative of the community and attract a disproportionate share of police resources. It is argued, for example, that police resources are drawn into low-crime, middle-class areas which results in police time being spent in areas which need them least (Donnison, Scola and Thomas, 1986). In addition, it is argued that crimes prevented in these areas are likely to be displaced into areas less suitable for NW which, in turn, reinforces social-economic inequalities.

A third criticism concerns the level of police control over NW programmes. It is argued that the public and the police might hold different perceptions of the nature of the problems in an area. For example, residents might be most concerned about people loitering in the streets, graffiti and noise from neighbours, whereas the police might wish to focus community attention on the problem of residential burglary (Lewis and Salem, 1981; Rosenbaum, 1986). A linked criticism is that some residents might object to any kind of involvement of the police in the community, including community efforts to prevent crime.

A fourth problem presented by many commentators, including the police, is the concern that NW might promote 'vigilantism'. It is official policy in the Metropolitan Police that NW should not include citizen patrols and that the existence of these or similar programme elements should be discouraged. There have been reports that citizen patrols do exist in the Metropolitan Police District, despite the official policy (Donnison, Scola and Thomas, 1986). The majority of police forces in Britain discourage citizen patrols because it is believed that they can lead to vigilantism and can lead to actions being taken which are not in the best interests of the patrollers, the residents or the police. Nevertheless, there is evidence that citizen patrols operate in this country without police approval, and at least one scheme has been implemented in Merseyside which has been accepted by the local police.

Other criticisms include the view that NW encourages neighbours to spy on each other, which can break down rather than restore communities. It is also feared that specific groups, or specific individuals within the group, will be selected out for special treatment and become ostracized. This concern was expressed in a newspaper article which reported a story of a teenager who had been branded by the local NW organizers as 'Yobbo of the month' residents were encouraged to keep records using an incident form and to telephone the area co-ordinator, 'every time they see the "Yobbo of the month' doing something anti-social': *(Daily Telegraph,* 28 July 1986). The youth's irate mother was reported as intending to take legal action over the distribution of the NW newsletter to over 500 homes in the area 'targeting her son as a trouble-maker.

Discussion

Evaluations of the operation of neighbourhood crime prevention initiatives have highlighted some of the problems associated with the implementation of NW-type schemes. The research has shown that there are systematic differences between participants and non-participants. With a few exceptions participants are more likely than non-participants to be socially advantaged, socially active and socially integrated. Neighbourhood schemes are less well supported by renters, by young people, by low-income people and by less well-educated people. It cannot be assumed, therefore, that NW will be universally accepted.

The research also suggests that even when schemes do exist, there will be active participation in them. The research has shown that the participation rates in some scheme areas are low, and that activity levels in some scheme areas are low. The evidence also suggest that there may be harmful unintended consequences of NW. It is possible that attendance at NW meetings might serve to heighten awareness to crime and exacerbate fear of crime. It might also weaken the feeling among residents that they are in control of their environment which might, in turn, weaken social control. Other concerns about the unwanted side-effects of NW are not documented in these the findings of evaluative research, but these find expression in journalistic accounts or private conversation. It is believed that NW can be socially divisive and serve to divert police resources from those who need them most to those who need them least.

PART III

THE LONDON
EVALUATION

5 Research Methods

Introduction
The idea for an evaluation of NW arose out of discussions between the Home Office Research and Planning Unit and the Metropolitan Police, who saw a need for an independent assessment of the effectiveness of the new NW programmes in London. In many ways these early discussions shaped the broad parameters of the evaluation before the Institute of Criminology entered the field. It was expected that the independent evaluation would investigate just one or two schemes to avoid replicating the evaluation of NW in London which was already being conducted by the Metropolitan Police, using police-recorded crimes as a data source. It was also expected that the research would comprise a detailed investigation and examine a broad range of outcome variables, including crime, fear of crime, public satisfaction with the police, reporting rates and clear-up rates.

A further factor which served to define the parameters of the research was the funds available to conduct it. At an early stage in the discussions between the Home Office and the Institute of Criminology, it was agreed that the evaluation should include crime and public attitude surveys. The funds allocated to conduct these surveys determined the overall scale of the project.

The research design
Within the framework of the broad parameters laid down during the early discussions between the Home Office and the Metropolitan Police it was necessary to decide on an appropriate research design. The first decision taken was that the research should be based on a quasi-experimental design. The main reasons for this decision was the recent and successful adoption of quasi-experimental designs among evaluators in the USA in the investigation of the effectiveness of community crime prevention programmes (Rosenbaum, 1986,1987; Brown and Wycoff, 1987). The second decision was that the research should be based on crime and public attitude surveys as the primary method of data collection. This decision was influenced by the recent growth of national and local crime surveys and the use of crime-survey techniques in the evaluation of community crime prevention programmes in the UK and USA (Cirel *et al.*,1977; Veater, 1984). There were clear advantages in using crime and public attitude surveys in terms of the wide range of outcomes that could be measured (e.g. reporting rates, fear of crime, police–public relations, etc.).

Quasi-experimentation
The choice of quasi-experimental design focused on three alternative models. These are defined by Cook and Campbell (1979) as: (1) the

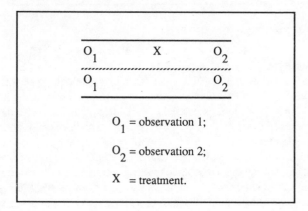

Figure 5.1   The untreated control group design with pre-test and post-test

untreated control group design with pre-test and post-test; (2) the untreated control group design with separate pre-test and post-test samples; and (3) the one-group design with separate pre-test and post-test samples.

One of the strongest quasi-experimental designs is the untreated control group design with pre-test and post-test; this is shown graphically in Figure 5.1.

A similar design is the untreated control group design with separate pre-test and post-test samples; this is shown graphically in Figure 5.2.

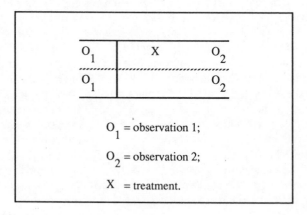

Figure 5.2   The untreated control group design with separate pre-test and post-test samples

The vertical line separating the fiist and second observations signifies that the two samples comprise different respondents. The main difference between the designs is that the former represents a panel survey (using the same individuals for each round of interviewing) and the latter represents a cross-sectional survey (using a separate random sample of individuals at each round of interviewing). One of the advantages of the panel survey design is that it allows an assessment of changes from one survey to another in relation to the same individuals. One of the advantages of the cross-sectional survey design is that it allows an assessment of change among groups of individuals (e.g. community or town).

An important drawback of the panel survey design is that the expected attrition rate of panel members from one survey to another is usually high. Research adopting this approach frequently reports no more than a 50 per cent re-contact rate from to post-test surveys (Rosenbaum, 1986). A significant problem associated with a low response rate is the possibility of systematic differences between respondents and non-respondents. This was an important consideration in relation to the current research because of a possible association between non-response and victimization. Conceivably people who were out of their homes for many hours a day were more likely than those who were at home all day to be the victims of burglary. It was for this reason that it was decided that a cross-sectional rather than panel design should be chosen.

The untreated control group design with separate pre-test and post-test samples (Figure 5.2) was chosen as the model for the evaluation of the impact of NW on crime. This design was not chosen for the evaluation of the impact of NW on public attitudes and behaviour. In order to achieve the number of interviews required and to attract market research companies from the funds available for survey work, it was necessary to reduce the scale of the research. This was done by using a shortened version of the questionnaire for respondents living in the control areas which excluded questions on

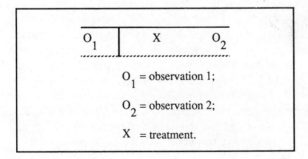

O_1 = observation 1;

O_2 = observation 2;

X = treatment.

Figure 5.3   One-group design with separate pre-test and post-test samples

public attitudes and behaviour. It was decided therefore to conduct this part of the evaluation using the one-group design with separate pre-test and post-test samples; this is shown graphically in Figure 5. 3. This design is not as strong as either of the models in Figures 5.1 and 5.2 and absence of a control group makes interpretation more difficult. Some of the weaknesses of the design can be ameliorated by extra effort in assessing the additional threats to internal validity.

Operationalizing the research design
Once the broad outline of the evaluation had been decided, it was necessary to make many further decisions about the way in which the design was to be implemented. The principal decisions concerned the number of NW programmes to evaluate, the number and nature of non-NW comparison areas and the number of completed interviews necessary for the analysis.

One of the important discussion points at the time of the research was the issue of the potential displacement effect of crime prevention measures. The issue of displacement was important because of the potential criticism that any reduction in crime in NW areas occurred as a result of crimes being displaced to nearby non-scheme areas. Evidence of success in terms of crime reduction could be dismissed on the grounds that it was the result of no more than a shift of crime from scheme to non-scheme areas. An assessment of the displacement effects of NW had been included in the research designs of the Seattle (Cirel *et al.,*1977) and the Bristol (Veater, 1984) evaluations. It was decided therefore that the London evaluation should include at least one area adjacent to an experimental NW area to measure and possible displacement effects, should the schemes prove to be effective.

Apart from the inclusion of a displacement area, it was also necessary to incorporate in the research design at least one control area. This was necessary in order to compare changes in the experimental areas with changes in a similar area without a NW scheme over the same period of time.

The number of NW schemes to evaluate, and the number of control and displacement areas to be included in the research design, was dependent primarily on the total cost of the surveys. The cost of the surveys was governed by the cost per completed interview and the number of interviews conducted. Provisional inquiries with market research companies revealed that about 3,000 interviews could be conducted from the funds available, which allowed 1,500 completed interviews in both rounds of surveys. It was estimated that about 350 interviews would have to be completed in each area in order to record sufficient victimizations to conduct a meaningful statistical analysis. This meant that there could be no more than four areas included in the survey and no more than two of these could be programme areas.

The Neighbourhood Watch areas
Because of the wide variation in the size and nature of the schemes in

London, there appeared little to be gained from selecting a typical or, in some way, representative scheme. It was possible that this could have resulted in a small scheme or one in an area with little crime, both of which might have generated too few victimizations to conduct meaningful significance tests. Instead it was felt that it was necessary to be in control of the kind of area evaluated and to select the kind of scheme which would best suit that evaluation.

It was also felt that the schemes chosen should match as closely as possible the popular concept of NW in order to avoid the criticism that the research had not evaluated NW, but some other programme. It was also felt that the schemes chosen should have the best possible chance of success in order to guard against the criticism that the research had not evaluated NW, but some limited or weak version of it. It could also be argued that if the most promising schemes were later shown to have little effect, it would not be expected that less promising schemes would be any more effective.

The experimental areas were selected with the assistance of the Metropolitan Police Crime Prevention Branch who compiled a list of all watch schemes launched in London since the beginning of the programme in 1983. Details of the date of the launch, the number of households in the watch area and the participation rate were included on the list.

The first stage of the selection involved choosing ten divisions which had implemented at least two schemes since 1983, covering 500 households or more, and registering participation rates of over 50 per cent. It was necessary to investigate a scheme of this size in order to obtain a sufficient number of victimizations to be able to conduct the statistical analysis. It was necessary to investigate schemes within divisions which had a record of achieving high participation rates in order to maximize the probability of a high participation rate in the experimental areas. The second stage involved contacting senior officers from these divisions by telephone or by letter and asking them whether they intended implementing similar schemes in the near future. Three of the original ten divisions reported that they were going to launch at least one scheme covering at least 500 households during the period specified. The third stage involved visiting the three divisions to discuss the proposals with local officers and touring the prospective NW areas.

The selection of the two experimental areas was dependent on the extent to which they matched our selection criteria. The list of criteria covered five broad categories: (1) the proposed programme; (2) the social and geographical structure of the area; (3) the rate and pattern of crime within the area; (4) the police; and (5) the NW co-ordinators. In order to evaluate a scheme which had a good chance rather than a poor chance of success it was felt necessary that the programme be as comprehensive as possible; the selection procedure therefore included establishing whether property marking and home security surveys were an intended part of the programme.

It was hoped that the site selected would have actual or symbolic boundaries which would demarcate it from other areas. It was necessary that the structure of the area and the type of dwellings within the area facilitated surveillance, thus low-rise rather than high-rise properties were more suitable. It was necessary that the area had an average or above average crime rate, to generate sufficient crimes to measure meaningful changes from one period to another. In order to determine crime rates over time, it was necessary to obtain summary data from police crime reports for the area over the preceding two-year period; and that crime rates were fairly consistent from one year to another. There was a danger in selecting an area which had recently experienced a temporary peak in crime, which would fall back to some more typical level following the launch of the NW scheme. It was also important that the number of known offenders living in the area was small as the programme depended on residents interacting (and sharing crime prevention information) which they might be reluctant to do if their neighbours were offenders.

During preliminary discussions with senior and local police on the divisions of the potential sites an assessment was made of their level of commitment to NW and their enthusiasm for the programme. It was essential to the evaluation that the programme was launched and implemented as planned, and successfully maintained for the 12-month experimental period. The attitude of local police towards the programme and their apparent level of commitment to it were necessary factors to be taken into consideration, for it was important that NW was not seen by the local police as merely an administrative chore undertaken to achieve division objectives.

Finally, the ability and enthusiasm of the potential area co-ordinators was to be assessed, to ensure that the experimental schemes were well managed. The design of NW in London places area co-ordinators in a key position in determining both the character and duration of the programme. For example, a sudden loss of interest by an area co-ordinator might result in the demise of the scheme.

Two experimental areas were chosen from the three divisions visited which best matched our selection criteria. One site was in Acton and the other in Wimbledon; however, the exact location of the schemes is not revealed in order to ensure confidentiality of the respondents who participated in the surveys.

The single displacement area was less difficult to choose simply because the choice was more limited. It was decided that the displacement area should adjoin one of the experimental areas along at least part of its boundary, and that there should be no plans for the implementation of NW in that area in the foreseeable future. It was not possible to guarantee that any of the areas adjoining the experimental site in Acton would remain NW-free during the forthcoming 12 months; consequently, this limited the choice of displacement area to the sites adjacent to the Wimbledon experimental area.

A site was chosen which had a similar social and geographic structure to the experimental area.

A control site was selected by matching the Wimbledon experimental area with a randomly chosen area of similar social composition (as measured using ACORN classifications) and roughly the same distance from the centre of London. As the Acton and Wimbledon experimental areas were almost identical in terms of ACORN classification, and in terms of distance from the centre of London, it was possible to use the single control area as a comparison for both. A list was compiled of all eligible areas and 12 were randomly selected from this list for provisional investigation. The investigations involved determining whether a NW scheme was in operation in the area, or planned; the crime rates and pattern of crime; and the number of households within the area. One area was chosen from the list of 12 which best matched the selection criteria. The site chosen was in Redbridge.

The crime surveys

The main method of data collection used in the evaluation was crime and public attitudes surveys. The surveys are perhaps more correctly referred to as censuses as an attempt was made to interview a representative of every household in the area. The main reason for doing this was to achieve sufficient numbers of victimizations to conduct the statistical analysis. Drawing a sample of households from the area would have increased the sampling error and exacerbated the problem of establishing statistically significant differences in victimization between areas and periods.

The sampling was done by a market research company who drew up a list of all households using the Electoral Register. It was necessary to add missing addresses using rating lists supplied by the local authority to complete the sampling frame. Further checks were made during the interviewing stage to establish the total list of households in the area. The interviewers were instructed to establish the number of households living at each address and attempt to interview a representative of each.

Each household on the list thus became initially eligible to be included in the survey. Addresses which were later found to be non-residences, vacant or demolished (or not found at all) were classified as ineligible and excluded from the sampling frame. Once a contact with a member of the household had been made, further inquiries were conducted to establish how long the members of the household had lived in the area. Households containing members who had not lived in the area for at least the previous 12 months were classified as ineligible and also excluded from the survey.

Respondents were selected for interview using the same procedure adopted in the first two British crime surveys. A single adult representative was chosen from each household by selecting from household members aged 16 years or over, using a Kish grid random selection procedure. Therefore, the final sample comprised a random and representative sample of adult members of households resident in the survey area.

Most recent surveys have adopted the same procedure, with the interesting exception of Bottoms, Mawby and Walker (1987), who used the Marchant–Blyth technique which allowed more than one respondent to be interviewed per household. Another recent variation in respondent selection procedure is choosing an adult representative by requesting to interview the member of the household whose birthday comes next. It is argued that such a procedure overcomes the problem of listing the names of every household member before selection can take place. Some residents might not wish to reveal this information at an early stage in the interview.

The first round of surveys began in May 1985 and was completed by early June. Fieldworkers employed by the market research company went into all four areas (2 experimental,1 displacement and 1 control) at about the same time. The NW schemes were launched in the middle of June in Acton, and at the beginning of July in Wimbledon (within two weeks of one another). One year elapsed before the second round of surveys was conducted in the same four areas; the second wave of interviewing began in July 1986 and was completed by early September .

The questionnaire
The style and substance of the questionnaire was similar to the questionnaire used in the first and second British crime surveys . The pre-test and post-test questionnaires were almost identical, apart from the addition of questions in the second round of surveys in the experimental areas, concerning public involvement in and attitudes towards the local NW schemes.

Examples of the kind of questionnaire used in the evaluation can be found in the technical reports of the companies commissioned to conduct the first and second British Crime Surveys (Wood,1983; NOP Market Research,1985) and in the reports of local crime surveys (Maclean, Jones and Young, 1986; Kinsey,1984). In order to provide an impression of the questionnaire used in the evaluation, it might be helpful to describe briefly its component parts.

The questionnaire was divided into five parts. The first part comprised an 'address record sheet' and a 'respondent selection sheet' which were used to record details of contacts made, and contacts not made.

The second part comprised the main questionnaire which contained 18 questions concerning residents' satisfaction with their area, social cohesion, fear of crime and feelings of safety, perceived probability of victimization and perceptions of area crime rates, and a further 24 screening questions concerning victimization. The screening questions included 6 questions designed to establish which screening questions to ask about (e.g. non car owners were not asked about car theft) and a further 18 questions about specific offence victimizations. The victimizations included in the screening questions were: vehicle theft, theft from a vehicle, damage to a vehicle, bicycle theft, burglary with theft, burglary with damage, attempted burglary, theft from a dwelling, theft outside a dwelling (excluding milk bottles), damage to dwelling, theft of milk bottles (not used when counting offences), damage to dwelling, theft from person, attempted theft from person, other theft, other damage, assault, threats and sexual assault (females only). The questions concerning offences were phrased in everyday language rather than legal crime categories: 'in the twelve months since the first of July 1985 has anyone got into this house/flat without permission and stolen or tried to steal anything.'

The third part was the 'victim form'. All offences identified in the screening questions of the main questionnaire, with the exception of theft of milk bottles from outside the dwelling, were initially eligible to be investigated in depth through the questions contained in the victim form. The main purpose of using victim forms in this way was to match reported victimizations with Home Office offence classifications, to ensure that only bona fide offences are included in the analysis. The victim forms also served to gather more information about the offence, such as details of losses, and whether the offence was reported to the police.

A distinction was made on the victim form between 'single' and 'series' offences. Again, this distinction is common to all surveys which use the victim-form method of identifying and counting offences. A *series* offence was defined as occurring when a number of similar incidents were reported by a respondent 'where the same thing was done under the same circumstances and probably by the same people'. One victim form was completed for each single and each series of offences up to a maximum of eight victimizations. This limit is higher than the number set in the first two British crime surveys in order to record as accurately as possible the number of multiple victimizations of key offences such as burglary and vehicle crime. If more than eight victimizations were reported, the interviewer was instructed to select eight offences from the list of screening offences in a preset order. Offences against the person were given priority over offences against the household.

The fourth part of the questionnaire was a 'follow-up' questionnaire, which contained additional questions concerning policing and NW. The main purpose in using a follow-up questionnaire, in addition to the main questionnaire, is that it separates specific questions from the main questionnaire which might be asked when interviewing some respondents but not others, or used in one round of surveys but not another. In the first round of surveys, for example, the follow-up questionnaire contained questions relating to whether residents were willing, in principle, to join an NW scheme. In the second round of surveys the follow-up questionnaire contained questions relating to respondents' actual participation in their local NW scheme.

The fifth and final part of the questionnaire was the 'demographic questionnaire', which recorded details of the respondent and other household members. Apart from the usual demographic questions concerning age, gender and background of the respondent, the questionnaire also sought details on the head of the household and other family members including the relationship of each family member to the respondent.

Counting crimes

The questionnaire contained details of victimizations reported in the form of screening question responses, and in the form of completed victim forms. In order to count these offences and to determine which were eligible to include in the statistical analysis, it was necessary to devise counting rules; some of these rules have already been discussed. Only victimizations recorded on the victim forms were considered as bona fide offences. Thefts of milk bottles were not included on victim forms. Each victim form contained details of one single offence or one series of offences. A maximum of eight victim forms were completed per respondent.

A number of other rules were followed in determining the final number of offences to be recorded, in each area, in each survey period. It is usual practice in the analysis of victimization data from surveys to stipulate a maximum number of series offences to be counted as individual offences. The usual maximum is 5 (Hough and Mayhew, 1983, 1985; Farrington and Dowds, 1985). The main reason for limiting the number of series offences is that they might have a disproportionate effect on the total number of crimes recorded. For example, one victim reported 40 acts of criminal damage to his vehicle (a milk roundsman} and another reported 50 cases of assault (a wife reporting assaults by a husband}. The impact of a large number of crimes would be particularly disruptive when comparing one period with another in relation to crime in fairly small communities.

Each single and series offence recorded on the victim forms was coded by staff trained by the market research company which conducted the surveys in accordance with Home Office counting rules. Over 50 coding categories were used to classify offences. Offences which could not be allocated to a category were excluded from the analysis. Offences that were coded as falling outside the surveys' coverage, or offences which were ambiguous, were also excluded from the analysis. The full list of offence categories used for initial coding is given in the Chapter 7.

A further attrition of offences occurred as a result of the decision to include in the analysis only those victimizations which occurred within the 12- or 13-month period before interview (the exact length of time varied between respondents because of the one-month interviewing period), and only victimization which occurred within the boundaries of the survey areas. Offences were included in the analysis if they were committed between July 1984 and June 1985 in relation to the pre-test surveys and between July 1985 and June 1986 in relation to the post-test surveys.

The samples

Eight separate surveys were conducted during the course of the project: four in the period before the launch of the schemes, and four one year following the launch. Details of the total number of households sampled and the eventual contact rate for each survey is shown in Table 5.1.

The total number of households identified includes additional households discovered during the course of the survey. Addresses were classified as ineligible if they were discovered to be vacant, demolished or non-residential. Households were classified as ineligible if the members of the household

Table 5.1 Response rates and sample sizes for the four survey areas

	Action experimental area	Wimbledon experimental area	Wimbledon displacement area	Redbridge control area
Pre-test				
total households	639	711	540	495
total ineligible	115	73	74	53
total eligible	524	638	466	442
interviewed	306	353	323	306
response rate	58%	55%	69%	69%
Post-test				
total households	702	710	570	557
total ineligible	179	95	87	44
total eligible	523	615	483	513
interviewed	309	400	332	330
response rate	59%	65%	69%	64%

had not lived in the area for at least one year prior to interview. The total number of eligible households comprises the number remaining, once both types of ineligible household have been subtracted from the total number identified. The response rate was calculated as the total number of interviews completed, divided by the total number of eligible households.

The overall contact rate was 62 per cent in the pre-test surveys and 64 per cent in the post-test surveys. The rates varied widely between areas with a range from 55 to 69 per cent in the first round and from 59 to 69 per cent in the second. These contact rates are generally lower than is usually recorded from random public attitude surveys and lower than that achieved on both

British crime surveys. The main reason given by the market research company for the lower than expected rates was that, in their experience, contact rates are always lower in urban and inner-city areas than over the country as a whole. The two main reasons for non-contact given on the completed address forms for non-contacts were 'refusal' and 'no contact after four or more call backs'.

It is possible that residents in urban areas, especially in areas with above average crime rates, are more likely to be suspicious of strangers knocking on their doors and are less likely as a result to agree to be interviewed or to answer the door in the first place. It is also possible that conducting a census in a small community over a short period of time creates special problems for fieldworkers not experienced in national sample surveys.

The characteristics of the respondents are summarized in the Appendix. Overall, the table shows little variation in the characteristics in the samples drawn from each area in the pre-test and post-test surveys. In Acton the main differences occurred in relation to marital status (more single respondents in the post-test); in the Wimbledon experimental area the main differences occurred in relation to income (more higher-income households in the post-test), tenure (more 'owners' in the post-test); and socio-economic status (more non-manual workers in the post-test); in the Wimbledon displacement area there were no significant differences; and in Redbridge the main differences occurred in relation to income (more higher-income households in the post-test).

The table also shows some interesting characteristics of respondents which were reflected in all or most of the samples. A slightly higher proportion of females than males were interviewed in each area and in each round of surveys. This might reflect the slightly greater proportion of females in the population as a whole, or it might be the product of the greater likelihood that females will be at home during the day and available for interview. Respondents tended to be married rather than single or 'separated, widowed or divorced', 'white' rather than 'non-white', home owners rather than 'renters', employed rather than unemployed and motor vehicle owners rather than non motor vehicle owners. The overall impression of the residents interviewed is that they are about average in terms of economic and social status.

Non-survey data collection

The crime and public attitudes surveys comprised the major source of data for the evaluation and the strongest evidence for the assessment of the effectiveness of NW. A number of other data were collected during the course of the research, however, to supplement the survey data or to cover additional aspects of the evaluation.

One of the additional elements of the evaluation was an examination of the impact of the programme on telephone calls for service from the public to the local police station and on the use of the emergency ('999') telephone system. It would be expected that if the NW schemes were effective in encouraging the public to report suspicious incidents to the police, this would be reflected in the number and type of calls made to the police. The examination of the number and content of telephone messages also helped assess the extent to which police–community relations had improved as a result of NW, and the extent to which the flow and quality of information received by the police had improved.

Telephone messages directed to the local station were recorded by hand on special station message pads as they were received and emergency call messages were recorded automatically on computer and dispatched to the local station in the form of a printer output. Both kinds of messages were kept by the local stations in their files for a period of at least 6 months before destruction. The stations involved in the research were requested to keep these messages and to make them available for analysis. The analysis required searching through all written and printed message sheets received by the subdivisional police stations and selecting out all calls made from residents in the research areas. This procedure was conducted for Acton and Wimbledon experimental areas, and for the Wimbledon displacement areas. A sample of station messages and emergency calls was collected for a 6- or 7-month period before the launch of the NW schemes and for the whole one-year period following their launch. It was not possible to include data for the whole of the 12-month period before the launch as message sheets were systematically destroyed after 6 months. Messages selected in this way were photocopied and returned to the files and the copies used as the raw data for computer coding and analysis.

A second additional element of the evaluation was an investigation of the resource implications of NW for the police in terms of police manpower and other costs. The inquiry also allowed an assessment to be made of the kinds of work that NW creates for the police and the nature and level of contact between the police and local co-ordinators.

Total salary costs were assessed by obtaining a detailed log of police time spent on NW tasks. This required asking all of the key police personnel who were in any way involved in work relating to the two NW programmes to complete activity sheets each time a NW task was performed. A NW task was defined as any activity that the officer would not have performed had the scheme not existed. The activity sheets requested information on the nature of the tasks performed, the date and time the task was performed, and how long it took to complete it. Activity sheets were completed by the home beat officer(s), the crime prevention officer(s), the police NW co-ordinator and any senior officers who made some input into the schemes (e.g. at the launch meetings.)

Total 'other' costs were assessed by asking the key NW officers to keep a record of all expenditures relating to the local schemes. These expenditures covered the cost of the initial launch meeting, the cost of publicity and other material distributed to residents, in the area and other running costs such as the costs of producing a regular newsletter.

A third source of non-survey data comprised semi-structured interviews with the local police and with the area and street co-ordinators running the scheme. In both experimental areas the key police personnel were interviewed at the end of the first scheme to determine their attitudes towards and beliefs about the operation and potential success of the programme. In one of the experimental areas (Acton) the area co-ordinator and six of the street co-ordinators were interviewed to obtain a more detailed view of their assessment of the first year of the scheme. Both police and co-ordinator interviews were tape recorded and transcribed verbatim.

Finally, non-survey data collection involved the miscellaneous acquisition of evidence in relation to the general monitoring of the development of the programmes. All written material produced by either the police or the civilian co-ordinators was, when available, collected. This included memoranda, minutes of co-ordinators' meetings and news-sheets and newsletters produced throughout the year. Conversations with the police and co-ordinators which had a bearing on the design or development of the schemes were noted and filed. It was also necessary to monitor closely other developments in the area which might effect crime in any way or might enhance or retard the impact of the programme. Local authority initiatives were watched carefully and efforts made to establish any structural changes to the area such as changes in pedestrian or vehicular access or changes to street lighting. Police initiatives were also carefully watched to determine whether any changes in policing might independently affect crime rates or public attitudes in the area. Evidence of policing initiatives which might substantially increase arrest rates of local offenders and additional crime prevention or police–community involvement initiatives were closely monitored.

6 The Programmes

Introduction
The programme implemented represents the treatment to be evaluated. It is important therefore that the exact nature of the treatment is made clear. This involves describing as fully as possible what happened in the experimental areas during the research period. This chapter is divided into three main sections: the first section describes the areas in which the schemes were implemented; the second section examines the design of the programmes; and the third section considers the residents and levels of participation in the NW scheme.

The areas
The Acton experimental area is situated in the Ealing Police Division and covers nine roads. The area adjoins a major trunk road on its western side and is within walking distance of a major route road on it southern side. Residential roads adjoin it on three of its four sides. The area is not often used as a through-route by pedestrians or vehicles, but it is used by outsiders as a place to park vehicles. A few years ago the problem of on-street parking led to the erection of traffic gates on roads near to the experimental site. No additional gates were erected during the pre-test or post-test periods. The housing stock comprises large Edwardian and Victorian houses, many of, which have been converted into flats or maisonettes. This was not, however, 'bedsitter-land' and a large proportion of residents own their own property. It is a developing area and house prices have increased rapidly over the past few years. The impression gained from walking around the site is that it is a quiet, well-ordered and well maintained community with tidy, well-kept streets and houses.

The Wimbledon experimental area is in the Merton Police Division and covers 13 roads and 2 halves of roads. The site adjoins a major route road on its western side and is bordered by a railway line on its northern edge. A busy main road cuts across the southern boundary. On its eastern side is the displacement area of similar housing stock. The area is not often used as a through-route by pedestrians or vehicles, although like the Acton site, it has a problem of on-street parking. A large car-dealing company is located just outside the area on its southern side. For some time, residents in that part of the area have complained about the use of on-street parking facilities by this company. The houses are dominantly Edwardian or Victorian, most of which are single-family homes and owner-occupied. The area has undergone major improvements over the last few years and there is substantial evidence of past and present home improvements.

The Wimbledon displacement area is very similar to the experimental site. It comprises 6 roads and 2 halves of roads and is located on the eastern edge of the experimental areas, bordered by the same railway line to the north and a stream to the east. It differs from the experimental area, in that the southern edge meets other similar residential roads, together with a lower proportion of owner-occupied residences and a higher proportion of converted flats or maisonettes.

The Redbridge control site covers 2 roads and 5 halves of roads. It is bordered by major roads at the north and east, and at the southern edge of the areas there are similar residences which stretch down to a high-street. The western edge of the area comprises residences and a park. The area is dominantly semi-detached and terraced houses, most of which are owner-occupied.

The programmes

Details of the NW programmes, and the way in which they were implemented, gives the clearest impression of the kind of 'treatment' being evaluated. This section examines both schemes in detail. Evidence is drawn from a number of sources including participant observation at public and co-ordinators' meetings, documentary evidence in the form of minutes, newsletters and other material, interviews with police officers and co-ordinators, and evidence from casual conversations.

The Acton NW scheme

The NW scheme in Acton was launched on the 17 June 1985 with a public meeting. The meeting was held in the evening in a church hall within the area. It was attended by two home beat officers, a home beat sergeant, two crime prevention officers, a NW police co-ordinator, a chief inspector, a civilian area co-ordinator, some street co-ordinators who had volunteered before the official launch of the programme and about 100 local residents. The potential area co-ordinator and street co-ordinators were pre-selected because the scheme was public initiated rather than police initiated and was launched at the request of this small number of local residents.

The meeting began about 8.00 p.m. with an opening address by the chief inspector, who outlined to the audience the need for the police and the community to work together in the prevention of crime. After about 10 minutes, the crime prevention officer showed a short promotional video recording of a programme about NW presented by Shaw Taylor, followed by a second programme by the same presenter on property marking. At 8.30 p.m. the chief inspector took the chair and asked the audience if they had any questions. The remaining hour comprised questions from the residents to the police and the police replies. The questions were wide-ranging and covered issues which included: the number of burglaries committed in the area, police response time, whether window stickers attracted burglars, the boundaries of the schemes, the place of residence of offenders who commit crimes in the area, the role of the street co-ordinators and the timetable for the erection of street signs. After the meeting, residents were asked by the area co-ordinator if they were willing to become street co-ordinators.

The first co-ordinators' meeting was held 10 days after the launch of the programme at the home of the area co-ordinator and was attended by all street co-ordinators, a home beat officer and a crime prevention officer. Co-ordinators' meetings were then held at approximately monthly intervals throughout the year. Meetings later in the year were sometimes attended by outside speakers who gave presentations to the group after the business of the meeting.

In preparation for the co-ordinators' meetings, the area co-ordinator, with the assistance of the home beat and crime prevention officers, produced a monthly newsletter. The newsletter reported on crimes in the area over the preceding month and any other issues relating to crime in the area that either the co-ordinators or the police wished to draw to the attention of the group. The newsletters were brought to the co-ordinators' meeting and distributed among the street co-ordinators, who later delivered them by hand to participants in their street.

Street signs were erected within 3 months of the launch of these schemes and were positioned on lamp-posts close to the entrance of every street in the area. The Metropolitan Police were willing to erect signs in the two experimental areas as soon as possible to assist the evaluation.

Residents marked the fact that they were members of the scheme by displaying NW window stickers on a ground-floor window or door pane. The area co-ordinator arranged, for the benefit of the research, periodic surveys of the number of stickers displayed. Three months after the launch of the scheme, a survey was conducted by the scheme co-ordinators and found that there were 257 window stickers visible from the street. This figure represented almost half of the eligible households in the area. A second survey conducted one month later showed that the number of window stickers had increased to 343.

One of the most important activities in the life of the NW scheme was the monthly meetings of co-ordinators. It is possible to gain some insight into the way the scheme operated and what it meant to the co-ordinators running it to describe in more detail what happened at these meetings. One approach to providing greater detail of these meetings is to describe what happened at one that I attended as a participant observer. It was felt prudent not to attend these meetings during the early stages of the programme as there was a danger of contaminating the character of the scheme. It was the general policy of the research to play down the fact that the programme was being evaluated and during the early stages of the scheme only the area co-ordinator and a small number of street co-ordinators were aware that the programme was being researched. It was felt that towards the end of the project the character of the scheme had consolidated and my attendance at these meetings would be less disruptive. The meeting attended took place after about nine months had elapsed since the launch date. Detailed notes were taken during the meeting, supplemented by additional notes made immediately afterwards.

The meeting was held at the home of the area co-ordinator in the early evening and street co-ordinators began arriving from 7.30 p.m. Within half an hour 18 street co-ordinators had gathered, plus the area co-ordinator and her husband, the local crime prevention officer and a fireman from London Fire Brigade who was an invited guest speaker. The meeting commenced at 8.15 p.m.

The formal business of the meeting included drawing up plans for a street party in the area to mark the first anniversary of the NW scheme. Details of whether the local police would agree to closing the street to traffic during the party were also considered and police plans for patrolling the area while residents were out of their homes discussed. The meeting considered the role of local children in the NW scheme, including the feasibility of a 'Kids' Watch'. A suggestion was also made to establish a 'safe-house' system in the area for the protection of local children. The issue of whether the local schools should be included more actively in the NW scheme were also debated and some co-ordinators volunteered to visit the headmaster of the local school.

The topic of the meeting then changed to crime and crime prevention issues, and the local crime prevention officer gave an update on the state of crime in the area. He reported that burglaries had fallen during the month before the meeting compared with the previous month. Less encouraging news was reported on the incidence of criminal damage and theft from outside of dwellings. The report included details on the way in which offences were committed. This was followed by advice on ways to prevent similar crimes being committed in the area, which included: securing property left in outbuildings, investigating noises heard at night and reporting them if necessary and marking pedal cycles. Questions from the audience concerned whether specific crimes in the area had been detected; whether burglars returned to a dwelling if they were unsuccessful on a first attempt; and whether internal doors should be locked.

The meeting concluded with the presentation by the local fireman, who gave his impressions of a day in the life of a London Fire Brigade officer. This was followed by questions concerning possible conflict of interest between fire brigade and crime prevention officers over such matters as street gates and vehicular access to residential areas. The date for the next meeting was set and the meeting drew to a close at 9.50 p.m.

Further insights into the nature and functioning of co-ordinators' meetings can be found in the minutes of the meetings. The structure of the minutes and of the meetings followed a regular format. The first issue covered in the minutes was the monthly report of the area co-ordinator. The special position of the area co-ordinator in the running of the scheme was highlighted in these reports, which showed her to be an important link in the chain of information from the police to the street co-ordinators and to the rest of the residents in the area. The area co-ordinator also was often the person to follow up suggestions made during earlier meetings and to report back progress. The kinds of issue discussed in the area co-ordinator's report included details of crimes in the area of special interest or relevance to the group (crime trends in general were discussed by the home beat or crime prevention officer), the management of street co-ordinators (ensuring a constant number) the management of the NW programme (such as developments relating to the availability of window stickers and street signs), issues relating to the production and publication of the local newsletter and suggestions for initiatives relating to the general quality of life in the area (e.g. the proposed 'Kids' Watch' and 'Safe House' schemes).

The next issue covered by the minutes was usually the monthly crime report of the home beat or crime prevention officer. This often included a summary of the number of burglaries and vehicle crimes reported to the police from residents in the area and in the adjacent areas over the preceding months. Additional information was often supplied on the time of the offence, the street and often the way in which the offence was committed. This was usually followed by one or two suggestions about ways to improve crime prevention efforts in the area.

The remainder of the minutes were usually reports of individual initiatives and actions taken to improve the functioning of the scheme or to improve the quality of life in the area in general. Such topics included plans for local children to attend lectures on ways to avoid unwanted approaches from strangers; how to obtain crime prevention advice; suggestions about locksmiths who might offer their services at a discount to NW members; the organization of a Christmas drinks party for co-ordinators and the police; developments on the 'Kids' Watch' and 'Safe House' schemes; and plans relating to the anniversary street party.

Another source of information about the workings of the scheme is the newsletters (and additional 'news flashes' produced between newsletters when necessary) which were produced monthly by the area co-ordinator and the local police in collaboration and distributed to all members of the scheme by the street co-ordinators. The newsletters usually covered two sides of A4-size paper, single spaced and produced using a stencil duplicator by the local police. The bulk of the newsletters presented details, of crimes in the area over the preceding month and often taking the form of presenting dates, street names, times, method of entry and goods or cash lost. This was normally followed by advice on what might be done to avoid repetitions of the offences and general crime prevention advice. Details on suspicious behaviour in the area were also reported including reports of bogus electricity men and suspicious tradesmen. Other changes in the area were reported which affected the quality of life such as the replacement of broken street lights by the local authority.

The Wimbledon NW scheme

The NW scheme in Wimbledon was launched on 1 July 1985, in a church hall, in the evening, within the NW area. It was attended by a home beat officer, a crime prevention officer, a police NW co-ordinator, a civilian area co-ordinator, a number of street co-ordinators who had already volunteered, a superintendent and about 100 local residents. The programme was public initiated, as was the Acton scheme, by the potential area co-ordinator and a small number of potential street co-ordinators who approached the local police with a request that a NW scheme be implemented in their area.

The meeting was opened at 8.00 p.m. by the superintendent who gave an introductory talk in which he pointed out that crime was rising in the area and that NW was an effective means of halting this trend. This was followed by a presentation by the crime prevention officer who spoke for over an hour on a wide range of issues relating to crime and crime prevention. The audience was then invited to ask questions which included: what should residents do when leaving their homes to go on holiday?; should inner doors be locked? are schools involved in NW?; how quickly is NW spreading throughout the division?; and would there be a replacement for the home beat officer when the usual officer was off-duty? The superintended concluded the meeting at 9.30 p.m. with another short speech. Attempts were made to recruit members of the audience as street co-ordinators when they left the hall.

The first co-ordinators' meeting was held on 9 October 1985, almost three months after the launch meeting, at the home of the area co-ordinator. The meeting was attended by the home beat officer, the area co-ordinator and a number of street co-ordinators. It was agreed at this first meeting that co-ordinators' meetings should be held at three-monthly intervals rather than monthly. In fact only three meetings were held during the course of the first year.

The area co-ordinator and the home beat officer were less active than their counterparts in Acton in the production of newsletters. It was intended that there should be one newsletter accompanying each co-ordinators' meeting. During the first, year of the scheme two newsletters were produced. The format of the newsletters was similar to the format of the Acton scheme newsletter, whereby the home beat officer provided details of crimes in the area and produced the newsletters after discussions with the area co-ordinator. The contents of the newsletters included: trends in crime in the area; successful arrests made; the importance of displaying NW window stickers; and advice on property marking.

The procedure for erecting street signs in the area was also fairly similar to that used in Acton. The Metropolitan Police were willing to erect the signs in the area as soon as possible to assist the evaluation. Street signs in the Wimbledon scheme area were set up within about three months of the launch of the programme and positioned at a convenient point at the entrance of every street leading into the watch area.

Surveys of the number of window stickers on display were conducted periodically by the home beat officer for the benefit of the research. The first survey was conducted 2 months following the launch of the scheme and revealed 124 window stickers visible from the front of the dwellings (those displayed at the rear were excluded from the survey), representing about one-fifth of eligible households in the area. A second survey conducted towards the end of the first year of the scheme revealed 184 homes displaying window stickers, representing about one-third of eligible households.

Information about the contents of the co-ordinators' meetings was collected by attending one of the meetings as an observer and by obtaining copies of the minutes. The meeting attended in Wimbledon was held at the home of the area co-ordinator. It was also attended by 3 street co-ordinators, the home beat officer and the area co-ordinator and her husband. The meeting commenced at 7.40 p.m. and was opened by the home beat officer, who began by discussing suspicious behaviour and the need for residents to report it to the police. He then presented details of crimes committed in the area since the last meeting. It was noted that vehicle crime had not reduced noticeably, and he hoped that the newsletter would warn residents that this crime was still frequently occurring in the area. He advised co-ordinators on the benefits of property marking and suggested that residents should be told to contact him if they needed help on this topic. He then asked for questions: the street co-ordinators were interested in finding out whether other areas had more burglary and vehicle crime than the scheme area; questions were also put to the home beat officer on what he knew about the type of offenders operating in the area; and the area co-ordinator asked if anything could be done about the telephone system to the local police station and reported that it regularly took 5 minutes to be connected, which she felt might deter residents from reporting suspicious incidents to the police. The home beat officer offered to look into all of the issues raised.

The discussion then moved away from crime reports to other issues which affected the area. It was suggested that a video should be made available for local children on the topic of resisting approaches from strangers, and interest was shown in obtaining educational material which might make the children and the residents of the area feel safer. Complaints were made about the problems of on-street parking as a result of the area being used by commercial vehicles. Complaints were also made about the condition and general appearance of non-residential buildings in the area and whether anything could be done to improve this. The meeting was concluded at 8.50 p.m. and the latest issue of the newsletter was distributed to the street co-ordinators to deliver to residents and to the remaining street co-ordinators not attending the meeting.

The minutes of the two meetings held during the first year (which I did not attend) suggested a similar format. An important element was the report by the police representative on crime in the area since the last meeting, which was typically followed by advice on ways to prevent such crimes continuing. The meetings also included discussions on specific issues which affected the general quality of life in the area. The problem of the use of on-street parking by commercial vehicles was mentioned at every meeting and the encroachment of building and other machinery on to pavements in the area was also extensively discussed.

The newsletters produced by the home beat officer and the area co-ordinator were also similar, in that most of the contents concerned reports of crimes committed in the area and suggestions about ways in which this might be prevented in the future. This was followed by general crime prevention advice including the use of NW window stickers and the benefits of property marking.

Similarities and differences

The preceding sections have aimed to present the evidence relating to the two NW programmes as objectively as possible. At this point, it might be helpful to comment on the two schemes a little more subjectively.

The first observation is that the area co-ordinator clearly played a key role in the design and management of both schemes. This was particularly noticeable in Acton in which the area co-ordinator provided almost the sole channel of information from the police to the other co-ordinators and to the residents. The area co-ordinator also held an important role as collaborator and joint editor of the newsletter and its contents. In itself, there is nothing wrong with the area co-ordinator playing an indispensable role in the management of the scheme. However, there is a danger that the scheme might become too dependent on this one person which might jeopardize the future stability of the scheme.

The second issue worth raising is that the business of NW in the two areas focused tightly on the area co-ordinator and the street co-ordinators. The regular meetings in the area were for the benefit of the co-ordinators alone and other residents were not invited. Consequently, other residents had little impact on the design or management of the scheme, and apart from looking out for anything suspicious and displaying a window sticker, played no other part.

The third point concerns the contents of the co-ordinators' meetings. What happens in these meetings has not been widely reported, and it is generally unknown what issues are discussed. One view is that the business of these meetings is dominantly crime-oriented and the extreme version of this view is that the focus on crime is excessive, generating or exacerbating fear of crime. Another view is that once the meetings become established, issues relating to crime tend to recede in importance and give way to discussions about more general problems facing residents in the area. A more extreme version of this view is that the meetings become no more than a means of diversion and entertainment for the participants.

It seems clear from the accounts presented above that none of these positions is wholly accurate. Crime and crime issues were discussed in both areas throughout the first year and were generally well balanced. Discussion about crime did not become unnecessarily morbid or excessive and there was little evidence that the police attempted to encourage crime awareness as a means of maintaining support for the schemes. (There was some evidence of moderate attempts by the police to heighten awareness of crime during the launch meeting as a way of motivating support for the programme.) These discussion were matched fairly equally with broader debate about the general well-being of the community. To some degree, the meetings in both scheme areas performed a social and entertainments function. But this was not the dominant purpose of the group and did not interfere with the normal business of the meeting.

The fourth observation is that the Acton NW scheme was, in many ways, a fuller and more comprehensive programme than the Wimbledon scheme. This fact was reflected in the number of co-ordinators' meetings held, the number of newsletters produced, the number of additional activities carried out by the group and the number of window stickers displayed in each area. Other differences between the two schemes in levels of participation will be discussed in more detail in the next section.

The participants

The nature of the experimental programmes can also be observed by examining participation rates among the local residents and the activities of participants. Various measures of participation are shown in Table 6.1.

Almost all of the residents interviewed were aware that a NW scheme had been in operation in their area over the previous year (element 1). About half of respondents in both Acton and Wimbledon were able to estimate accurately, to the nearest month, how long the scheme had been running. There is strong evidence therefore that programme awareness was high and the message that some kind of treatment had been implemented had reached the target population.

Few residents actually attended the launch meeting (element 2). It would appear therefore that direct attendance at the launch meeting was not an important means of spreading knowledge about the existence of the scheme. A much higher proportion of householders received at least one copy of the NW newsletter (element 3). About two-thirds of residents in Acton and one-fifth of residents in Wimbledon knew their street co-ordinator, either by name or by sight (element 4). The proportion of respondents who knew their

*Table 6.1   Involvement of residents in the programme elements
in the two experimental areas (percentages)*

Element	Acton experimental area			Wimbledon experimental area		
	Yes	No*	Total (n = 400)	Yes	No	Total (n = 309)
1 Know NW in area†	95	5	100	90	10	100
2 Attended launch	13	77	100	17	73	100
3 Received newsletter	89	11	100	46	54	100
4 Knew co-ordinators	61	39	100	21	79	100
5 Knew beat officer	28	72	100	15	85	100
6 Participant	62	38	100	44	56	100
7 Displayed NW sticker	64	36	100	40	60	100
8 Displayed PM sticker	8	92	100	24	76	100
9 Home security survey	5	95	100	3	97	100
10 Looked out	47	53	100	40	60	100

* The category 'No' includes 'don't know' and 'missing' responses.
† The meaning of the element labels is described in the text.

local home beat officer, either by name or by sight was generally lower (28 and 15 per cent in Acton and Wimbledon respectively), and only 22 and 6 per cent of respondents in Acton and Wimbledon respectively said that could recall the name of their home beat officer (element 5).

More encouraging results could be found in the proportion of residents who defined themselves as 'participants' (element 6). Respondents were asked whether they would say that they were a member of, or participant in, the local NW scheme. Sixty-two per cent of respondents in Acton, and 44 per cent in Wimbledon, defined themselves as programme participants. About the same proportion of residents in both areas said that they had displayed a NW window sticker during the previous 12 months (element 7). The difference in the proportion of respondents in Acton displaying a NW sticker and defining themselves as a participant is probably due to a small number of residents switching from being participants to non-participants during the year.

Respondents who considered themselves members of, or participants in, the NW programme were asked why they joined. The reasons given are summarized in Table 6.2. The question was open-ended and the response categories were created by data coders employed by the market research company. The first three reasons in rank order of importance were the same

Table 6.2   *Reasons given for joining the NW scheme (open-ended)*
             (percentages)

	Acton experimental area (n = 191)*	Wimbledon experimental area (n = 174)
Good idea	30	28
Protection–self	14	11
Protection–all	17	17
Prevent crime	24	31
Mutual help	20	20
Family joined	6	2
Other	5	5

*Respondents sometimes gave no reason or more than one reason.

for both areas. The most frequent reason given for joining the NW scheme was that it was a good (or excellent) idea, without further elaboration. The second reason in order of frequency of citation was that NW would prevent crime, and the third was that NW enabled members of the community to help one another.

Respondents who claimed that they were not participants in the scheme were asked to give their reasons for not joining. Their responses are shown in Table 6.3; again, the question was open-ended, allowing the respondent

Table 6.3   *Reasons given for not joining the NW scheme*
             (open-ended) (percentages)

	Acton experimental area (n = 118)*	Wimbledon experimental area (n = 226)
No time	16	10
Missed launch	3	11
No encouragement	6	16
Not at home much	18	7
Old/disabled	10	5
Not aware of NW	3	15
Not interested	11	7
Other	6	7

*Respondents sometimes gave no reason or more than one reason.

to say what they wanted. The major categories formed were not the same in the two area. The three main reasons for not joining in Acton were 'not at home', 'no time' and 'not interested'. The three main reasons given in Wimbledon were 'no encouragement', 'not aware' and 'missed launch'.

The three main elements of the comprehensive NW package as defined by the Metropolitan Police are (1) NW, whereby the public look out for suspicious incidents and report them to the police; (2) property marking; and (3) home security surveys. Just under half of respondents in Acton, and a slightly smaller percentage in Wimbledon, said that they had deliberately looked out for anything suspicious in their area during the preceding 12 months (element 10). Only 20 per cent of respondents in Acton, and 5 per cent in Wimbledon, said that they deliberately looked out for anything suspicious because of the existence of the NW scheme. Most of the residents noting that they looked out said that they would have done so anyway, whether or not the NW scheme had been in operation.

The main purpose of the drive by the Metropolitan Police to encourage residents to look out for anything suspicious is that they report what they see to the police. How successful were residents in seeing anything suspicious, and how successful were they in reporting these incidents to the police? A total of 146 interviewees in Acton, and 159 in Wimbledon, mentioned that they had deliberately looked out for anything suspicious in the preceding 12 months. Seventy (48 per cent) of these in Acton, and 72 (45 per cent) in Wimbledon, said that they had seen something suspicious. Respondents who had seen something suspicious were then asked whether they had reported it to anyone. A total of 37 residents (25 per cent) in Acton and 24 (15 per cent) in Wimbledon claimed that they reported the incident. When asked about whom they had they reported the incident to, 27 (18 per cent) in Acton, and 18 (11 per cent) in Wimbledon, said that they had reported it to the police; the remainder said that they had reported it to the area or street co-ordinator, to a neighbour or to someone else.

These findings show a considerable attrition in the process of reporting suspicious incidents to the police. In total, only 9 per cent of respondents in Acton, and 5 per cent in Wimbledon said that they reported anything suspicious to the police during the course of the previous year.

The second and third element of the comprehensive NW package comprised property marking and home security surveys. Eight per cent of residents in Acton, and 24 per cent in Wimbledon, said that they had displayed a property marking sticker in their windows during the last 12 months (element 8). The higher rate in Wimbledon was due to the particular interests of the local home beat officer and the efforts he had put in before the launch of the scheme in encouraging residents to mark their property. About half of the residents who said that they had marked their property said that they did so because of the existence of the NW scheme, and the other half stated that they would have done so anyway. Only 5 per cent of respondents in Acton, and 3 per cent in Wimbledon, reported that they had a security survey in the preceding 12 months (element 9).

The findings presented above concern the nature and level of activity both of participants and non-participants. It would be expected that levels of NW-related activity would be lower among non-participants than participants, and that this would reduce the overall level of involvement for residents in the area as a whole. It is relevant therefore to describe separately the nature and level of activity among participants and non-participants. Involvement in each of the NW elements by participants and non-participants is shown in Figure 6.1.

The figure shows a greater proportion of participants than non-participants involved in each programme element. While most of the differences are self-evident, it might be helpful to highlight some of the variations. Overall, few residents attended the launch meeting, although in Wimbledon more than one-third of participants attended the opening public meeting. Almost all households interviewed in Acton reported receiving a copy of the NW scheme newsletter. The newsletter was less well circulated in Wimbledon. About three quarters of participants in Acton knew their street co-ordinator by name or by sight. About one-third of participants in Acton said that they knew their home beat officer by name or by sight, compared to one-fifth in Wimbledon. Over 80 per cent of participants in both areas reported displaying a NW window sticker, and almost half of participants in Wimbledon reported displaying a PM window sticker. Over half of participants in both areas reported looking out for suspicious incidents over the preceding year.

The bar charts in Figure 6.1 give a more optimistic impression of the nature and level of the programmes in the two areas, showing higher levels of involvement in the schemes among participants. It has been argued throughout this section that levels of participation and involvement were not as high as might have been expected. Comparing the activities of participants and non-participants provides a more favourable impression of the activities of the programmes. There remains the problem of low levels of implementation of property marking and home security surveys which comprised two-thirds of the total NW package. The programmes were not as comprehensive or as embracing therefore as might have been expected from two potentially promising NW areas. Nevertheless, the programmes touched, in some way, a large proportion of households in the area, and it can be argued that some kind of treatment programme had been implemented in these two area and that this is capable of being evaluated.

The final section of this chapter examines the question of who participates in NW. A breakdown of participation by 12 individual and social independent variables is provided in the Appendix. The age category containing the highest proportion of participants was 41–50 years, comprising 80 per cent participants in Acton and 59 per cent in Wimbledon (compared with 62 and 44 per cent respectively for the samples as a whole). Both the very young and

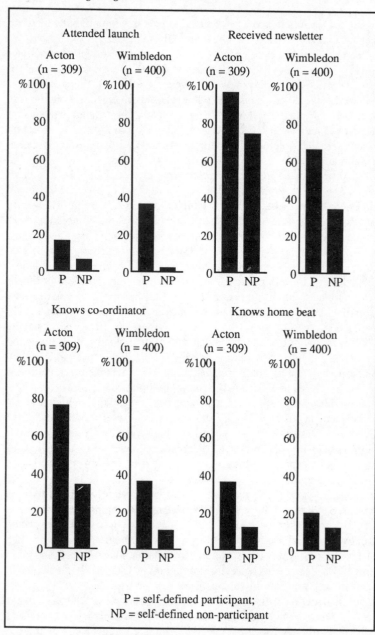

*Figure 6.1   Percentage of participants and non-participants (self-
            defined) involved in selected element of the NW
            programmes*

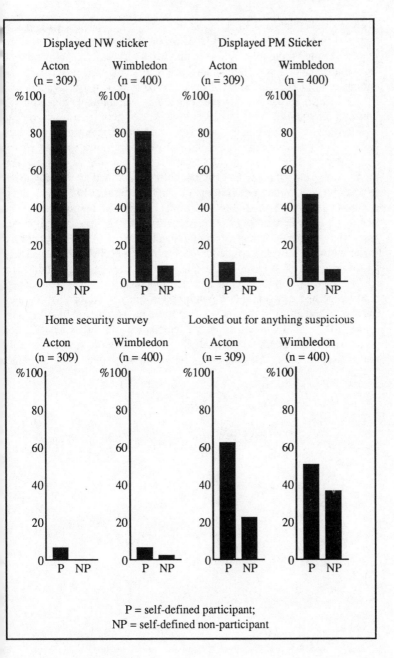

Figure 6.1 (continued)

the very old were less likely than the middle-age groups to consider themselves as participants. A higher proportion of females than males reported being a member of the programme in both areas. Respondents who were married were more likely than those who were single or separated, or widowed or divorced, to be participants. The majority of married respondents in both areas reported that they had joined the programme. People living in houses were more likely than those living in flats, maisonettes or rooms to say that they were members. Owner-occupiers more frequently reported participating in the scheme than renters. There was no consensus in terms of skin colour and participation. More whites than non-whites in Acton and more non-whites than whites in Wimbledon claimed to be members. Households containing one or more children were more likely than those containing no children to be participants. Employed respondents more frequently reported that they were members of the scheme than unemployed respondents, and households with high incomes more frequently recorded participating in the programme than households with low incomes. There was no consensus in terms of the relationship between participation and socio-economic status. In Acton more non-manual than manual respondents reported being members, and in Wimbledon more manual than non-manual residents claimed to be members. There was no association in either area between the age at which respondents completed full-time education and participation. Households containing more than one adult were more likely than those containing a single adult to report being members of the scheme.

7 The Results: Victimizations

Introduction

The primary aim of NW in London is to reduce crime. This chapter presents the findings of the evaluation on the impact of two NW programme on crime in their areas. The chapter is divided into two main sections: the first examines the impact of the programmes using police crime reports,and the second investigates their effect using crime surveys of reported victimizations

Police recorded crimes have been included in the analysis because, despite their weaknesses, they provide an alternative data source which can be compared to the results obtained from the crime surveys. They also provide additional data on crimes committed in the experimental areas for a number of years before the pre-test surveys.

Police-recorded crime

Comparison with survey crimes

Police crime reports and reported victimizations obtained from crime surveys measure different things. Police crime reports are collected on a subdivisional basis and include crimes committed within the subdivision against victims who live in the subdivision and elsewhere. Crime surveys collect data on an area basis and include crimes committed within the area and elsewhere against victims who live in the area.

The crimes reported in the analysis which derive from the crime surveys have been adjusted to include only offences against victims living in the NW areas who were victimized in those areas (victimizations elsewhere have been excluded). Crimes reported in the analysis which derive from police crime reports have not been adjusted and include offences against victims living in the area and elsewhere who were victimized in the area.

In the case of offences such as burglary where the place of the offence and the place of residence of the victim are the same, the difference is not problematic. In the case of offences such as theft from or of a vehicle where it is possible that the owner lives outside of area, the difference should be borne in mind when comparing results.

Classifying offences

The coding frame for police-recorded offences was the same as that used for victim-reported crimes in the crime survey. Usually the offences were coded directly from the crime reports as defined by the police. Offences classified as 'attempted' have been included in the following tables along with the completed offences. Offences classified by the police as 'no crime' have been excluded from the analysis. In order to make the crime report data as comparable as possible with the survey data, police recorded offences which do not fall within the survey offence categories have been excluded from the analysis. Typical offences excluded were: driving while disqualified; handling stolen goods; indecent exposure; unlawful sexual intercourse; possession of offensive weapons; non- residential burglary; and non-residential theft.

Trends in police-recorded crime
The total number of police-recorded crimes falling in the pre-test and post-test periods in the two experimental areas is shown in Table 7.1. The offences included represent the most frequent crimes committed in residential areas and those crimes that NW is most likely to be effective in reducing. Few offences fell outside the survey's coverage (an average of 4 offences per period per area). Offences against the person (assault, theft from the person, robbery, sex offences and threats) have been collapsed into the single category of 'personal offences'.

The total number of police-recorded crimes in the Acton NW area increased by 40 per cent from the pre-test to the post-test period. The greatest percentage increase was in the offence of criminal damage. The greatest increase in numbers of offences resulted from increases in vehicle crime.

Table 7.1   *Police-recorded crime: Acton and Wimbledon experimental areas* (July 1984-June 1986)

	Acton experimental area			Wimbledon experimental area		
	pre	post	%change*	pre	post	%change*
Property offences						
TOMV†	7	14	+100	13	16	+23
TFMV§	11	15	+36	23	19	-17
Bicycle theft	0	1	na	4	0	na
Burglary	25	23	-8	23	15	-35
Theft from dwelling	4	9	na	6	3	na
Criminal damage	7	16	+129	7	13	+86
Person offences	3	2	na	5	1	na
All offences	57	80	+40	81	67	-17

*Pre-test = July 1984-June 1985; post-test = July 1985-June 1986
†TOMV = theft of motor vehicle
§TFMV = theft from motor vehicle
na = not applicable when either value is below 5

Theft from a motor vehicle increased by one-third, and theft of a motor vehicle doubled. Small reductions occurred in the number of burglaries and in offences against the person. There is little immediate evidence from police-recorded crimes therefore that the NW scheme had a noticeable impact on crime. The small reductions in burglary (from 25 to 23 offences) and offences against the person (from 3 to 2 offences) are unlikely to be the product of a programme effect.

Changes in police-recorded crime in the Wimbledon experimental area present a more favourable picture. The total number of crimes recorded in the area fell by 17 per cent from the pre-test to post-test periods. This decrease was largely the result of a fall in the number of recorded burglaries and thefts from motor vehicles. Over the same period, thefts of motor vehicles and criminal damage both increased. The reduction in the offence of burglary is the most encouraging finding from this table. It is marred, however, by the small numbers involved (a reduction of just 8 offences from the pre-test to post-test period) and by increases in other offences. Overall, the figures shown in Table 7.1 do not convey the message that since the implementation of NW there has been a clear and substantial reduction in crime.

One reason for failing to be impressed by these figures is that it is to be expected that the rates of specific crimes will fluctuate by a small amount from year- to- year. The tables show no evidence that any substantial impact has been made on these normal annual fluctuations. An examination of police-recorded crime rates over a longer period tends to support the conclusion that the measured changes represent no more than normal year-to-year fluctuations. Figures 7.1 and 7.2 present the movements in the form of a line graph of the total number of police-recorded crimes for the two experimental areas in the years 1983 to 1986.

Movements in crime in the Acton experimental area show that the number of recorded offences follows a cycle of peaks and troughs. By the middle of the pre-test period (January 1985), the number of offences had reached a deep trough. From the beginning of 1985 to the launch date in June and onwards to the end of 1985, the total number of police-recorded crimes increased sharply. There was no evidence of a halt in this trend until the average monthly rate had reached its normal peak. From the middle of the post-test period the monthly crime rate began to fall. Such a move was in keeping with normal cyclical patterns and the upturn towards the end of the experimental period suggests that the downward trend might be temporary.

The pattern of recorded crime in Wimbledon also failed to show evidence of a change in normal fluctuations following the launch of the NW scheme. During the months immediately after the launch the crime rate gradually fell. An examination of the movements in monthly crime rates during the pre-test period suggests, however, that such a fall was part of normal fluctuations. Monthly crime rates had peaked around the middle of the pre-test period and

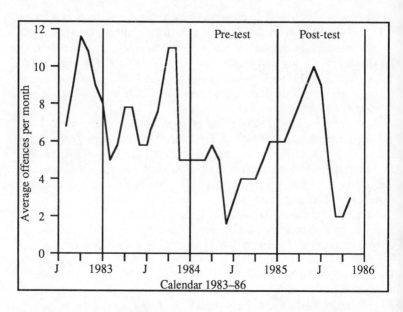

Figure 7.1   Acton experimental area police recorded crime (3-month moving average)

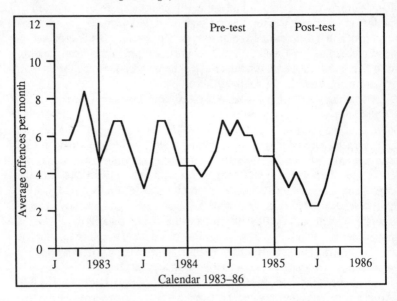

Figure 7.2   Wimbledon experimental area police recorded crime (3-month moving average)

slowly declined over the second half of this period. The decline continued throughout the launch and continued until the middle of the post-test period. From the middle to the end of the post-test period crime rates rose steadily to a normal peak value.

It is difficult to be convinced by the possible argument that the reduction in the first half of the post-test period was the result of the NW scheme. Why did the scheme fail to halt the increase in crime in the second half of the post-test period? Why should it be more effective at its birth and during the period before the maximum number of window stickers had been displayed, and before the NW street signs had been erected than in the period after?

The impression that police-recorded crime shows little evidence of success is further strengthened by an examination of crime rates in the displacement and control areas. Evidence of a NW success in terms of crime reduction cannot be based alone on evidence of changes in crime rates in the experimental areas. Instead a comparison must be made between changes in the experimental areas with changes in comparable areas without NW schemes in operation. The main comparison that must be made to determine a programme effect is between the experimental and the control area.

The displacement area cannot be used as a pure control area because there is a probability that patterns of crime in the displacement area will be

Table 7.2　　*Police-recorded crime:Wimbledon displacement and Redbridge control areas (July 1984-June 1986)*

	Wimbledon displacement area			Redbridge control area		
	pre	post	%change*	pre	post	%change*
Property offences						
TOMV†	10	14	+40	33	24	-27
TFMV§	14	12	-14	17	8	-53
Bicycle theft	1	3	na	1	2	na
Burglary	25	20	-20	12	8	-33
Theft from dwelling	8	5	-38	3	0	na
Criminal damage	11	12	+9	6	3	na
Person offences	5	1	na	4	1	na
All offences	74	67	-9	76	46	-39

*Pre-test = July 1984-June 1985; post-test = July 1985-June 1986
†TOMV = theft of motor vehicle
§TFMV = theft from motor vehicle
na = not applicable when either value is below 5

affected by patterns of crime in the experimental area to which it is adjacent. The contamination effect of the experimental area on the displacement area will occur only if NW is effective. If there is no reduction in crime in the experimental area, there should be no displacement of crime to the adjacent area. Under such conditions the crime rate in the displacement area would be independent of the crime rate in the experimental area, and movements of crime in the displacement area might be used as contributory evidence in determining whether NW resulted in a crime reduction effect. The crime rates for the displacement and control areas are shown in Table 7 2.

If the NW scheme had the effect of reducing crime, it would be expected that the displacement area either would show an increase in crime (NW was effective but displaced crimes to the adjacent areas) or follow normal crime trends (NW was effective and did not displace crime to the adjacent areas). The table shows that crime in the displacement area decreased from the pre-test to the post-test by 9 per cent. This was largely the result of reductions in theft from motor vehicles, burglary, household theft and offences against the person. Theft of motor vehicles and criminal damage both increased slightly over the same period. The absence of an increase in crime in the displacement area could be the result of NW working and not displacing crime, or NW not working and not displacing crime.

In order to register a NW success in terms of crime reduction, it would have to be shown that crimes reduced more in the experimental areas than in the control area. The control area was the Redbridge site. The table shows that the total number of recorded offences fell in the control area by 39 per cent from the pre-test to the post-test period. With the exception of bicycle theft, every offence category showed a reduction over the experimental period. The reductions in crime were considerably greater than occurred in the Metropolitan Police District as a whole over the same period. It would not be expected that crime rates in selected and matched areas would be the same as in London as a whole. Nevertheless, such a substantial reduction in an area which implemented no crime prevention programme over the experimental year is hard to explain.

It might be helpful in explaining the changes in crime rates in the displacement and control area over the experimental period to look at the line graphs of monthly crime rates over a longer period of time (Figures 7.3 and 7.4).

The line graphs of crime in the displacement area show that the crime trend (ignoring seasonal cycles) is roughly flat over the pre-test and post-test periods. There is no evidence of a sustained increase in crime following the launch of the scheme in the experimental area. Similarly, there is no sign from the line graphs that the normal monthly cycles have been disrupted by the implementation of the NW scheme in the adjacent area.

The line graphs show that the pattern of crime in the Redbridge control area appears to move regularly over the period prior to the launch date of the

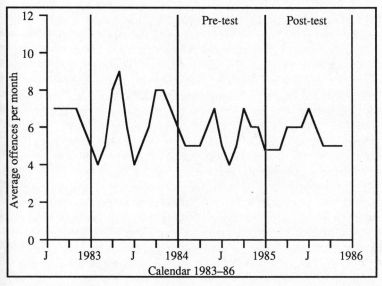

Figure 7.3   Wimbledon displacement area police- recorded crime (3-month moving average)

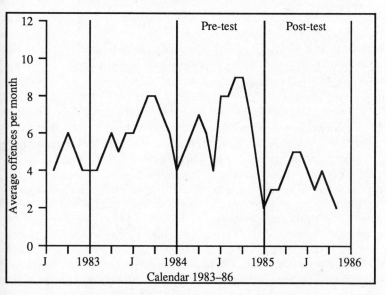

Figure 7.4   Redbridge control area police- recorded crime (3-month moving average)

NW schemes in Acton and Wimbledon but changes noticeably in the experimental year. The annual cycle of peaks and troughs were all lower in the post-test period than in previous years. The reduction in the post-test period might be the result of general reductions in crime for London as a whole over this period (which was not, however, the case); it might be the result of general reductions in crime for areas of a similar social, demographic and crime structure as the Wimbledon experimental area and its Redbridge control site (fairly unlikely); or it might be the result of changes in crime-generating factors peculiar to that area (the most likely explanation). The reduction in crime rates in the post-test period appears to be untypical and reflective of a change in the area.

It is obviously more difficult for the experimental area to compare favourably with a control area, which itself has undergone a period of crime reduction. Nevertheless, the control area indicates that there was no increase in crime in an area of similar composition to the Wimbledon and Acton experimental sites. Therefore, the increase in crime in Acton and the small decrease in crime in Wimbledon must be measured not against an increasing rate in similar areas (as indicated by both the control and the displacement areas), but against a static or possibly falling rate. Such a comparison does not provide favourable or convincing evidence of an NW success in terms of crime reduction.

Crime detection

The detection of crime is not presented in the policy literature as a primary aim of NW. It is understood, however, that the effort to encourage residents to look out for and to report suspicious incidents to the police might result in a greater number of arrests.

It was not possible in the time available to collect details on offences cleared-up which were committed in the experimental area. It was possible to obtain data on the clear-up rates for the subdivisions as a whole for the pre-test and post-test periods. NW schemes were being launched in the subdivisions of both experimental areas at a regular rate. Consequently, the proportion of residents living in a NW scheme within the subdivisions was increasing over time. It would be expected therefore that if NW improved clear-up rates, this would be reflected in the clear-up rates for the subdivision as a whole. The possibility of some countervailing influence simultaneously reducing clear-up rates by as much or more than NW was increasing them seemed unlikely over the relatively short period of the research. The clear-up rates for a package of four offence types over the pre-test and post-test period is shown in Table 7.3.

The clear-up rates for all four offences either remained stable or decreased from the pre-test to the post-test periods in both areas. There is no indication from this table that the spread of NW schemes in the experimental subdivisions led to an improvement in the rates of detection for the offences investigated.

Table 7.3   *Clear-up rates of four selected offences in the Acton and Wimbledon subdivisions (percentages)*

	Acton experimental area		Wimbledon experimental area	
	pre	post*	pre*	post*
TOMV†[2]	5.8	5.8	9.0	8.0
TFMV§ [3]	4.1	3.7	7.8	4.3
Burglary	7.1	4.4	11.1	6.3
Criminal damage	10.4	8.0	6.9	5.6
Total all offences	7.1	5.7	8.3	5.7

*Pre = July 1984-June 1985; post = July 1985–June 1986
†TOMV = theft of motor vehicle (includes unauthorized taking)
§TFMV = theft from motor vehicle

Source: Table compiled from data provided by Metropolitan Police Statistics Branch

Survey-reported crime
The analysis of police-recorded crimes was included to provide comparative evidence on the impact of NW of crime and to provide additional information on movements in crime in the areas not covered by the crime surveys. Police-recorded crime data is not wholly suited to assessing programme impact because of possible variations in public reporting and police recording practices over the experimental period. This problem is especially poignant when the programme being investigated is specifically designed to influence public reporting practices. The main research findings on the impact of NW on crime derive, therefore, from the results of the crime surveys. The following analysis of the crime survey data is divided into two main sections: the first section presents the findings in the form of bivariate analyses, and the second section presents the findings using multivariate analyses.

Bivariate analysis involves presenting the findings in their summary form as simple cross-tabulations. This form of analysis has the advantage that the data can be presented simply and descriptively; it also has the advantage that it can bring the reader closer to the data, revealing its general nature and any provisional trends. However, it has the disadvantage that it cannot be used adequately to test the effectiveness of the programme. Changes from the pre-test to the post-test surveys in crime rates could be the result of differences between pre-test and post-test samples. Some people or households are more prone to victimization than others. A change in the proportion of high to low-risk respondents in the pre-test and post-test samples could independently affect the number of victimizations reported.

Multivariate analysis has the advantage that differences between pre-test and post-test can be simultaneously controlled. It has the disadvantage that the reader is more detached from the data and is dependent on statistical tests and on the interpretations of the researcher to assess the results of the research. The clearest picture can be presented by using both kinds of analysis.

Bivariate analysis
Offences included   The main questionnaire contained screening questions relating to 18 types of offence. The offences identified by the screening questions, with the exception of theft of milk bottles from outside the dwelling, were recorded in detail on the victim forms and coded by trained data processors in accordance with Home Office counting rules. The full list of the 56 offence types used in the initial coding is given in the Appendix. Seven of these offences were excluded from the analysis because they fell outside the survey's coverage (19,39,49,59,69,89 and 99) and a further 4 offences were excluded because they were ambiguous (48,54,68 and 87). The final list of 45 offence types and the major offence groupings used in the analysis are presented in Table 7.4.

Survey-reported crime   The aim of this first section of results is to assess whether the NW programmes had any impact on crime. There are a number of ways in which levels of crime can be expressed. An important distinction often made in analyses of survey-reported crime is between the 'prevalence' and 'incidence' of victimization. The prevalence of victimization is the proportion of all residents or households in a specified area who experience at least one victimization over a specified period. The primary use of the measure is to determine the proportion of the population touched by crime. The incidence of victimization is the total number of crimes reported or recorded expressed as a number or as a rate (e.g. number of offences per 100,000 households per year). The primary purpose of expressing victimizations as a rate is to provide a measure of total offences committed, including multiple victimizations.

The following analysis is based on a division of all crimes into household crimes (e.g. burglary, theft from the home, damage to the home and theft of or from a vehicle) and crimes against the person (e.g. assault, robbery and sexual attack). As the total number of crimes against the household considerably exceeds the number of crimes committed against the person, the impact of NW on crime is assessed largely by its measured impact on household crime.

Table 7.4 Classification of offences used in the analysis

Household offences	Code	Description
Theft of motor vehicle	60	Theft of car/van
	62	Theft of motorbike/scooter/moped
Theft from motor vehicle	61	Theft from car/van
	63	Theft from motorbike/scooter/moped
Bicycle theft	64	Theft of pedal cycle
Burglary	50	Attempted burglary to a non-connected garage/outhouse
	51	Burglary dwelling (nothing taken)
	52	Burglary dwelling (something taken)
	53	Attempted burglary dwelling
	57	Burglary from non-connected garage/outhouse (nothing taken)
	58	Burglary from non-connected garage/outhouse (something taken)
Theft dwelling	55	Theft in a dwelling
Other household theft	65	Theft from outside dwelling (excluding theft of milk bottles)
	56	Theft from meter
Criminal damage	80	Arson
	81	Criminal damage to motor vehicle (£20 or under)
	82	Criminal damage to motor vehicle (over £20)
	83	Criminal damage to home (£20 or under)
	84	Criminal damage to home (over £20)
	85	Other criminal damage (£20 or under)
	86	Other criminal damage (over £20)
	88	Attempted criminal damage

(Continued)

Table 7.4 (Continued) Classification of offences used in the analysis

Property Offences	Code	Description
Assault	11	Serious wounding
	12	Other wounding
	13	Common assault
	21	Attempted assault
Theft from person	43	Snatch theft from person
	44	Other theft from person
	45	Attempted theft from person
Robbery	41	Robbery
	42	Attempted robbery
Sexual offences	31	Rape
	32	Serious wounding with a sexual motive
	33	Other wounding with a sexual motive
	34	Attempted rape
	35	Indecent assault
Threats	91	Threats to kill/assault
	92	Sexual threat
	93	Other threats or intimidation
	94	Threats against respondent made to someone else

The prevalence of victimizations (the proportion of households reporting one or more victimizations) in each of the survey areas for the pre-test and post-test periods is shown in Table 7.5. The main findings relate to the last two rows showing the prevalence of all household and all personal victimizations. The table shows that in both NW areas the prevalence of household victimizations increased from the period before the launch to the period after the launch. There is no immediate evidence therefore that the NW areas experienced a decline in the prevalence of household offences over the experimental period. The prevalence of household victimizations increased in the displacement area and decreased in the control area.

The prevalence of reported victimization against the person also increased in both experimental areas. By comparison, the prevalence of crimes against the person decreased in both the displacement and control areas.

Changes in prevalence of particular types of household offences show that the broad trends described above are reflected in most of the offence subcategories. In Acton all household offence types increased from the pre-test to the post-test surveys, and in Wimbledon only burglary declined in

Table 7.5   *Households victimized one or more times in the pre-test and post-test periods in the four survey areas (percentages)*

	Acton experimental area		Wimbledon experimental area		Wimbledon displacement area		Redbridge control area	
	pre	post	pre	post	pre	post	pre	post
n =	306	309	353	400	323	332	306	330
Theft of vehicle	1	2	1	1	1	1	1	1
Theft from vehicle	3	4	3	6	6	5	3	2
Criminal damage to vehicle	4	8	6	10	6	7	4	3
Burglary of dwelling	6	8	5	4	7	6	3	2
Other criminal damage	2	4	2	5	5	7	3	2
All household offences	17	26	20	23	25	29	15	11
All personal offences	1	5	2	2	4	3	1	2

Table 7.6   *Mean offence rate per household in the pre-test and post-test periods in the four survey areas*

	Acton experimental area		Wimbledon experimental area		Wimbledon displacement area		Redbridge control area	
	pre	post	pre	post	per	post	pre	post
n =	306	309	353	400	323	332	306	330
Theft of vehicle	0.01	0.03	0.02	0.01	0.01	0.01	0.01	0.01
Theft from vehicle	0.04	0.05	0.04	0.07	0.07	0.06	0.04	0.02
Criminal damage to vehicle	0.05	0.11	0.08	0.16	0.09	0.10	0.06	0.03
Burglary of dwelling	0.08	0.10	0.06	0.05	0.09	0.07	0.04	0.03
Other criminal damage	0.23	0.05	0.03	0.09	0.11	0.16	0.04	0.03
All household offences	0.23	0.43	0.28	0.43	0.48	0.48	0.22	0.15
All personal offences* [2]	0.03	0.13	0.06	0.08	0.13	0.13	0.04	0.09

*Personal offences have been weighted to standardize the responses and to express personal offences as a rate per household.

prevalence. The small reduction of burglary in Wimbledon of only one percentage point was not statistically significant.

Comparing the prevalence of victimizations between the two periods is helpful in describing the spread of crime across households, but it tells us little about multiple victimizations and the total number of victimizations experienced. Table 7.6 shows the mean offence rates per household for the two survey periods.

In both experimental areas the incidence (the total number of offences reported) of both household and personal victimizations increased from the pre-test to post-test surveys. In the displacement area the rate of both types of offence remained constant, and in the control area the rate went down for household offences and up for offences against the person. Again, these results provide no immediate evidence of a NW success in terms of crime reduction. In fact the changes are directly contrary to what might have been expected as evidence of an NW success.

The signs are no more hopeful in relation to particular types of offence. In Acton the incidence of all offences increased from the pre-test to the post-test periods. In Wimbledon the incidence of all offences increased with the exception of theft of a vehicle and burglary. The reduction in the rate of theft of a vehicle was a result of a decrease of offences from the pre-test to the post-test period. The reduction in the rate of burglary was a result of a decrease of 4 offences from the pre-test to the post-test period. The reduction in the rate of burglary was a result not of an actual decrease in the number of offences, but of a greater number of completed interviews achieved in the post-test survey.

Overall, the tables show increases in prevalence and incidence of victimization in both NW areas during the experimental period. The increase in incidence was partly a result of a greater proportion of households being victimized, and partly a result of an increase in the number of victimizations per household. In other words, there were increases in both single and multiple victimizations.

The percentage of all households victimized more than once increased from the pre-test to the post-test surveys from 28 to 42 per cent of all victimizations in Acton, and from 31 to 49 per cent of all victimizations in Wimbledon. Surprisingly, no increase in multiple victimizations occurred in either the Wimbledon displacement or Redbridge control area. In fact multiple victimizations decreased from 53 to 41 per cent of all victimizations in the Wimbledon displacement area, and from 31 to 26 per cent of all victimizations in Redbridge.

The preliminary findings are not very encouraging. The prevalence and incidence of victimization increased in both experimental areas and (apart from a small increase in incidence in the Wimbledon displacement area) either remained the same or went down in the displacement and control areas. These findings are almost exactly the opposite of what might have been hypothesized by proponents of NW.

Victimization and subgroups It is possible that while the programme might not be effective for the population as a whole, it might be effective for specific subgroups. No attempt was made by either the police or the co-

Table 7.7   *Mean offence rate per household of household offences by selected sub-groups*

	Acton experimental area		Wimbledon experimental area		Wimbledon displacement area		Redbridge control area	
	pre	post	pre	post	per	post	pre	post
n =	306	309	353	400	323	332	306	330
Age of Respondent								
16–20	–	0.40	0.33	0.52	0.78	0.67	0.17	0.20
21–30	0.24	0.45	0.39	0.52	0.56	0.54	0.36	0.23
31–40	0.21	0.63	0.39	0.52	0.55	0.41	0.35	0.13
41–50	0.30	0.47	0.31	0.59	0.63	0.57	0.14	0.13
51–60	0.25	0.36	0.17	0.32	0.29	0.58	0.18	0.14
60+	0.13	0.15	0.08	0.19	0.13	0.34	0.22	0.05
Gender								
male	0.27	0.44	0.38	0.47	0.67	0.60	0.26	0.11
female	0.20	0.42	0.20	0.39	-.32	0.38	0.18	0.18
Race								
white	0.24	0.42	0.29	0.46	0.47	0.53	0.33	0.26
non-white	0.14	0.46	0.21	0.34	0.54	0.31	0.11	0.11
Marital status								
single	0.19	0.42	0.34	0.37	0.49	0.46	0.33	0.26
married	0.23	0.46	0.32	0.50	0.47	0.58	0.21	0.12
S.W.D.	0.30	0.37	0.10	0.35	0.51	0.29	0.10	0.06
Income								
Under £10,000	0.18	0.35	0.21	0.35	0.45	0.42	0.18	0.11
£10,000	0.34	0.57	0.40	0.47	0.56	0.61	0.28	0.14
Socioeconomic group								
non-manual	0.26	0.50	0.27	0.55	0.53	0.52	0.26	0.15
manual	0.19	0.33	0.28	0.33	0.46	0.46	0.19	0.14
Employment status								
in work	0.28	0.48	0.36	0.50	0.54	0.55	0.25	0.19
not in work	0.15	0.33	0.16	0.31	0.38	0.38	0.17	0.07

Table 7.7 (Continued)   Mean offence rate per household of household offences by selected sub-groups

n =	Acton experimental area		Wimbledon experimental area		Wimbledon displacement area		Redbridge control area	
	pre 306	post 309	pre 353	post 400	per 323	post 332	pre 306	post 330
Age completed education								
under 16	0.23	0.40	0.26	0.44	0.48	0.50	0.18	0.13
16+	0.24	0.46	0.29	0.42	0.48	0.45	0.26	0.16
Tenure								
owner	0.28	0.55	0.28	0.46	0.55	0.51	0.23	0.14
renter	0.15	0.25	0.27	0.36	0.38	0.46	0.13	0.16
Dwelling type								
house	0.27	0.49	-0.27	0.45	0.59	0.50	0.22	0.14
flat/rooms	0.21	0.38	0.30	0.39	0.31	0.45	0.09	0.15
Car ownership								
owner	0.29	0.57	0.35	0.59	0.54	0.64	0.26	0.16
non-owner	0.13	0.18	0.15	0.15	0.40	0.27	0.08	0.09
No. of children								
0	0.21	0.38	0.24	0.40	0.40	0.56	0.16	0.12
1	0.35	0.71	0.37	0.70	0.43	0.31	0.37	0.22
2	0.21	0.45	0.42	0.34	0.74	0.32	0.17	0.02
3+	0.33	0.44	0.14	0.41	0.94	0.48	0.36	0.29
No. of Adults								
1	0.19	0.42	0.17	0.23	0.46	0.33	0.11	0.20
2	0.29	0.48	0.29	0.48	0.40	0.59	0.28	0.12
3+	0.21	0.35	0.38	0.56	0.66	0.45	0.17	0.13

ordinators to target specific groups. Nevertheless, NW might have a different impact on different groups for other reasons. In order to test this hypothesis, comparisons were made of each of the demographic and personal variables included in the questionnaires in terms of the mean reported victimization rate for household offences. A similar breakdown in relation to personal victimizations has not been attempted because of the small numbers involved. The results of the comparisons are shown in Table 7.7.

In Acton all subgroups registered an increase in the rate of reported household victimizations from the pre-test to the post-test period. In Wimbledon all subgroups with the exception of two (non-car owners and respondents in households which include two children) registered an increase in the rate of household victimizations. Overall, there is little evidence from the table that specific subgroups experienced a reduction in victimizations rates following the introduction of NW.

Victimization and NW participation   The bivariate analysis has not yet shown any evidence of an NW effect on crime, when investigating NW area samples as a whole or when investigating various sample subgroups. It is still possible, however, that there might be a NW crime effect which is experienced only by participants in the NW scheme. Over the experimental period crime rates might have decreased among participants and increased among non-participants.

As the samples were cross-sectional, rather than panel, it was not possible to compare the victimization rates of participants and non-participants in

Table 7.8   Mean offence rate per household of household offences for participants and non-participants

	Acton experimental area post-test	Wimbledon experimental area post-test
n =	309	400
Participation		
participant	0.44	0.47
non-participant	0.41	0.40

both rounds of surveys. Data does exist, however, on victimization rates of participants and non-participants in the post-test period.

Table 7.8 shows that the mean victimization rate for household offences was greater for participants than non-participants in both NW areas. The difference is slightly greater for the Wimbledon scheme area than for the Acton scheme area.

It is reiterated that the data refer only to post-test differences and participants might also have been more highly victimized than non-participants in the pre-test period. It is also worth noting that there are important social and demographic differences between the two groups (see Chapter 6). It is interesting that many of the social and demographic variables associated with participation are also associated with victimization. Participants were more likely to be young (but not too young), house dwellers, owner-occupiers, living in households with one or more children and employed. The most highly victimized respondents tended also to be young, house dwellers, owner-occupiers, living in households with one or more children and employed.

The individual contribution of social and demographic factors and participation in the NW scheme can be explored more fully using multivariate analysis. However, the preliminary findings of the bivariate analysis do not suggest that participants were better protected against crime than non-participants.

Reporting rates   One of the aims of NW is to improve the flow of information from the public to the police. An important element of this flow of information to the police is the reporting of crime. To a greater or lesser extent, the police encourage residents in NW areas to report victimizations to them. The widely held belief that reporting rates increase in NW areas is sometimes used as an explanation of weak reductions, or even increases, in the rates of police-recorded crime following the launch of NW schemes. The use of crime surveys enables an assessment to be made of changes in reporting rates from one time period to another.

A question was included on each victim form inquiring whether the offence was reported to the police. As only one victim form was used to record information about series offences, it was necessary to weight these responses by the most recent offence. The percentage of all crimes reported to the police during the pre-test and post-test periods is shown in Table 7.9.

The percentage reporting rates for specific offence types need to be treated with caution as they are based on a small numbers. The offence of 'theft of a motor vehicle' and 'offences against the person' have been omitted from the table because the small numbers involved makes percentage comparisons meaningless. In addition, specific percentages relating to the remaining offences have been excluded when the values on which they were based fell below the value 10. The strongest findings that can be presented concern changes in reporting rates for total household offences. The total includes all household offences and not just those shown in the table.

Reporting rates for all household offences in the Acton experimental area increased slightly by just three percentage points from the pre-test to the post-test period. In the Wimbledon experimental area the total rate decreased by one percentage point. The initial impact of these findings is that reporting rates did not increase substantially in the NW areas. Comparing reporting rates with those in the displacement and control areas does little to improve this assessment. In order to compare favourably with the displacement and control area, it would have to be shown that reporting rates in both areas declined sharply during the experimental year. In fact reporting rates for household offences fell by four percentage points in the Wimbledon displacement area and increased by seven percentage points in the Redbridge control area.

Table 7.9 *Reporting rates for specific offence types in the pre-test and post-test surveys in the four research areas*

	Acton experimental area		Wimbledon experimental area		Wimbledon displacement area		Redbridge control area	
	pre	post	pre	post	pre	post	pre	post
n =	306	309	353	400	323	332	306	330
Theft from vehicle	45	43	23	24	54	42	36	–
Burglary dwelling	55	73	55	65	60	74	–	–
Criminal damage	19	19	8	10	24	18	3	6
All household offences	37	38	30	29	37	32	23	27
n =	71	132	97	172	156	161	65	47

*This category includes all household offences, not just those shown.
Note: Percentages not recorded if the number falls below the value 10.

The most encouraging findings in the table relate to reporting rates for burglary which increased in both experimental areas. Unfortunately, the foundations of this favourable result are weak. First, the numbers are small. The increase in the percentage of offences reported from the lower rate to the higher rate represents the reporting of six extra offences in Acton and two extra offences in Wimbledon. Secondly, the reporting rate for burglary also increased in the Wimbledon displacement and the Redbridge control area. There is no evidence from this table that the change in rates in the NW areas were both positive and substantially better than reporting rate improvements in similar areas without a NW scheme.

Multivariate analysis
An important disadvantage of bivariate analysis is that it cannot adjust for differences in the pre-test and post-test samples. Multitvariate analysis can control for some of the differences between the samples and produce a more valid measure of changes in victimization rate between the two periods.

Choice of method   The choice of statistical method is dependent on the nature of the dependent variable (the variable to be explained) and the nature of the independent variables (the variables used to explain the dependent variable). The dependent variable in the current analysis is 'victimization'. This is expressed either as a dichotomous variable (0 or 1 or more offences) or as a scale (0, 1, 2, 3, etc.) (interval scale variables). The main independent variables are 'area' (whether it was an NW or non-NW area) and 'period' (whether it was before or after the launch of the scheme) (nominal scale variables). The most appropriate multivariate test for interval scale dependent variables with nominal scale independent variables is the analysis of variance (Cook and Campbell, 1979). The main programme used for the following analyses is the SPSSPC+ package, ANOVA (analysis of variance with covariates). (All calculations were duplicated using a log-linear technique (GLIM) to guard against possible violations of the assumptions underlying the test.)

Method of determining a programme effect   The analysis required creating a number of pooled data sets, each comprising data from two selected areas for the pre-test and post-test surveys . Two 'dummy variables' were added to the data to register whether the area was an NW area (experimental) or a non-NW area (displacement or control) and whether the period was the pre-test (wave 1) or the post-test (wave 2). Pooled data sets were created for the following comparisons: Wimbledon experimental area vs Redbridge control area; Acton experimental area vs Redbridge control area; Wimbledon experimental area vs Wimbledon displacement area; and Acton experimental area vs Wimbledon displacement area.

The test for an NW effect in relation to victimization cannot be determined solely by looking at the differences between the pre-test and post-test or between the experimental or non-experimental areas. As the data sets are pooled, a comparison between victimizations for the pre-test and post-test periods would mask the effect of the type of area and a comparison between type of area would mask the effect of the survey period. It is necessary therefore to assess the effect of NW by looking at the interaction between area and period. Evidence of a successful programme effect would be when the interaction term made a positive and significant contribution to the explanatory power of the statistical model.

The covariates and factors used in the analysis were those most frequently used as 'controls' in the analysis of victimization data. These are largely demographic variables because they must be capable of affecting the dependent variable (victimization rate) without being affected by the key explanatory independent variable (the experimental programme). The following independent variables were entered initially into each equation: age of respondent, household income, age respondent completed full-time education, number of adults in the household, number of children in the household, socioeconomic group, gender, marital status, tenure, race and employment status.

Survey-reported crime   The main results of the ANOVA analysis of reported victimizations is shown in Tables 7.10 and 7.11. The tables shows the independent contribution of the interaction term in explaining the incidence and prevalence of reported household crimes and the incidence

Table 7.10   *Impact of interaction between area being NW or non-NW and pre-test or post-test surveys on reported victimizations (experimental vs control areas)**

	Acton experimental area vs Redbridge control area		Wimbledon experimental area vs Redbridge control area	
	F.	Sig.	F.	Sig.
Incidence of household offences	12.6	0.000	8.7	0.003
Incidence of personal offences	0.5	n.s.	0.0	n.s
Prevalence of household offences	11.5	0.001	2.8	n.s.

*ANOVA procedure for SPSSPC+
n.s. = not significant.

of personal crimes. The prevalence of offences against the person has not been included in the table because the number of households affected is too small to generate a sufficiently powerful explanatory model.

The comparison between the Acton and Wimbledon experimental areas and the Redbridge control area reveals that the interaction between the area being NW or non-NW and the pre-test or post-test surveys contributed significantly to explaining the incidence of total household offences in relation to both the Acton and Wimbledon comparisons. In neither of the comparisons was the change in victimization rates in the direction predicted by proponents of NW. The comparison between the experimental areas and the control in relation to the incidence of household victimizations is shown up clearly in Figure 7.5.

The mean rates shown in the figure are adjusted to compensate for differences in social and demographic differences between the samples. In order to provide evidence of a possible NW effect, it would have to be shown that the two adjusted mean victimization score lines crossed, or at least converged, from the pre-test to the post-test. In fact the figure shows that the lines diverged. The mean household victimizations increased from the pre-test to the post-test in Acton and Wimbledon and decreased in Redbridge. The figure shows, then, that even after controlling for the effects of

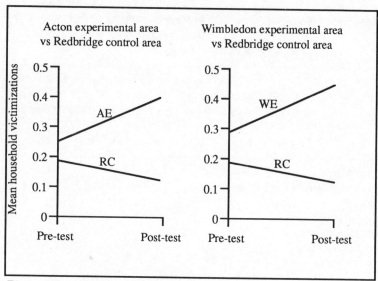

Figure 7.5   *Changes in adjusted mean number of household victimizations from pre-test to post-test surveys (experimental vs control area)*

independent variables, the change is in a direction opposite to that hypothesized.

The main purpose of conducting surveys in a displacement area was to monitor possible displacement of crime from the adjacent NW area if the scheme was found to be effective. There is little evidence from the analysis that either NW schemes achieved an absolute reduction in crime or achieved a relatively more favourable change in crime compared with a similar control area. The function of the displacement area becomes redundant when there is no evidence of an NW effect. It is possible therefore to use the displacement area as a surrogate control.

The main reason for wanting to use a surrogate control is, it could be argued, that the Redbridge control area behaved untypically over the experimental period and the reduction in crimes recorded was not an accurate reflection of movements in crime in similar areas. It is accepted that an unexpected reduction in crime in the control area makes it more difficult for the experimental areas to compare with it favourably. It seems unlikely, however, that alternative control areas would have experienced an increase in victimization rates of an order that would enable the NW areas to show a programme effect. Nevertheless, the question arises of the likely effect of an alternative control comparison.

The main justification of using the Wimbledon displacement area as a surrogate control is that it reduces (rather than increases) the probability of generating a type I error (showing there is no effect when there is). It is possible that there was an undetectable NW effect which had no impact in preventing the overall increase in victimization in the area but had some impact in preventing it rising as high as it might have done. It is possible that the small number of offences prevented in the experimental area were displaced to the displacement area. Under these conditions, a comparison between the experimental and the displacement area would tend to increase the probability of showing an NW programme effect. Hence the main justification for using the displacement area as a surrogate control is that either it has no effect on the comparison (when there is no real NW preventative effect) or favours the NW area in the comparison (when there is a NW preventative effect).

The comparison between the Acton and Wimbledon experimental areas and the Wimbledon displacement area is shown in Table 7.11. The table shows that the interaction between whether the area was NW or non-NW, and whether the survey was the pre-test or the post-test, did not contribute significantly to explaining the incidence or prevalence of household offences or the incidence of personal offences in relation to either the Acton experimental area or the Wimbledon experimental area comparisons. The direction of change is shown graphically in Figure 7.6.

Table 7.11   Impact of interaction between being NW or non-NW and pre-test or post-test surveys on reported victimizations (experimental vs displacement areas)*

	Acton experimental area vs Redbridge control area		Wimbledon experimental area vs Redbridge control area	
	F.	Sig.	F.	Sig.
Incidence of household offences	2.5	n.s.	1.8	n.s.
Incidence of personal offences	1.3	n.s.	0.1	n.s.
Prevalence of household offences	0.5	n.s.	0.1	n.s.

*ANOVA procedure for SPSSPC+.
n.s. = not significant.

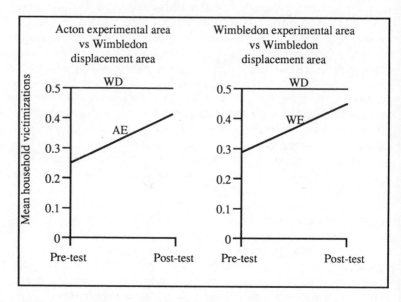

*Figure 7.6   Changes in adjusted mean number of household
victimizations from the pre-test to post-test surveys
(experimental vs displacement areas)*

In order to provide evidence of a programme effect, the two adjusted
mean victimization score lines should diverge (as the surrogate control rate
was higher in the pre-test than the experimental area rate). In fact the lines
converged. Once again, the comparison provides evidence which shows
that the (surrogate) control area performed more favourably over the
experimental period than the experimental area after controlling for the
effects of independent variables.

Victimization and participation   It was noted in the bivariate analysis,
above, that the NW programme might produce a crime reduction effect that
was experienced only by participants in the scheme. A corresponding or
greater increase in crime among non-participants might mask this effect
when looking at the sample as a whole. There was no evidence in the
bivariate analysis, however, that participants experienced lower rates of
victimization than non-participants in the post-test period. In fact, the rate of
household victimizations was higher for participants than non-participants.
It was argued, however, that the two groups differ in social-demographic
characteristics which were linked to the probability of victimization. One
way to disentangle the effect of participation on victimization rates from the

effect of other social-demographic variables is to conduct a multivariate analysis.

It should be noted that the analysis of differences between participants and non-participants was not built into the research design. The decision was made to examine the effect of NW on areas rather than individuals and the cross-sectional survey design was chosen to achieve this. It is nevertheless interesting to look at differences between these two groups.

The results of the multivariate analysis showed that after controlling for social-demographic differences between the two groups there was no significant difference between participants and non-participants in the incidence of household victimization.

Summary
This chapter has investigated various aspect of the relationship between NW and victimization. Most of the evidence points in the direction of no favourable NW impact on crime.

Data from police crime reports showed that crimes committed in the Acton NW area increased and crimes in the Wimbledon NW areas decreased during the first year of the schemes. An examination of trends in police recorded crime over the three-year period preceding the launch, and over the one-year period following the launch, failed to reveal improvements in crime trends.

Data from the crime surveys showed that the prevalence (proportion of households victimized at least once) and incidence (total number of offences expressed as a rate per household) of household victimizations increased in both experimental areas. The prevalence of personal victimizations increased in Acton and remained constant in the Wimbledon experimental area, and the incidence of personal victimizations increased in both experimental areas. The results of the multivariate analysis confirmed that there were no discernible benefits from being a resident in a NW area, in terms of levels of household victimization.

There was no evidence that specific subgroups of the sample experienced a significant reduction in victimization rates over the experimental period. All subgroups in the Acton NW area experienced an increase in victimizations following the launch of the schemes. All subgroups in the Wimbledon NW area experienced an increase in victimizations with the exceptions of non car owners and households containing two children. The main differences recorded among subgroup members concerned the extent of the increase.

The rate of household victimizations was no different for self-defined participants in the NW scheme than for non-participants. The bivariate analysis showed in the first year of the scheme that the rate of household victimizations for participants was slightly higher than that for non-participants. The multivariate analysis failed to reveal any difference between the two groups in terms of victimization rates.

The chapter also examined the impact of NW on reporting rates and on clear-up rates. Again, the results were not particularly favourable. Reporting rates increased in the Acton area by a small amount and decreased in the Wimbledon experimental by a large amount. The clear-up rate of selected offences committed in the subdivisions covering the NW schemes either remained stable or decreased from the pre-test to the post-test period.

Overall, the results of the crime analysis are not encouraging. Most of the findings suggest that residents in the NW areas experienced either no better or worse rates of victimization than their non-NW counterparts.

8 The Results: Public Attitudes and Behaviour

Introduction

It is clear from the main policy documents that NW in the Metropolitan Police District was intended to fulfil a number of functions, apart from the goal of lowering crime rates. The *Force Instructions* (Assistant Commissioner 'A' Department, 1983) identified reduction in the fear of crime as a primary aim of NW; its additional purposes are elaborated in the official guidelines (Russell, n.d.). Apart from crime reduction, it was hoped that NW would improve contact between the police and the public, encourage residents to become more actively involved in crime prevention and stimulate contact between neighbours.

In order to assess the impact of NW on these additional aims, it was first necessary both to identify and operationalize the kinds of change expected. The choice of topics for evaluation was influenced by the NW publicity material which presented the aims of NW, and by the kinds of issue covered in similar social surveys which aimed to investigate public perceptions of the police and of their neighbours and area. The key issues selected for investigation were: (1) fear of personal victimization; (2) fear of household victimization; (3) perceived probability of personal victimization; (4) perceived probability of household victimization; (5) satisfaction with the area; (6) social cohesion; (7) home protection behaviour; (8) evaluation of police service; and (9) police contact.

Constructing analytic scales

The nine issues to be investigated represent not so much single questions, but more multidimensional concepts. The concept of the fear of crime, for example, cannot satisfactorily be reduced to a single question as it comprises notions of personal safety, as well as specific worries about particular offences. A more satisfactory method is to construct analytic scales which compress responses to a number of questions and to present them in the form of a unidimensional continuum.

The method adopted of selecting and scaling items was similar to that used by Wycoff and Skogan (1985) and Rosenbaum, Lewis and Grant 1985). Both authors used Principal Component Factor Analysis and the Reliability procedure within SPSSX (a statistical package for mainframe computers: SPSS Inc., 1986). The main purpose of the factor analysis was to ensure that the scales were single-factored, or unidimensional, and measured one underlying concept. The main purpose of the Reliability procedure was to ensure internal consistency between the scale items and positive correlation.

Table 8.1   Items used in the construction of analytic scales

Scale:	Item:
Fear personal victimization	1 How safe do you feel walking alone in this area after dark? Would you say you feel... 2 Most of us worry at some time or other about being the victim of a crime, and I should like you to tell me how worried you are about being the victim of different types of crime. Could you tell me how worried you are about: (a) being mugged and robbed; (b) being attacked by strangers; (c) being insulted and bothered by strangers.
Fear household victimization	(Main question as Q.2, above): (a) having your home broken into and something stolen; (b) having your home or property damaged by vandals.
Probability of personal victimization	1 I am going to read out a list of crimes and, for each one, I should like you to tell me [from this card] how likely you think this crime is to happen to you in the next year: (a) being mugged and robbed; (b) being attacked by strangers;
Probability of household victimization	(Main question as Q.1, above; (a) having your home broken into and something stolen; (b) having your home or property damaged by vandals.
Satisfaction with area	1 Overall, how satisfied or dissatisfied are you with living in the area? 2 How would you feel about moving from this area? Would you be pleased or sorry, or would you have mixed feelings?

Table 8.1 (continued)   Items used in the construction of analytic scales

Scale:	Item:
Social cohesion	1 In some neighbourhoods people do things together and try to help one another, while in other areas people mostly go their own way. In general, what kind of neighbourhood would you say you live in: (a) is it one where people mostly help each other? (b) or where people mostly go their own way? 2 In your neighbourhood how difficult is it for you to tell a stranger from someone who lives there? 3 Thinking of the people who live in the area, how many would you regard as your friends or acquaintances?
Home protection	1 The last time you were away from home for more than a few days did you: (a) ask someone to come and stay in it? (b) ask someone to come in to make sure things were all right? (c) ask someone to keep an eye on your home?
Police evaluation	1 How would you describe the police when you have wanted help from them? (I am talking about your recent experience rather than your experience in the past.) 2 How would you describe the attitude of the police on any occasion when they have approached you? (Again, I am talking about your recent experience.) 3 Taking everything into account, would you say the police in your area do a good job or a poor one?
Police contact	1 When did you personally see a police officer on foot in your area?

The scales were constructed from a pooled data set, comprising the full set of the pre-test and post-test data for the two experimental areas. An initial list of items (specific questions and their response data) from the questionnaire was compiled for each of the nine concepts under investigation. Various combinations of initially eligible items were assessed using factor analysis until the best combination was attained (single-factored and strongly loaded on the principal factor). The items were then assessed for reliability. Once the scale items had been selected, they were combined into a single scale by adding the unweighted scores. More precisely, scale scores were calculated by summing the valid (non-missing) values of the items and dividing the total by the number of valid (non-missing) values. This allowed scale scores to be generated when one or more of the item values was unknown.

The items used in the construction of the nine main scales used in the analysis are shown in Table 8.1. The items shown represent the final list – i.e. after initially eligible questions had been excluded as a result of poor factoring or poor reliability. One scale was based on four items (fear of personal victimization); two scales were based on three items (social cohesion and police evaluation); four scales were based on two items (fear of household victimization) probability of personal and household victimization, and satisfaction with the area; and two scales were based on one item (home protection behaviour and police contact). The reliability of the scales containing more than one item ranged from 0.54 (social cohesion) to 0.83 (fear of personal victimization) as calculated using Cronbach's Standardized Alpha (SPSS Inc., 1986).

Bivariate analysis
The analysis of the impact of NW on public attitudes and behaviour is divided into two main sections: bivariate analysis and multivariate analysis. The main reason for dividing the results in this way has been discussed in Chapter 7. Bivariate analysis involves presenting the findings in summary form, which has the advantage that it brings users closer to the data. It allows summaries of the data to be presented clearly, and it fully reveals the general magnitude and direction of the results. However, in order to make realistic comparisons between the pre-test and post-test surveys, it is necessary to control for demographic and other differences between the samples. This is done more effectively by using multivariate analysis.

Changes in public attitudes and behaviour
Changes in the mean scale scores from the pre-test to the post-test surveys for the two experimental areas are shown in Table 8.2. The scales have been re-coded, where necessary, to provide directionality. Low scores represent unfavourable outcomes, and high scores favourable outcomes. A movement from a lower score to a higher score from the pre-test to post-test surveys represents a movement in a favourable direction.

Table 8.2   *Mean public attitude and behaviour scale scores for the pre-test and post-test period*

	N	Acton experimental area		Wimbledon experimental area	
		pre	post	pre	post
Fear of personal victimization	4	2.65	2.70*	2.55	2.64*
Fear of household victimization	4	2.35	2.54*	2.30	2.36*
Probability of personal victimization	6	3.92	3.95*	3.90	3.89
Probability of household victimization	6	3.71	3.78*	3.71	3.67
Satisfaction with area	4	3.14	3.25*	3.01	3.08*
Social cohesion	4	2.05	2.16*	2.19	2.24*
Home protection	2	1.79	1.77	1.82	1.89*
Police evaluation	5	3.79	3.81*	3.62	3.59
Police contact	5	3.56	3.11	2.49	2.15

* Move in a favourable direction.
N = number of values in the scale.

In Acton the mean scores of seven of the nine scales moved in a favourable direction from the pre-test to post-test periods, and in Wimbledon the mean scores of five of the nine scales moved in a favourable direction. In both areas the fear of personal and household victimization decreased (shown as an increase in scale mean value), and in Acton the perceived probability of personal and household victimization decreased (respondents reported lower levels of probability). No reduction in perceived probability of personal or household victimization were measured in Wimbledon. Both areas showed improvements in residents' satisfaction with the area and in the social cohesion. Involvement with others in home protection behaviour increased in Wimbledon, but decreased in Acton. Public evaluation of the police improved in Acton, but failed to do so in Wimbledon. Police contact as measured by recent sighting of a police officer in the area decreased in both areas.

The results of these changes shown in mean scores over the experimental period are more encouraging than the changes in mean scores in relation to victimization rates in the areas. The reduction in the fear of personal and household victimization is a particularly welcome sign, in that a reduction in fear of crime was one of the twin aims of NW in the Metropolitan Police District. The results are marred slightly, however, by the apparent reduction in the recent observation of police officers in both areas.

Public attitudes and behaviour and subgroups
It it possible that the impact of the NW programme on public attitudes and behaviour might be differentially effective in relation to specific subgroups of the population. It is important to investigate therefore not only whether NW has an impact on attitudes and behaviour for the population as a whole, but also whether it has an impact on population subgroups. A summary of the major differences in attitudes and behaviour among subgroups is shown in the Appendix in Table A.2.

The table shows that the age distribution of fear of crime, and perceptions of the probability of victimization, are almost identical for Acton and Wimbledon. Older respondents are more fearful than middle-aged and younger people and perceive the risks of victimization as higher. Conversely, older respondents tend to be more satisfied with their area; have a stronger sense of social cohesion; are more involved with others in home protection; and have a higher regard for the police .

There are also strong differences between males and females in attitude and behaviour scores which are reflected in the surveys from both areas. Females are more fearful than males but more satisfied with their areas, and they are more likely to be involved with others in home protection and to rate the police highly. Routine differences can also be observed between respondents in terms of skin colour. Black respondents are more fearful than whites, are less involved with others in home protection and evaluate the police less favourably. Married and separate, and widowed and divorced, respondents are more fearful of victimization than single respondents. Low-income workers, manual workers and unemployed residents are more fearful of crime and perceive the risks of victimization as higher than their better-off counterparts. The latter, however, are more likely to be satisfied with their area; to believe that the area is cohesive; to involve others in home protection; and to evaluate the police highly. Finally, people living in households with three or more adults are less fearful (in Wimbledon but not in Acton), and more satisfied with the area, the community and the police (in both areas) than people living in single or two-adult households.

A number of relationships are suggested by the pattern of the data. There is some suggestion that the most fearful groups are the least powerful and the most socially disadvantaged groups. Old, female, non-white, low-income, manual workers and unemployed respondents are the most fearful groups in both experimental areas. There is also some indication from the pattern of the data that the least powerful and most fearful groups are also the most satisfied with their area, most integrated within it, the most likely to be involved with others in home protection and the most satisfied with the

Table 8.3   Changes in mean scale scores for all scales, by slected subgroups

	Acton experimental area									Wimbledon experimental area								
	FP	FH	PP	PH	SA	SC	HP	PE	PC	FP	FH	PP	PH	SA	SC	HP	PE	PC
Age																		
16–20	-	+	-	-	+	+	-	-	+	+	+	-	+	-	-	+	+	-
21–30	-	+	+	+	+	+	-	-	-	+	+	-	-	+	+	+	+	-
31–40	+	+	-	-	+	+	-	+	-	-	-	-	-	+	+	+	-	-
41–50	-	-	-	+	+	+	+	+	-	+	+	+	+	-	-	+	-	-
51–60	+	+	-	+	+	+	+	-	-	+	-	-	-	+	+	+	-	-
61+	+	+	+	+	+	+	-	+	+	+	+	+	+	+	+	+	+	+
Gender																		
male	+	+	-	+	+	+	-	-	-	-	-	-	-	+	+	+	-	-
female	-	+	+	+	+	+	-	+	-	+	+	-	-	+	+	+	+	-
Race																		
white	+	+	+	+	+	+	-	+	-	+	+	+	-	+	+	+	-	-
non-white	+	-	+	+	+	+	-	+	-	+	-	-	-	+	+	+	+	-
Marital status																		
single	-	+	-	-	+	+	-	-	-	+	-	-	-	-	-	+	-	-
married	+	+	+	+	+	+	+	+	-	+	+	+	-	+	+	+	-	-
s.w.d.	-	+	-	-	+	+	+	+	-	+	+	+	+	+	-	+	-	+
Income																		
under £10,000	+	+	+	+	+	+	-	+	-	+	+	+	+	+	+	+	+	-
£10,000 or more	+	+	-	-	+	+	-	-	-	-	-	-	-	+	+	+	-	-
Socioeconomic group																		
non-manual	-	+	+	+	-	+	-	+	-	-	-	-	-	+	+	+	-	-
manual	+	+	+	+	+	+	-	-	-	+	+	+	+	+	+	+	-	-
Employment status																		
in work	-	+	-	-	+	+	-	+	-	+	-	-	-	+	+	+	-	-
not in work	+	+	+	+	+	+	-	-	-	+	+	-	-	+	-	+	+	+
No. of adults																		
1	+	+	-	-	+	+	+	+	-	+	+	+	-	+	+	+	-	-
2	+	+	+	+	+	+	-	+	-	+	+	+	-	+	+	+	+	-
3+	+	+	+	+	+	+	-	-	-	+	-	-	-	+	+	+	-	-

Notes:

FP, PP, PH, SA, HP, PE, PC = the nine scale headings (abbreviations).
A plus denotes an improvement, and a minus no improvement from pre-test to post-test surveys.

performance of the police. The main exception to this trend is among non-whites, who evaluated the police less highly in both surveys.

A summary of the changes in mean scale scores from the pre-test to post-test surveys for selected subgroups is shown in Table 8.3. The first impression gained from the table is that overall changes for the populations as a whole were not always reflected in the movements of all subgroups. A plus sign in the table represents an improvement, and a minus sign an absence of improvement in the attitude or behaviour from pre-test to post-test surveys. Here 'improvement' is used to denote the kind of change among populations generally considered desirable (e.g. a change from high fear of crime levels to low fear levels).

Older respondents (61+) registered changes in a favourable direction in relation to every attitude and behaviour scale in Wimbledon, and in eight of the nine scales in Acton. In Acton the youngest age-group (16–20) recorded the lowest number of attitudinal or behavioural improvements, whereas in Wimbledon the middle-aged recorded the lowest number. Females showed a greater number of improvements than males in both areas and married and separated, widowed or divorced, respondents recorded a greater number of positive changes than single respondents. Low-income households, manual workers and unemployed respondents registered a greater number of favourable changes than high-income households, non-manual workers and employed respondents.

It is interesting that all of the major differences in change in attitudes and behaviour among subgroups occur among those groups which are traditionally regarded as the least powerful and least socially advantaged. The relationship is not wholly consistent as non-whites were no more likely than whites to show favourable changes in attitude and behaviour over the experimental period. The greater improvements among married rather than single respondents, and among multiple adult households rather than single adult households, suggests a somewhat more complex explanation of differences than simple differences in status, wealth and power.

Fear of victimization
The association between fear of crime and age revealed in the literature is borne out in the current survey (Clarke and Lewis, 1982; Giles-Sims, 1984; Lindquist and Duke, 1982; Maxfield, 1987). Scores relating to fear of personal victimization were consistently lower (showing higher fear levels) for respondents aged 51–80 and 61 and over. There was some indication, however, that the relationship between age and fear of personal victimization was not linear, but 'U'-shaped, with high fear levels recorded by both the very young and very old. The relationship is apparent but less striking in relation to fear of household crime. In Acton the most fearful age-group was the youngest category in both surveys, and in Wimbledon the most fearful groups were the two oldest categories. The middle-aged groups (31–40 and

41–50) groups consistently revealed lower fear levels than the other age-groups.

The association between fear of crime and gender revealed in other crime surveys is also borne out in the current surveys (Riger, Gordon and Bailly, 1978; Ortega and Myles, 1987). Females consistently recorded lower scores (revealing higher fear levels) for fear of personal crime, and for fear of household crime, in all four surveys.

A consistent trend in fear of personal and household crime scores is also revealed in relation to the respondent's race (more precisely the respondent's colour). In both experimental areas non-white respondents invariably reported higher fear of crime levels than white respondents.

In three of the four surveys the highest levels of fear of personal crime were expressed by respondents who were separated, widowed or divorced. In two of the four surveys the highest levels of fear of household victimization were also reported by this group. This finding reflects the results of earlier surveys of victims of burglary which showed those groups to be most concerned about their victimization (Maguire and Bennett, 1983). Single respondents almost invariably reported the lowest levels of fear.

A further, almost consistent, relationship between fear and subgroup categories can be found in relation to income. In seven of the eight fear of crime comparisons lower-income respondents reported higher fear levels than higher-income respondents. Manual workers almost invariably reported higher levels of fear of personal and household victimization than non-manual workers. Similarly, respondents employed in full-time or part-time employment regularly expressed lower fear levels than respondents who were unemployed. Single adult households reported higher fear levels than respondents from multiple adult households in five of the eight comparisons made.

Probability of victimization

A similar pattern emerges between age and perceptions of the probability of victimization as appeared between age and fear of victimization. The younger age-groups consistently reported lower probabilities of victimization (higher scale scores) than older age-groups. In six of the eight surveys the 16–20 age-group reported the lowest probability levels, and in all eight surveys either the 51–60 year-old or the 61+ year-old subgroup recorded the highest probability levels. The finding supports other research which shows an age–victimization paradox (highest expectation of victimization and lowest actual victimization among the oldest subgroups) (Garafola, 1979; Lindquist and Duke, 1982).

The relationship between gender and fear of crime was also reflected in perceptions of the probability of crime. Females consistently reported higher probability levels than males for both personal and household victimizations. Non-white respondents consistently rated the probability of personal and household victimizations higher than white respondents. In five of the eight surveys separated, widowed and divorced respondents reported higher levels of certainty of victimization than single or married respondents. In all eight surveys single respondents reported the lowest levels of certainty of victimization. The relationship matches closely reports of other surveys and the findings relating to fear of crime.

A strong relationship also existed between perceptions of certainty and income. Respondents from low income households consistently reported higher levels of probability of victimization than respondents from high-income households. The relationship was also evident in relation to socioeconomic groups, where manual workers consistently reported higher levels than non-manual workers. The relationship with employment status is less clear, with half the surveys showing higher expectations of victimization among unemployed workers and the other half showing higher expectations among employed workers. Respondents from single adult households more frequently recorded higher expectations of victimizations than respondents from multiple adult households.

Satisfaction with area and social cohesion
Apart from one or two digressions, the associations between age and satisfaction with the area and sense of social cohesions was almost linear. The two youngest age-groups invariably reported the lowest levels of satisfaction with the area and lowest assessments of social cohesion in the area. Conversely, the oldest age-group reported the highest levels of satisfaction in the majority of surveys and the highest levels of social cohesion in the majority of surveys.

There was no consistent relationship between gender and area satisfaction or sense of cohesion. Males registered higher satisfaction with the area than females in one of the two surveys in Acton, and in one of the two surveys in Wimbledon. Males registered higher sense of social cohesion in both surveys in Acton, and in one of the two surveys in Wimbledon.

Almost invariably, non-white respondents reported higher levels of satisfaction with the area and a greater sense of social cohesion than white respondents. In Acton whites registered more favourable responses only in relation to perceived satisfaction with the area in the pre-test survey. In Wimbledon whites scored lower levels of satisfaction and sense of cohesion in all surveys.

Single respondents scored lower in terms of perceived satisfaction and sense of social cohesion than either married or separate, widowed or divorced respondents. There was no clear distinction between married and separated, widowed or divorced respondents.

There is some evidence that residents from lower-income households were more satisfied with their area and felt a greater sense of social cohesion than residents from higher-income households. Manual workers were more likely than non-manual workers to report higher levels of satisfaction and a greater sense of social cohesion. Further, unemployed respondents were more likely than employed respondents to say that they were satisfied with the area in which they lived and felt a sense of cohesion. Respondents from households with multiple adult members were more satisfied and experienced a greater sense of social cohesion than respondents from single adult households.

Involvement in home protection

Involvement with others in home protection behaviour was more prevalent among older residents than among younger ones. Females were consistently more likely than males to report that they were involved with others in home protection. Whites were consistently more likely than non-whites to say that they looked after each other's homes when they were away for a few days. Single respondents were far less likely to report that they asked people to look after their homes when away. In every comparison home protection behaviour involving others were more frequent among married respondents. No consistent relationship could be found between income, socioeconomic status or employment status and involvement with others in home protection behaviour. The highest levels of home protection behaviour were recorded among respondents from multiple adult households. Single adult household recorded lowest levels in three of the four surveys.

Police evaluation and contact

There is a clear tendency for older rather than younger respondents highly to evaluate the police. The lowest ranking occurred among 16–20-year-olds in both surveys both in Acton and Wimbledon, and the highest ranking occurred among 51–60 or 60+ year-olds in both surveys in Acton and in one survey in Wimbledon. The trend is less clear in relation to recency of sighting of a police officer in the area where the highest scores tended to fall among the middle-aged groups.

Female respondents consistently rated the police more highly than male respondents. Higher scores were recorded for females in both surveys in both areas. Male respondents were more likely than female respondents to report a recent sighting of a police officer in their area.

Invariably, white respondents rated the police more highly than non-white respondents. In Acton non-whites were more likely than whites to report a recent sighting of a police officer in the area, whereas in Wimbledon whites were more likely than non-whites to have recently observed the police.

The relationship between marital status and police evaluation was constant for all surveys. Respondents who were separated, widowed or divorced rated the police most highly; married respondents rated the police second highest; and single respondents rated the police least highly. An identical relationship existed in Acton in relation to recency of police observation with separated, widowed and divorced respondents more likely to report a recent sighting than either married or single respondents. No clear relationship existed, however, between marital status and police contact in Wimbledon.

There is some evidence that higher-income groups rated the police more highly than low-income groups, but there is no clear relationship with either socioeconomic group or employment status. There was no consistent relationship between number of adults in the household and either police evaluation or police contact.

Public attitudes and behaviour and NW participation

The previous analysis has shown that changes observed from the pre-test to the post-test surveys for the population as a whole were not necessarily reflected in changes for particular subgroups. Some subgroups recorded favourable attitude or behaviour changes over the experimental period, while others did not. It is possible therefore that there might also be systematic differences between participants and non-participants in the NW scheme. It might be expected, for example, that participants would benefit more from the scheme than non-participants and would show more favourable changes during the first year of the programme.

It has been already noted that it was not possible to conduct a panel survey of residents which would have resulted in interviewing the same individuals in both rounds of surveys. It is not possible therefore to compare the pre-test scores with the post-test scores for individual participants and non-participants. However, it is possible to compare the results of the two groups in the post-test surveys.

The mean scale scores for participants and non-participants are shown in Table 8.4. For the purpose of analysis, participation refers to self-defined participation in the scheme.

In Acton participants invariably recorded lower scale scores than non-participants for the fear of crime and perceived probability of crime scales. In other words, participants were more fearful and perceived a higher risk of victimization than non-participants. In Wimbledon participants and non-participants differed less systematically in fear of crime, although participants reported higher levels of probability of both personal and household victimization than non-participants.

In both Acton and Wimbledon samples, participants were more satisfied with their area than non-participants and reported a greater sense of social cohesion. Participants were also more involved with others in the protection of their home. In both areas, participants rated the police more highly than non-participants, and participants reported more recent sightings of police officers in their area.

Table 8.4   *Mean public attitude and behaviour scale scores for pre-
test and post-test periods for participants and non-
participants*

	Acton experimental area		Wimbledon experimental area	
	P	NP	P	NP
Fear of personal victimization	2.58	2.91	2.64	2.64
Fear of household victimization	2.38	2.80	2.78	2.42
Probability of personal victimization	3.90	4.03	3.66	3.67
Probability of household victimization	3.70	3.91	3.66	3.67
Satisfaction with area	3.28	3.19	3.13	3.03
Social cohesion	2.29	1.96	2.27	2.21
Home protection	1.85	1.64	1.93	1.86
Police evaluation	4.01	3.47	3.61	3.58
Police contact	3.26	3.04	2.13	1.92

P = participant; NP = non-participant.

The overall impression given from this table is that participants are more worried about crime than non-participants; are more socially and psychologically attached to their areas; and more strongly supportive of the police. Such a picture matches well the popular stereotype of the NW participator.

Multivariate analysis
The analysis so far has been based on simple cross-tabulations of the data. The presentation of the results, in summary form, has the advantage that the broad trends in the data can be observed without recourse to complicated statistical notation. It is not easy, however, to separate real changes in public attitudes and behaviour from changes in the characteristics of the pre-test and post-test samples. It is necessary therefore to control for differences between pre-test and post-test samples by using multivariate analysis.

Choice of method
Some of the issues involved in choosing an appropriate statistical test have been discussed in Chapter 7. The main consideration in this choice is the nature of the dependent variable (the variable to be explained), and the

nature of the independent variables (the variables used to explain the dependent variable).

Strictly speaking, the coded responses to attitudinal questions do not constitute interval scale variables (one of the essential prerequisites of most parametric tests). It cannot be assumed, for example, that the interval between the values 'very certain' and 'fairly certain' is the same as the interval between 'fairly uncertain' and 'very uncertain'. However, current analysis is mainly based not on the responses to individual questions, but on the values of composite scales created by adding together the scores of a number of variables. It could be argued therefore that the analytic scales approximate interval scale variables.

The independent variables used in the analysis are mainly social and demographic variables, which almost invariably constitute nominal scale variables. The most appropriate statistical test for interval scale dependent variables and nominal scale independent variables is the analysis of variance. The following analysis is based on the SPSSPC+ programme ANOVA. (All calculations were duplicated using a log-linear technique (GLIM) to guard against possible violations of the assumptions underlying the test.)

Method of determining a programme effect

It has already been discussed that the stronger research design using both experimental and control areas could not be adopted in the assessment of NW on public attitudes and behaviour. Questions on these issues were included therefore only in the questionnaires used in the experimental areas.

The method of determining a programme effect was based on a comparison of pre-test and post-test responses. The main disadvantage of this method is that it is not known whether any changes observed in the experimental areas also occurred in similar non-NW areas over the same period. It is possible, however, to draw on other evidence to assess the likelihood of changes observed in the experimental areas occurring elsewhere. Pre-test/post-test designs can produce interpretable results if care is taken in assessing the various threats to internal validity.

The method of determining a programme effect was essentially the same as that used in the analysis of the impact of NW on victimization. A pooled data set was created using pre-test and post-test data for both experimental areas. A 'dummy' variable was added to register whether the period was the year before the launch of the NW scheme (wave 1) or the year following the launch (wave 2). The aim of the analysis was to generate a linear model of independent variables which best explained the dependent variable. The independent variables used in the analysis were largely social and demographic variables and included: age of respondent, household income, age respondent completed full-time education, number of adults in the household, number of children in the household, socioeconomic group, gender, marital status, tenure, race and employment status. The programme was considered to be (potentially) effective (prior to interpretation), when the dummy variable which represented the period of the survey explained a significant amount of the variance of the dependent variable.

Public attitudes and behaviour

The statistical significance of the changes between the pre-test and post-test surveys in relation to the nine factors investigated is shown in Table 8.5. The bivariate analysis showed that, in Acton, changes occurred in a favourable direction in relation to seven of the nine scales, and in Wimbledon, changes occurred in a favourable direction in relation to five of the nine scales. The table shows that statistically significant improvements occurred in relation to three of the scales in Acton, and in relation to two of the scales in Wimbledon; and that statistically significant, unfavourable movements occurred in one of the scales in Acton and one of the scales in Wimbledon.

The main favourable findings of the analysis are that the introduction of the NW schemes had a potential impact (i.e. subject to interpretation) on fear

Table 8.5   *The impact of whether the survey was the pre-test or the post-test on public attitude and behaviour in the two NW areas*

	+/-	Acton experimental area (n = 615) F	sig. of F	+/-	Wimbledon experimental area (n = 753) F	sig. F
Fear of personal victimization	+	0.5	n.s.	+	0.70	n.s.
Fear of household victimization	+	6.49	*	+	1.63	n.s.
Probability of personal victimization	+	0.09	n.s.	-	0.85	n.s.
Probability of household victimization	+	1.29	n.s.	-	0.12	n.s.
Satisfaction with area	+	4.34	*	+	4.31	*
Social cohesion	+	4.76	*	+	1.47	n.s.
Home protection	-	0.28	n.s.	+	7.89	*
Police evaluation	+	0.41	n.s.	-	0.26	n.s.
Police contact	-	4.04	*	-	19.93	*

+ = a change in a favourable direction; - = a change in an unfavourable direction.

* = significant; n.s. = not significant.

of household crime, residents' satisfaction with their area and sense of social cohesion in Acton, and on residents' satisfaction with their area and home protection behaviour in Wimbledon. There is evidence therefore that residents in the NW areas experienced some favourable changes in attitudes and behaviour following the launch of the NW scheme. These changes were independent of changes in the social or demographic characteristics of the pre-test and post-test samples and were larger than might have been expected by chance.

The bivariate analysis also showed changes in an unfavourable direction in two of the nine scales in Acton, and in four of the nine scales in Wimbledon. The table shows that the deterioration in home protection behaviour in Acton, and the increase in the perceived probability of victimization and the deterioration in police evaluation in Wimbledon, were not statistically significant and could have occurred as a result of differences between the samples or as a result of random variations from year to year. The decline in the recency of observations of police officers was significant in both areas and represents a research finding that needs to be explained.

Public attitudes and behaviour and subgroups
It was shown in the bivariate section that changes in attitudes and behaviour from the pre-test to the post-test period were not uniform for all population subgroups. It is possible that while there might be no discernible improvement in specific attitudes and behaviours for the population as a whole, there might be significant improvements for population subgroups.

A summary of the results of the analyses is shown in Table 8.6. The table includes information on scales for which there was no overall potential programme effect.

In order to test this hypothesis, additional data files were created for each subgroup, and each new data set was tested using the same analysis of variance procedure as used for the population as a whole. A successful programme effect was defined as occurring when the dummy period variable, which identified the period of the survey, was statistically significant (at the 0.05 probability level).

In Acton there was no significant change in fear of personal crime from pre-test to post-test surveys among any of the subgroups. In Wimbledon there was a statistically significant reduction in fear of personal victimization among females. For the sample as a whole fear of household victimization decreased significantly in Acton. Fear of household victimization did not decrease significantly in Wimbledon for the sample as a whole, but the reduction was in relation to the subgroup females, whites, separated, widowed or divorced and low-income respondents, and for those living in single adult households.

The perceived likelihood of personal victimization failed to decrease significantly for the sample as a whole in both areas. The only significant

Table 8.6   *Changes in mean scale scores for selected scales by subgroups*

	Acton experimental area					Wimbledon experimental area					
	FP	PP	PH	HP	PE	FP	FH	PP	PH	SC	PE
Age											
16–20	-	-	-	-	-	+	+	-	+	-	+
21–30	-	+	+	-	+	+	+	-	-	+	+
31–40	+	-	-	-	+	-	-	-	-	+	-
41–50	-	-	+	+	+	+	+	+	+	-	-
51–60	+	-	+	+	-	+	-	-	-	+	-
61+	+	+	+	-	+	+	+	+	+	+	+
Gender											
male	+	-	+	-	-	-	-	-	-	+	-
female	-	+	+	-	+	[+]	[+]	-	-	+	+
Race											
white	+	+	+	-	+	+	[+]	+	-	+	-
non-white	+	+	+	-	+	+	-	-	-	+	+
Marital status											
single	-	-	-	-	-	+	-	-	-	-	-
married	+	+	+	+	+	+	+	+	-	+	-
s.w.d.	-	-	-	+	+	+	[+]	+	+	-	-
Income											
under £10,000	+	+	+	-	+	+	[+]	+	+	+	+
£10,000 or more	+	-	-	-	-	-	-	-	-	+	-
Socio-economic group											
non-manual	-	+	+	-	+	-	-	-	-	+	-
manual	+	+	+	-	-	+	+	+	+	+	-
Employment status											
in work	-	-	-	-	+	+	-	-	-	+	-
not in work	+	[+]	+	-	-	+	+	-	-	-	+
No. of adults											
1	+	-	-	+	+	+	[+]	+	-	+	-
2	+	+	+	-	+	+	+	+	-	+	+
3+	+	+	+	-	-	+	-	-	-	+	+

Note:

FP, PP, PH, SA, HP, PE, PC = the nine scale headings (abbreviations).
A plus denotes an improvement, and a minus no improvement from pre-test to post-test surveys.
Statistically significant differences (P<0.05) are identified by enclosing the symbol in parentheses.

reduction observed for subgroups was among unemployed respondents in Acton. There was no significant reduction in the perceived likelihood of household victimization in either area or for any of the subgroups. There were no significant changes for subgroups in relation to home protection behaviour or police evaluation in Acton, nor in perceptions of social cohesion or police evaluation in Wimbledon.

Summary

This chapter has assessed the impact of NW on public attitudes and behaviour, focusing on nine specific aspects of public attitudes and behaviour which have been hypothesized in the literature as being affected by the implementation of NW programmes. The analysis was based on analytic scales which were constructed from the responses of (usually) more than one question in order to represent more faithfully the underlying concept under investigation.

The results of the bivariate analysis show that there were a number of changes in public attitudes and behaviour which could be construed as favourable and supportive of the hypothesized aims of NW. In Acton there were overall improvements in relation to the fear of personal and household victimization; the perceived risk of personal and household victimization; satisfaction with the area; in a sense of social cohesion; and evaluations of police performance. There were no improvements in home protection behaviour and police contact as measured by the recency of observation of a police officer in the area. In Wimbledon there were overall improvements in fear of personal and household victimization, satisfaction with the area, sense of social cohesion and home protection behaviour. There were no improvements in the perceived risks of personal or household victimization, evaluation of police performance or police contact.

The results of the bivariate analysis alone cannot determine the effectiveness of the programme because of the problem of social and demographic differences between pre-test and post-test samples. Nevertheless, the consistency and nature of the improvements in both areas are striking. It would seem unlikely that general improvements in fear of crime, satisfaction with the area of residence and sense of social cohesion were improving throughout London as whole or in similar areas during the same short period of time. The initial impressions gained from these findings is that the results are encouraging and suggestive of a programme effect.

The results of the multivariate analysis were somewhat more sobering. Only three of the seven favourable changes in mean scale scores in the Acton surveys, and only two of the five favourable changes in the Wimbledon surveys, were statistically significant. The results undermine, to some extent, the fairly uniform general improvements recorded in the bivariate analysis. Nevertheless, the substantial improvements in Acton in fear of personal crime, area satisfaction and sense of social cohesion are important changes which should be welcomed. Similarly, the overall improvements in Wimbledon in area satisfaction and home protection behaviour are also significant changes in the community which should not be discounted.

A bivariate analysis was also conducted on the differential distribution of the specific public attitudes and behaviours among various subgroups of the sample and on variations in the direction and magnitude of change among these subgroups from pre-test to post-test surveys.

The analysis of the differential distribution of attitudes and behaviours showed that there were important differences between the groups in terms of fear of victimization. Females consistently expressed higher levels of fear of personal and household victimization than males and also reported higher levels of perceived certainty of personal and household victimization. Fear of crime, and the perceived probability of crime, were also consistently higher for older rather than younger respondents. The results confirm the evidence from other research which shows an age and gender paradox, whereby females and the elderly are the least victimized groups, but are most fearful of victimization.

The major objective of the bivariate analysis of subgroups was to determine whether there were any improvements in attitudes or behaviour from the pre-test to post-test period among subgroups of the populations. The results showed that there were consistent variations between groups. Older respondents recorded a greater number of favourable changes than younger respondents in both Acton and Wimbledon. Females showed a greater number of improvements than males in both areas. Low-income households, manual workers and unemployed respondents also registered a greater number of favourable changes than their counterparts.

There is some indication from the pattern of these findings that most of the changes occurred among the social disadvantaged or least powerful subgroup. The relationship does not hold true for all comparisons, however, as white respondents experienced a greater number of improvements than non-white respondents and married respondents recorded a greater number than single respondents. There is also some indication that improvements more frequently occurred among groups whose attitudes and behaviours were the least favourable in the pre-test surveys. Respondents who were older, female, in low-income households, manual workers or unemployed each recorded high levels of fear and perceived the risks of victimization as high and showed the greatest reductions in fear from pre-test to post-test periods.

The results of the multivariate analysis showed that few of the changes from the pre-test to post-test were statistically significant. There were important and significant improvements in fear of personal and household victimization among females in Wimbledon and significant reductions in fear of household crime among whites, respondents who were separated, widowed or divorced, respondents from low-income households and respondents from single adult households also in Wimbledon. There were significant improvements in perceptions of the likelihood of personal victimizations among unemployed respondents in Acton.

Overall, the analysis has shown some potentially encouraging findings. The reduction in fear of household crime among residents in Acton is perhaps the most significant of the results from this section. The reduction in fear of personal and household victimization among females in Wimbledon is also a welcome result. There are also, however, some equally discouraging findings. The significant reduction in police contact as measured through recency of observation of a police officer in the area is worrying. It is also of some concern that there was no overall significant reduction in fear of personal victimization for the samples as a whole in both areas. Before any conclusions can be drawn, however, it is necessary to consider the validity of the findings in order to determine to what extent the favourable (and unfavourable changes) can be justly attributed to the existence of the NW programmes.

9 The Results: Calls, Conversations, Commitments and Costs

Introduction

This chapter presents the findings of four additional areas of investigation which were not covered in the crime and public attitudes surveys. The first comprises an analysis of differences in the nature and number of telephone calls made by residents living in the NW areas to the local police during a period before and after the launch of the scheme. The second is an analysis of the transcripts of semi-structured interviews conducted with area and street co-ordinators and with some of the police involved in running the schemes. The third is an analysis of the nature of the tasks performed by the police in administering the NW programme. The fourth is the total manpower and other costs involved in launching and implementing the schemes during their first year.

Telephone calls by the public to the police

The main purpose of investigating telephone calls by the public to the local police stations is to determine the impact of the NW schemes on the flow of information from the public to the police. A central aim of NW in London is for the public to become the 'eyes and ears' of the police and to report suspicious behaviour to them. It is assumed that this would provide the police with relevant and current information which might result in the arrest of offenders and reduce crime. Therefore, it is important to determine whether this central element and key mechanism of NW was activated in the experimental programmes.

Telephone messages from the public to the police comprise direct calls to the local police station and 999 or emergency calls. The calls to local police stations are processed and recorded by a duty officer responsible for dealing with incoming calls. At the time of the research (before the CAD computerized system had become fully operational), telephone messages were recorded (by hand) on station message-pads. Emergency calls were processed by the switching centre at Scotland Yard and redirected to the relevant local stations in the form of a printer output.

The local stations were requested at an early stage in the research not to destroy any incoming messages. It is the normal practice in the Metropolitan Police for local stations to store message-pad forms and emergency-call printouts for a period of six months and then destroy them. As a result of this request, messages were made available for a period of approximately seven months before the launch of the NW schemes and for the whole one-year period following the launch. Details from the message-pad forms and the emergency-call printouts were recorded and coded for computer analysis.

Messages were selected from the total batch covering the subdivision as a whole. Telephone calls to the police were included in the analysis when they were made by members of the public living in the NW areas. All relevant messages held by the police were included and the final data base comprised a 100 per cent sample of all station and emergency call messages received at the local stations over a continuous seven-month period before the launch of the NW schemes and a twelve-month period following the launch. In order to make the pre-test and post-test periods comparable, the analysis was limited to messages received in the seven-month period before the launch of the schemes and in the same seven-month period following the launch.

A summary of the number of calls received during pre-test and post-test periods is shown in Table 9.1. The total number of station messages received during the seven-month period following the launch of the NW schemes was less than the total number received during the same seven-month period before the launch in both experimental areas. The total number of emergency calls also reduced from pre-test to post-test periods in Wimbledon, although the number increased in Acton. Overall, the total number of telephone calls from residents in the two NW areas to the local police decreased in both areas following the launch of the NW schemes. Therefore, there is little indication from these figures that the that the implementation of NW had any favourable impact on the total number of calls to the local police.

Telephone calls from the public to the police cover many topics from reports of road accidents to notification of crimes. It would not be expected

Table 9.1   *Telephone messages received by local police stations during a seven-month period before launch of NW scheme and during the same seven-month period after launch*

| | Acton experimental area | | | Wimbledon experimental area | | |
	pre	post	% change	pre	post	% change
Station messages	64	51	-20	50	49	-2
Emergency calls	25	35	+40	53	27	-49
All telephone calls	89	86	-3	103	76	-26

that the implementation of NW would have an impact on every type of call for service from the public. It would be expected, however, that if the schemes were effective, residents in a NW area would be more willing to report suspicious incidents and behaviour to the police. Changes in the total number of various categories of telephone calls are shown in Table 9.2.

In Acton there were reductions in three of the four categories of station messages from the pre-test to post-test periods. Only reports of crimes committed in the area increased over the experimental period. There is no evidence from the table that the number of reports of suspicious incidents increased as hypothesized following the launch of the NW scheme. The number of emergency calls relating to suspicious behaviour or incidents did increase from the pre-test to post-test period. It should be noted, however, that the numbers involved are small and the 60 per cent rise shown in the table resulted from an increase of just 3 additional calls during the post-test period.

Table 9.2   *Telephone messages received by local police stations during pre-test and post-test periods, by type of incident*

	Station messages		% change	Emergency calls		% change
	pre	post		pre	post	
Acton experimental area						
Crime report	15	19	+27	6	5	-17
Suspiciousness	17	13	-24	5	8	+60
Disturbance, dispute, complaint	20	9	-55	8	13	+63
Accident, hazard, other	12	10	-17	6	9	+50
All	64	51	-20	25	35	+40
Wimbledon experimental area						
Crime report	12	23	+92	18	10	-44
Suspiciousness	11	8	-17	11	4	-64
Disturbance, dispute, complaint	15	9	-40	11	8	-27
Accident, hazard, other	12	9	-25	13	5	-62
All	50	49	-2	53	27	-49

Notes:
Crime report = reports of crimes.
Suspiciousness = suspicious behaviour or incidents.

In Wimbledon the total number of station messages received in the seven-month period following the launch of the scheme was lower than in the same period before the launch in three of the four categories. The total number of emergency calls decreased over the same period in all four incident categories.

It should be noted that the number of calls made by the public to the police is a function of the number of incidents occurring in the area (e.g. noise from neighbours, domestic or disputes or youths acting suspiciously) and the willingness or inclination of the public to report these incidents. The total number of crime reports is a function of both the number of crimes committed and the willingness of the public to report them. The lack of evidence of an increase in reports to the police of suspicious incidents or behaviour might be the result of a failure of the NW schemes to motivate residents to report incidents to the police at a greater rate, or of a reduction in the number of suspicious acts eligible for reporting. The knowledge that crime increased in both areas from the pre-test to the post-test period makes the latter explanation the less convincing. The most plausible explanation is that the NW schemes failed to motivate residents to increase their reporting rates.

Station messages and emergency-call printouts contain useful information on the date, day and time of the message. It is possible that although there were no overall improvements during the post-test period as a whole, there might have been changes in the date, day and time of reporting.

It is possible that the end-of-year figures for the area might have masked a gradual improvement in the number of calls received during the course of the project. The number of incident calls (station messages and emergency calls) received by the local police stations for each month during the two seven-month periods is shown in Figure 9.1.

In Acton the trend in the number of calls received each month moved downward in the post-test period. There is no evidence therefore that the NW scheme had an impact in the second half of the year, which was masked by a lack of impact in the first half of the year. In Wimbledon the number of incident calls increased slowly throughout the second half of the post-test period. However, the number of calls received was lower for almost every month in the post-test period than for the equivalent month in the pre-test period. There is no indication from the figure that there was any important increase in the number of calls received throughout the year which could be attributable to the NW programme.

The time of day distribution for all telephone calls to the local police stations is shown in Table 9.3. The peak periods for calls from the public in Acton were between 12 noon and 6.00 p.m. (pre-test) and between 6.00 p.m. and midnight (post-test) and in Wimbledon between 6.00 p.m. and midnight in both periods. There is no suggestion from these figures of any major change in the time of day distribution of telephone calls from the public to the police over the course of the experiment.

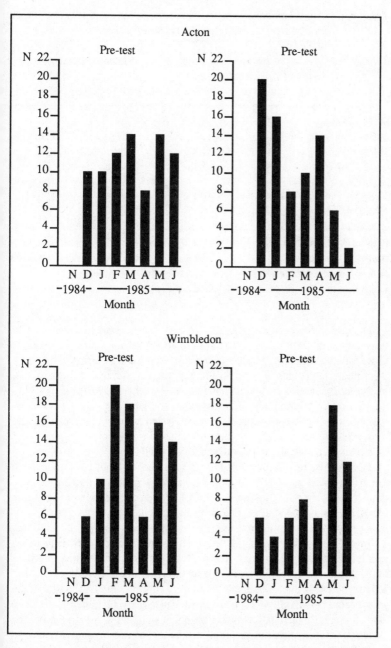

*Figure 9.1   Total number of station messages and emergency calls
received by local police station, by month*

*Table 9.3   Total number of telephone messages received by local
police stations, by time of day (percentages)*

Time (hour)	Acton experimental area		Wimbledon experimental area	
	pre	post	pre	post
0001–6000	13	17	16	16
6001–1200	22	24	22	16
1201–1800	34	27	24	30
1801–2400	31	32	38	38
Total %	100	100	100	100
Total n	89	86	103	76

Pre = a seven-month period from November to June prior to the launch
of the NW scheme.
Post = a seven-month period from November to June in the year
following the launch of the NW scheme.

The station message forms and the emergency call printouts also contain
information on police actions taken in relation to the call and the result of
those actions. The completed forms provide important information not only
on potential changes in the public reporting behaviour following the
implementation of NW, but also on potential changes in police response to
these reports. Unfortunately, the forms were completed fairly idiosyncratically
and information was often not recorded systematically or routinely. The
most reliable piece of information about the police response is the number
of officers sent and the method of transport used.

The number of officers sent in response to calls from the public is an
important indicator of police response, in that it might serve to consolidate
or undermine the potential impact of the NW programme. It is accepted that
the number of officers sent to deal with an incident is not solely a product of
police goodwill or the desire to improve or maintain police–public relations.
The number of officers sent will be affected by the strength of officers in the
subdivision, the number on duty and available for deployment, the seriousness
of the incident and the number of other calls for service outstanding. It would
be expected, however, that there would be a commitment on the part of the
police to show that they were fulfilling their side of the bargain by providing
visible evidence that something was being done. It would be expected
therefore that (all other things equal) the number of officers sent in response
to a call from a resident following the launch of the NW scheme would either
be the same or greater than in the period before the scheme.

The message and emergency call forms do not contain direct information on the number of officers dispatched. A typical format is to write the station number of the foot officers sent and the station number of any cars or vans sent. It is possible to estimate from this information the total number of officers sent by making some assumptions about the number of officers dispatched in vehicles. The estimates used are based on counts of one officer for each foot officer mentioned, 1.5 officers for each car sent (Panda-cars usually contain one officer, and area cars two officers) and two officers for each van sent. The total number of officers sent is shown in Table 9.4.

In Acton the average number of officers sent to deal with a call for service from the public was typically either one or one and a half. The number of calls to which no police officers were sent increased from the pre-test to the post-test period. The number of calls to which two or more officers were sent decreased following the launch of the NW programme. In Wimbledon the average number of officers sent to deal with calls for service was also typically one or one and a half. There was no change in the percentage of calls to which no officers were sent from the pre-test to the post-test period and no change in the percentage to which two or more officers were sent.

Table 9.4   Total number of police officers sent in response to telephone messages received by local police stations (percentages)

	Acton experimental area		Wimbledon experimental area	
	pre	post	pre	post
0	9	23	9	9
1 or 1.5*	65	55	78	80
2 or 2.5	21	15	7	7
3 or more	5	6	6	4
Total %	100	100	100	100
Total n	89	86	103	76

*The figures include 0.5 of an officer because the number of officers dispatched by car was estimated at 1.5.

There is no evidence from these estimates that more officers were dispatched to incidents following the launch of the NW schemes. In fact there is some evidence that in one of the areas the number of officers dispatched substantially decreased during the programme period.

In summary, the analysis of telephone messages from the public to the police has shown that the total number of station messages decreased from the pre-test to the post-test period both in Acton and Wimbledon and the total number of emergency calls increased in Acton and decreased in Wimbledon. Overall, the number of telephone contacts between the police and residents in the NW areas decreased following the launch of the NW schemes. Station messages relating to crime reports increased from the pre-test to the post-test, while all other categories of calls, including reports of suspicious behaviour, decreased in both experimental areas. There were no significant changes in the distribution of telephone calls received in terms of month of the year or time of day. There was no evidence that the police responded more favourably to calls for service following the launch of NW in terms of whether officers were dispatched, or in terms of the number of officers dispatched. Overall, the analysis of telephone calls from residents in the NW areas has failed to reveal any beneficial effects following the launch of the programmes.

Conversations with the police and the public

In addition to the crime and public attitudes surveys on residents' perceptions of the functioning and effectiveness of NW, extended interviews were conducted with some of the key police and public personnel responsible for managing the schemes. The main aim of using an additional research technique was to obtain qualitative and descriptive evidence on the operation of the NW schemes and to generate accounts of some of the changes that might have been perceived to have taken place among people close to the administration of the programme. It should be emphasized that the views expressed are those of the key management personnel and (apart from the co-ordinators) are not necessarily the views of the residents living in the areas.

The interviews were semi-structured and a checklist of questions to be covered was used during the interviews. The responses were tape recorded and later transcribed verbatim. Interviews were conducted with the crime prevention officer and the local home beat officer in Acton and Wimbledon, and with the area co-ordinator and six street co-ordinators in Acton. Different interview schedules were used for the four main types of active member of the schemes (crime prevention officer, home beat officer, area co-ordinator and street co-ordinator). The questions covered the role of each member in managing the scheme, the nature and amount of work done, their perceptions of the effectiveness of NW, and their views on the benefits and drawbacks of the programme.

Police managers

The way in which the police manage NW schemes in the Metropolitan Police District varies, to some extent, from division to division. In both the Acton and Wimbledon subdivisions the overall monitoring of the implementation and operation of NW was conducted by a police NW co-ordinator. The day-to-day administration of particular schemes is more typically the function of the local crime prevention officers (CPOs) (perhaps one CPO, or a CPO plus deputy) and the home beat officers (HBOs) (perhaps one or two HBOs per scheme).

The division of tasks between the CPO and the HBO varied considerably between the two experimental areas. In Acton the CPO played an active role in both initiating and managing the scheme on a day-to-day basis. The HBO played a much less active part in the launch of the programme, but was heavily involved in the administration and maintenance of the scheme. The CPO and HBO regularly met and discussed the running and progress of the scheme. In Wimbledon the CPO played an active part in initiating the scheme, but played almost no role in the day-to-day running of the programme, once it was implemented. Almost all of the day-to-day management of the scheme was the task of the HBO and the CPO; HBO rarely met or discussed the scheme, once it had been launched.

Crime prevention officers   Differences in the part played by the CPOs in administering the NW programmes was revealed most fully in the semi-structured interviews. In particular, the CPO in Wimbledon saw his task as launching and overseeing a large number of schemes *en bloc* and having little responsiblity for the day-to-day running of particular schemes. The CPO in Acton shared the view that his task was launching and overseeing NW on the subdivision, but he also felt responsible for, and played an active part in, the administration of individual schemes. The responses to the questions reveal this difference in orientation.

Neither CPO felt that the adoption of NW in their divisions had altered their job in any fundamental way, but both agreed that it meant more work for them. The Acton CPO believed that they were simply doing more of the same:

> I think there's no difference in the work we're doing but we're just doing more of a particular type of thing. We're certainly covering more meetings and talking to people generally about security. Generally speaking, I'd say we're not doing anything different at all, it's just an expansion on what we've done all along.

The main additions to the work load was their attendance at launch meetings and an increased number of requests by the public for home security surveys and property marking. Both felt that it was difficult to meet the needs of the public in this respect and were aware that they were unable to fulfil their commitments to support the NW programmes. This was expressed most forcibly by the Wimbledon CPO:

> NW has meant an increased number of requests for crime prevention surveys. At the moment there are one hundred and five schemes operating covering over thirty-five thousand residents and they have all been invited to ask the crime

prevention officer if they'd like a free survey. So we're trying to keep up with that side of it, but to be quite honest we can't do it.

Neither officer said that they were claiming much overtime as a result of these additional NW tasks. The usual method for dealing with evening and other additional hours spent on administering NW programmes was to credit hours worked to their time-off card and take the time off owed to them without claiming for it.

When asked whether the introduction of NW in the division had improved their job as CPOs in any way, they both noted the benefits of becoming better known. The Acton CPO emphasized contact with the local communities and the increased willingness of the public to approach the police. The Wimbledon CPO noted the importance of being known by the local communities and also by officials and professionals in other agencies with whom the police deal:

> I am much more widely known for a start. My name is on every bit of paper that goes out to all these schemes, so we're talking about over thirty thousand people have my name and telephone number. Yes, I'm much more widely known and when I do articles for local papers, of course, they accept that fact. It's made my job easier from that point of view and if I pick up the phone and I want to talk to local authorities of anything they all know me.

The CPOs were also asked if the adoption of NW in their divisions had made their job harder in any way. Apart from the additional work involved, there were few complaints about the introduction of NW. The Acton CPO was emphatic that nothing could be lost by implementing NW in a police division:

> Certainly not, I'm all for public contact and this we're getting. We as crime prevention officers are able to get our message across far greater.

The main advantages of NW seen by both CPOs was the increased contact with and communication between themselves and the local communities. Both felt that the level of contact with the public had improved. Most of the additional contacts resulted from the administration of security surveys and property marking and the establishment of new schemes. The Acton CPO argued that both the number and quality of contacts had improved:

> In the field of security we've had a lot more response from that area than I think we've ever had before. As you no doubt appreciate, most people tend to come to us after something has happened to them. But with this particular NW, as with many others, we're getting a lot more contact by their own volition. They're coming along to us before something has happened as a result of their NW newsletters and the things that are happening locally.

Once again, the importance of being known to the local residents was emphasized as an important mechanism which broke down some of the barriers which had previously prevented residents from contacting them:

> The people know who we are before we get there. They know who they are going to speak to before they pick up the phone. They are not dealing with a faceless person or a nameless person.

The next series of questions concerned the CPOs perceived effectiveness of the schemes. Both were optimistic that the schemes had been effective and had reduced crime. The Wimbledon CPO was less aware than the Acton CPO of the progress of the experimental scheme because of his more generalist approach to administering NW. Nevertheless, he spoke about the likely effectiveness of the programme on the basis of his general perceptions:

> I can only treat it the same as all the others. Every scheme that I check has showed at least a forty odd per cent reduction in all crimes. Now I can't see that one will be any different.

The Acton CPO's optimism was tinged with an element of doubt as he was aware that the number of police-recorded crimes in the area had increased over the post-launch period. He hoped that this increase was a result of an NW success in encouraging greater crime reporting:

> I think crime has decreased. Obviously, that's my opinion. I think that the number of reported crimes has gone up because we're trying to persuade people to report things so we know what's actually happening in the area. I think most crimes have fallen. I think the only crimes that seem to have gone up maybe are motor vehicle crimes, but that's an impression not a fact.

They were then asked whether they felt that the perceived reductions in crime were the result of the existence of the NW scheme or something else. If they considered it a result of the NW scheme, they were asked why they thought so and by what mechanism NW had reduced crime. The answers to these questions were interesting, in that they revealed in detail the officers' conceptions of the processes by which NW might be effective in preventing crime. The Acton CPO emphasized contact and communication:

> I think it's the fact that people are dealing more with people they know. I'm a great believer in contact and I think communication is what NW is about. It's about communication between us and the public and the public amongst themselves. That's certainly improved in the ... scheme and in many of the other schemes that we've got. Certainly, in the vast majority of the schemes, it seems to have improved this communication and contact. So I think that certainly it has improved the overall communication and this has improved matters generally.

The Wimbledon CPO mentioned improvements in public attitudes and their willingness to report incidents to the police:

> There are a lot of people who are for one reason or another at home during the day at the high crime time. They've got a little bit more enthusiasm perhaps pumped into them by going to meetings. They are told that it's not an offence to be nosey and things of that nature. They've been asked or pleaded with by people like me from the platform to react and respond and they are responding. In fact we've got some that make so many regular visits to the police station offering help and things like that even their presence out on the street would reduce crime. I simply lecture to them on these grounds. I say you people know who are committing these crimes and in the past you washed your hands; you will not tell us who it is. Let's start from tonight. So, I think it's public attitudes that have changed.

The responses to the questions concerning the perceived advantages of NW and its benefits in the experimental areas also focused on improved levels of police contact with the public. The Acton CPO mentioned improved communication as a result of the police becoming individuals and personalities rather than as anonymous officials. The Wimbledon CPO noted the improved levels of awareness of residents of the existence of each other. He saw additional advantages to such a change which stretched beyond crime reduction to greater self-help, which might be most beneficially received by the elderly and handicapped who were often isolated in communities.

Neither officer could find many disadvantages with the particular schemes in their areas. The additional workload was cited once again as the main drawback to NW, but both felt that they could cope with this and that it was a small price to pay for the overall benefits gained. However, both officers mentioned possible drawbacks in terms of the effective implementation of the schemes. The Wimbledon CPO felt that too few people were marking their property:

> What I would like to be able to do is mark their property. We had fifty thousand pounds worth of property in this station and I crawled all over it with lamps and I never found one bit marked and a lot of it came from neighbourhood watch areas; it's really annoying. When you tell them they look at you and you say, 'Please, if you can't afford the sixty pence for a pen I'll buy you one'.

The Acton CPO was concerned about the ability of the police to cope effectively with the number of telephone calls from the public:

> Well, the only disadvantage, and this is a personal view, is that we have generated a lot more calls to our communications room. Obviously, I feel that we should be in a position to deal with the public as they would expect. In other words, they want prompt replies. Well, it's not always possible because of varying workloads either through the information room at Scotland Yard or at the local station.

The issue of possible weaknesses of the NW schemes was explored at greater length in the remaining questions. The CPOs were asked their views on the long-term plans for the two experimental areas and how long they thought they might last. The Acton CPO was generally hopeful about future developments of the scheme but recognized the problem of maintaining interest:

> There is always a problem with trying to maintain interest. Crime prevention is very much a question of people doing something about it while they are thinking of it. For whatever reason, once they decide that it's not important, once that attitude creeps in, which it can do I think, you need to keep it topical and keep their interest going and certainly [the area co-ordinator] has and her team have done just that: they've managed to keep the interest there. They seem to come up with some unique ideas to keep the interest going. So, I would suggest the life expectancy of it would be quite a long time. [The area co-ordinator] is certainly community oriented and will continue to push either neighbourhood watch or something else in the future. I would hope that neighbourhood watch will continue.

The Wimbledon CPO also felt that NW in the experimental area and in the division as a whole had a long future:

> Well, I can't see an end to the present thinking on the residents' side. Can I give you an example. In another scheme in Wimbledon they had a change of home beat officer who was concerned that they'd not held their regular co-ordinators' meetings. In fact he said that the area co-ordinator was not showing any interest. So I simply typed out a letter saying I would like all residents to meet me for a public meeting to discuss the closure of the neighbourhood watch scheme. There was a tremendous turnout and forty five people volunteered to take over the role of co-ordinator. So in an area like that there's something magic about this neighbourhood watch thing. Whether it's justified or not I couldn't say.

They were questioned further on maintenance and continuing support for NW, and they were asked if there was anything more that the police could be doing to increase the chance of survival of the schemes. The Acton CPO felt that the police were doing all that they could do to maintain NW in the division by continuing to attend co-ordinators' meetings and providing additional publicity material when available. The Wimbledon CPO thought that there could be greater police input:

> Yes, I think we all need more input. We need to make it something more than just a crime battle; we need to make it something that is accepted as part of a good neighbourhood: to look after others, to work together, maybe to organise things together. But at the moment I am afraid that it's a long-term battle. It's not really got the resources it should have. They're saying here that we will come to the end of our resources when we get to one hundred and sixty schemes. It won't be long before we reach that figure and I can see no slackening off.

The interview concluded with a discussion on the police role in implementing, administering and maintaining NW schemes. Both officers could see problems in the way in which NW had been managed, and both were concerned that in many respects the police had not, and could not, deliver the goods. The Wimbledon CPO emphasized the inability of CPOs to keep up with the requests to launch new NW schemes:

> We are still doing six new neighbourhood watch schemes a month and it's not slackened. There are forty-four schemes waiting to start. None of them will be done before August because annual leave starts. So that's the backlog and it doesn't seem to be decreasing.

He also felt that the CPO had been placed in the position of front runner in implementing NW schemes without being given sufficient guidelines or resources to complete the task:

> There is no general policy from what I can see. Different areas have got different ideas on neighbourhood watch schemes. Every crime prevention officer that I've spoken to has said that there is a big increase in neighbourhood watch schemes and I can understand that because your name is up front. I think the general idea of neighbourhood watch is a magnificent idea but not enough resources have been put to it. If you want it more effective that's what you've got to do. The police are now questioning the costs, the financial costs, of NW schemes.

The Acton CPO saw problems in not giving the schemes the support they need and the danger of making promises which cannot be fulfilled:

> It's all very well starting schemes but if we cannot maintain them or back them up and give them the support we should be doing then I can see absolutely no point in starting them in the first place. We are going along and saying or telling them what to expect from NW and if we're not in a position to back it up then I feel strongly that we are letting the public down.

Home beat officers   The home beat officers (HBOs) were responsible for the day-to-day management and administration of the NW schemes. The HBOs were more likely than the CPOs, for instance, to call informally at the home of the area co-ordinator to discuss the running of the scheme. The HBOs more frequently attended the regular co-ordinators' meetings and were often involved in planning and organizing them. It is possible therefore that the HBOs' perspectives on the local schemes were different from those of the CPOs, who had a slightly more distant view of the schemes.

The schedule used for the HBO interviews was very similar to that used for the CPOs and covered the same topics. The first question concerned changes that might have occurred in the work of the HBO as a result of the adoption of NW in their divisions. Neither officer felt that the introduction of NW had altered their work in any fundamental way. The Acton HBO thought that his role as a police officer had moved slightly more in the direction of being a social worker but did not feel that this was a bad thing:

> Really there's no change except that, if anything, I'm doing more in the line of social work. There have been more contacts, certainly with the elderly, about security. They want to get security advice from the horse's mouth, as it were, rather than just taking advice from the newsletter. I obviously have to keep an eye on the crime books which is very good for me as my knowledge of day-to-day crime in the areas has improved.

Neither officer reported working more overtime or longer hours as a result of the scheme.

There was a consensus that NW had improved their jobs as HBOs, and both officers cited greater contact with the public as an example. The Wimbledon HBO believed that the existence of the NW scheme had enabled him to contact residents in the area whom he would not have contacted previously:

> It has certainly given me more contacts with members of the public; people in the normal run of events I wouldn't have had cause to meet or visit. I would not have come into contact with them had the scheme not been in operation.

The Acton HBO noted the value of being better known as a result of the scheme – as did both CPOs – and emphasized the benefits of local residents knowing one's name.

> Yes, more people know me as a result of neighbourhood watch. My name is mentioned by them. So I get a call from someone because he's heard my name, heard that I'm the home beat officer. He has a general picture of what I'm like. So that's a sort of improvement. I'm getting known to many more people. You meet one person and you are introduced to half a dozen more. If I was to put my finger on anything in particular it would be the contact, the public contact, it has improved tremendously.

The principal way in which it was felt that NW had made the work of the HBO harder was in terms of workload. Neither officer said that they worked longer hours as a result of the scheme, but both reported that the work was more intense when they were on duty. The two responses were very similar:

> The workload has increased by virtue of the fact that because there's more contact there is obviously a higher workload; one directly follows from another. Whenever you do anything there's always got to be a pen and paper at the end of it.

> I'm under pressure and the same goes for most home beats who've had neighbourhood watch schemes. There is never a day when I don't get a call from one of the schemes. I have five on my beat and it's a lot of people to keep happy.

Certainly as far as I can see my job has become a little bit more stressful. I'm having to rush about more than I would have done otherwise.

The next series of questions concerned police–public contact. Both officers said that they had spoken to more residents in the NW areas than in the past and felt that a greater number of residents had initiated the contact. Both felt that most of the public-initiated contacts could be defined as no more than a chat to pass the time of day. More serious topics, which included crime and crime prevention matters, were less frequent. The officers were then asked whether reports of suspicious incidents or behaviour had increased in the area following the launch of the NW scheme. Neither officer felt that the flow of useful information from the public had increased very much. The Acton HBO was least optimistic about the quality of information gathered by the home beats during public contact:

> A few times people have reported something but I've got to say that despite the fact that we are asking people to call the police direct at the moment they see something they think is suspicious, a lot of the time it's left for the neighbourhood watch meeting. They save up all their news to tell me a month after it has happened. Obviously, I, in a very nice way, say don't you think it would have been a good idea to tell me about that there and then. But I'm afraid it doesn't happen, so, really, I'm only getting a few calls.

Neither officer claimed that the schemes were wholly effective in reducing crime in the areas. The Acton HBO believed that the only possible reduction that he was aware of was in residential burglary:

> There has been a drop in the number of burglaries reported but there has been an increase in beat crimes reported. Those are the crimes that you obviously know are the minor crimes. Some of those crimes wouldn't have been reported had we not had a neighbourhood watch scheme. So I would imagine at the end of the day, despite falling burglary, the crime figures would probably be up.

The Wimbledon HBO believed that most crimes had decreased in the area with the exception of motor vehicle crime:

> I think it's decreased. I think the only one which hasn't decreased is motor vehicle crime. I think burglaries have gone down as far as I'm concerned.

The next question concerned possible reasons for the changes observed. The Acton HBO was asked why he thought crimes in the area had not reduced as much as might have been expected. In his response, he noted problems of public apathy and the difficulty or inability of NW to change people's behaviour:

I actually wonder if people really do take notice of what's in those newsletters, simply because there are so many examples, like the two burglaries last month where windows were left open in the house. Now how many times have we got to tell people not to leave windows open? It gets back in my mind that neighbourhood watch in my opinion hasn't really done masses to prevent crime; it's simply improved relations between the public and the police.

The Wimbledon HBO was more optimistic about the success of the scheme, and he attributed that success to people looking out for suspicious behaviour:

I think it's a result of the scheme because people are becoming more aware. There is more awareness of what's going on in the streets. I can't actually say hand-on-heart that it's NW that's done it.

Both officers felt that the NW scheme had improved the level of contact between local residents and between the police and residents. The Acton HBO was convinced that the improvements observed in levels of social interaction between residents in the area must ultimately have an impact on levels of crime:

One outstanding thing that I've noticed is that people have got to know their neighbours. At the recent street party I chatted to people I hadn't met before. And, rather than come up to me and start talking about the crime aspect, they were talking about the social aspect. They were now talking about the fact that they now know the three people opposite them. Because they've got to know them, they've got to know their cars and things like that. So in a way, promoting the social aspects in the long run will help crime. Neighbourhood watch has promoted better community relationships and perhaps in the long run that may assist crime prevention.

Neither officer could think of any major disadvantages to the schemes in their areas. It was felt that the existence of the schemes had resulted in an additional work additional work but added the proviso that he would like some evidence that there was a worthwhile end-product:

My work has increased and I actually wonder what real results. We won't know until we've seen the figures and seen what people have to say. I've worked damn hard this year, but I wonder to what end. I wonder if there has been a real improvement.

Each officer was asked about the future prospects of the schemes and their potential life expectancy. Both HBOs felt that the schemes would continue until the area co-ordinator lost interest. Neither officer was particularly optimistic about the long-term survival of the schemes, should the area co-ordinator pull out. The Acton HBO placed particular emphasis on the central role of the area co-ordinator, and on the need to obtain some evidence of success to maintain her enthusiasm:

I do feel that they are looking for a drop in the crime rate, they really are. Now if we go and report to them the fact that burglaries have gone up, motor vehicle crime has gone up, beat crime has gone up, I wonder how they will take it. It will continue as long as the area co-ordinator runs it. She has given strong leadership and if she decides to leave I wonder if it would be run at all. My own view is that I'm doubtful as to the future of it.

Public managers

Semi-structured interviews were conducted with both area and street co-ordinators to determine their reasons for becoming involved in the NW programme and their perceptions of it. No interviews were conducted with co-ordinators from the Wimbledon scheme area because of the limited time available to complete the project and write the report. The following sections are based therefore solely on interviews conducted with co-ordinators of the Acton scheme.

Area co-ordinator   One of the important issues relating to the implementation of NW schemes is the motives of people for wanting a scheme in their area. Some of the issues raised in the US research concern whether those motives are public-minded or private-minded (Lavrakas, 1981); whether they relate specifically to crime or to other problems in the area (Lavrakas and Hertz, 1982); and whether they concern problems that actually exist or that simply might exist in the area (Lavrakas, 1980). The responses of the area co-ordinator suggest that her motives were dominantly private minded in relation to the problems of crime, and were directed at crimes which might occur in the future rather than were occurring in the present:

> I didn't know anything about Neighbourhood Watch at the time. The reason I was interested was because, every time I picked up a local paper, crime seemed to be getting nearer and nearer. There seemed to be more and more crime in the area. I'm concerned because I'm a mother of two young children and it all just seemed to fit together at the time. I was worried about crime in the local streets. It just seemed to be getting nearer and nearer. I thought, 'Well, this seems a good thing to do'.

Wishing to have a scheme established in the area is not quite the same as wishing to start and run a scheme oneself. There is obviously some mechanism which links a perceived need for NW with the decision to volunteer to establish and administer it. The area co-ordinator explained her reasons for volunteering to establish and run the scheme as follows:

> I started talking to the home beat officer and that's how the whole thing came about. The idea came into my mind. No one else I'd spoken to at the time had ever heard of neighbourhood watch and I suppose it was more or less assumed that as I'd already spoken to the home beat officer about it that I should do it.

The area co-ordinator was next asked about some of the activities that the co-ordinators had been engaged in. One of the main formal elements of the scheme was the regular meeting of area and street co-ordinators. The area co-ordinator was asked what she saw as the principal aims of the regular meetings. In her response she stressed the benefits of social interaction within the group:

> The obvious aim is to disseminate information and to generate enthusiasm. It's also just a nice feeling of togetherness. We're like one big family now, it's lovely. Everybody has got to know everybody else. I mean, you join this group and you've immediately made twenty seven new friends. Basically, it's great.

One particularly interesting feature of the Acton scheme during its first year of operation was the decision among the co-ordinators to hold a celebration anniversary street party to mark the end of the first year of the scheme. The area co-ordinator notes in her description of the party that this was the only event held during the year which included the rest of the residents in the area:

> We had the street party because we were one year old in June and we celebrated the fact by having a street party to which all members of the watch scheme were invited. We fed one hundred and forty three children and, I didn't do a head count, but I suppose there must have been about three hundred and fifty people there. It was a fantastic afternoon and everybody has since said, 'When are we going to have another one?' It was a community thing and it was great fun. The home beat officer jumped out of a birthday cake which did a lot of good. He made of fool of himself and people enjoy that don't they. He was a good sport. The only other activities we've had have been basically amongst ourselves: Christmas parties for the co-ordinators and leaving parties for the various co-ordinators who have gone. I suppose the next thing will be a public showing of the video that was made at the street party.

The area co-ordinator believed that the scheme had been beneficial to the community over the first year in a number of ways. She believed that it had improved relationships between the local police and the residents in the area:

> Well I suppose a typical comment at the street party, talking about our street officer, was 'Gosh, he really is like one of us isn't he?' Someone wearing a uniform must come from the planet Mars. So in that sense it's done a marvellous thing. I think on the whole the main thing is people like to see policemen walking the streets. So many people have said to me, 'If only we could get back to that era again when you continuously saw a policeman walking the streets. If only the police could clout the young kid round the ear when he does something instead of the kid having to go to court'. It's the old philosophy but it works.

She was less certain about the effect of the scheme on crime, and felt that increases in recorded crime were inevitable because people were encouraged to report offences to the police:

> Once people get the hang of neighbourhood watch and they become part of it your figures will obviously increase because people are going to start reporting things that they normally would never bother to report. Burglary has certainly decreased. Whether it keeps like that I don't know. But when you get people reporting that their off-side wing mirror has been taken when normally they wouldn't bother. I think next year will be the telling year not this year.

Another benefit noted was the improved relationship between residents in the area:

> People seem more friendly. I don't know whether that's my imagination. Certainly, a great many people have said to me, 'I've lived here for eight years, or fifteen years, and I've at long last got to say hello to the chap who lives over the road'. I've said to them, 'Why haven't you said hello before?' and they say, 'Because you don't like to bother people'. It seems incredible, but it's a fact.

The area co-ordinator believed – as did the CPOs and HBOs – that there were no drawbacks to NW apart from the hard work involved:

> I can't think of any and I don't say that because I'm biased. I honestly can't think of any at all except that it's a lot of hard work.

Street co-ordinators   Interviews were also conducted with six of the street co-ordinators of the Acton scheme. The interviews were held before one of the co-ordinators' meetings at the home of the area co-ordinator during the first year of the scheme. The six co-ordinators comprised about half of the co-ordinators attending the meeting that evening and were selected on a first-come-first-served basis.

One of the main aims of interviewing the street co-ordinators was to find out their reasons for taking on the responsibility of running the scheme. The motives cited combined a desire to reduce crime in the area with a wish to create a stronger community spirit. The main reason given for volunteering themselves, rather than leaving it to others to volunteer, was a sense of personal responsibility and a desire actively to support the scheme. The six responses are reproduced in full below:

> Well, I'd just retired and I had time on my hands and, as I say, it's a good way of meeting people.

> I thought it was a good thing. I thought that it would help, which it has done.

> The person who approached me was very energetic and enthusiastic about the situation. She explained it to me and I thought that if she was willing to put a bit of energy into my neighbourhood I don't see why I shouldn't put in a bit myself.

Well, I had read about, it actually, how they'd been doing it in the United States. I'd lived over there for ten years and I thought, 'If it can be successful over there, it can be here'. So I thought I'd have a go.

Well, I suppose you call it civic duty.

It started with my husband, but I took over. I thought the whole idea was an excellent idea to try to create a community feeling. I just wanted to support it.

Most of the street co-ordinators were convinced that crime had reduced in the area over the preceding year and believed that the NW scheme had contributed to the decline. A number of other perceived benefits of the scheme were also cited; many of the co-ordinators were impressed by the new level of friendship that had developed among residents in the area:

Everybody's friendly and everybody helps one another. I mean we had a great party a fortnight ago. It just proves it. There were hundreds of people there and they were just saying what a great scheme it was. Everyone was for it.

More friendliness. It helps you to meet your neighbours.

I think the friendliness of everybody on my patch is fantastic. I'll give you an example. When we were planning the street party we had to have a raffle to raise money. We had no prizes. I went over to all of my people and I said, 'It's all for the street party'. They would say, 'Oh yeh, we'll have two pounds' worth'.

I think it makes you more aware of your neighbours. It's just to check everybody and to be more aware of who lives around you.

Few street could think of any serious disadvantages to the programme. Some criticisms were raised however about the problem of nosiness and the problem of controlling the spread of confidential information:

There are some people who think that we are being nosy. I don't agree with that.

I have seen people in this meeting who don't exactly mix with the best kind of people. I say to them, 'This information we have got is very private and to let nobody else know'. I mean, we know where crime is being committed. If this should get into the wrong hands or the wrong people. It's not something that you want to discuss with Tom, Dick or Harry in the pub .

Summary

Interviews with key police and public personnel responsible for managing the two experimental schemes revealed widespread and strong support for NW. The interviews also revealed that there was a stronger belief in the efficacy of the schemes in improving contacts between the police and local residents, and between the residents themselves, than in bringing about a reduction in crime.

The CPOs felt that their workload had increased slightly but did not see this as a serious problem. They believed that the most important advantage of NW in their areas was the improved levels of contact with the public. They were uncertain about whether crime rates had reduced in the experimental areas and also about the life expectancy of the NW schemes. Both officers felt that there were important problems in the management of NW in terms of the police being able to fulfil their share of the bargain.

The HBOs also felt that their workload had increased as a result of the implementation of NW in their areas and indicated that this was an unimportant problem. They believed that one of the most significant advantages of the NW schemes was the increased level of contact with the residents in the areas. Neither officer felt that these contacts had resulted in an increase in the flow of useful information. They were uncertain about whether crime rates had reduced in the experimental areas. They were also uncertain about the long-term prospects of the schemes and felt that their future depended on the continued support and enthusiasm of the existing area co-ordinators. The interviews with the area co-ordinator revealed that the reasons for establishing the schemes were private minded, crime-oriented, and directed at the future rather than the present. Another reason for taking on the responsibility of the scheme was that she was the right person in the right place at the right time. The area co-ordinators believed that one of the most important advantages of the scheme was the greater level of interaction between residents living in the area and between residents and the local police. She was less certain, however, about the effect of the scheme on crime rates in the area.

The main reasons given by the street co-ordinators for volunteering to help administer the scheme was a belief that it would provide an opportunity to meet people; a belief that it was a good thing; a desire to support the work of the area co-ordinator; and feelings of duty. The most frequently mentioned benefit of the scheme was the new friendships established. Most of the street co-ordinators felt that crime had been reduced.

The interviews with the key personnel managing the NW programmes revealed striking similarities in their perceptions and attitudes towards the scheme. One important theme which emerged from these conversations was that NW was well liked by all those involved in its administration. A second theme was the belief that the most important benefit of the NW programmes during their first year of operation was the improved contact and social interaction between the police and the residents, and among the residents themselves. A third theme was the apparent uncertainty about the efficacy of the scheme in terms of reducing crime.

Tasks performed by the police
The analysis of tasks performed by the police in administering NW arose out of the investigation of the cost of NW. In order to investigate the manpower costs of administering the two NW schemes, it was necessary to ask officers

to complete activity sheets each time they performed an NW task. NW tasks were defined as activities relating to the NW area that the officer would not have performed, had the scheme not existed. The completed activity sheets provided not only useful data on the manpower costs of NW, but also a detailed breakdown of the work done by the local police in administering the experimental schemes during the first year of their operation.

Activity sheets were completed by all police officers who performed any tasks associated with the implementation or running of the schemes. This resulted in at least one activity sheet being completed by: the home beat officer; the crime prevention officer; the NW police co-ordinator; the home beat sergeant; the chief inspector; and the station superintendent. The officers were asked to complete one activity sheet each time they performed a task which related to the establishment or functioning of the experimental NW scheme. They were requested to include only tasks which were related to the scheme, which they would not have performed had the scheme not existed. The activity sheets included spaces for the officer's name and number, the date the task was completed, the length of time spent on the task in hours and minutes, together with a description of the task. A breakdown of the number of hours spent on selected NW activities is shown in Table 9.5.

In both areas, the greatest number of hours worked performing NW tasks was recorded by the home beat officers, and the second greatest number of hours was recorded by the crime prevention officers. Other officers made only a small contribution to the running of the scheme in terms of hours worked. The work of the senior officers in the subdivisions was limited almost entirely to attending the launch meeting.

In Acton the most time-consuming activity for the HBO was telephoning and visiting the area and street co-ordinators; and the second most time-consuming task was arranging and attending co-ordinators' meetings. In Wimbledon the most time consuming activity recorded by the HBO was property marking; and the second most time-consuming task was responding to contacts from residents (most of which concerned parking and other vehicular problems). The difference between the workloads of the two officers can perhaps be best explained by the particular interest of the Wimbledon HBO in promoting property marking and dealing with local parking and other problems associated with vehicles in the area which preceded the establishment of the NW scheme. Therefore, it would be estimated that the workload of the Acton HBO was more typical of the activities performed by HBO's responsible for a NW scheme.

The work of the CPOs was less wide-ranging. In Acton the greatest number of hours worked by the CPO was involved in organizing special area events which comprised mainly the organization of a mobile security exhibition and assisting with the street party. The next most time-consuming activities were evenly divided between planning and attending the launch meeting; planning and attending co-ordinators' meetings; and conducting

Table 9.5   Time spent by police officers on tasks relating to the experimental NW schemes (hours)

Task	Acton experimental area			Wimbledon experimental area		
	HBO	CPO	Other	HBO	CPO	Other
Plan or attend launch meeting	2.0	4.0	4.0	2.5	9.5	8.0
Plan or attend co-ordinators' meeting	16.5	4.0	6.0	6.5	4.0	0.0
Personal or telephone call to co-ordinators	24.9	1.0	0.0	14.0	0.0	0.0
Personal or telephone call to other residents	1.3	0.0	0.0	0.0	0.0	0.0
Prepare or distribute newsletters	1.3	0.0	5.0	0.0	0.0	0.0
Home security surveys	0.0	5.5	0.0	0.0	8.0	0.0
Property marking	0.0	0.0	0.0	43.0	0.0	0.0
Responding to resident contacts	3.2	0.0	0.0	30.3	0.0	0.0
Special area events	10.3	11.0	0.0	0.0	0.0	0.0
Street signs	0.0	1.8	1.3	0.0	4.0	0.0
Other	5.3	0.0	0.5	3.0	0.0	0.0
Total	64.8	27.3	16.8	99.3	25.5	8.0

Other = NW police co-ordinator, home beat sergeant, chief inspector and superintendent.

home security surveys. In Wimbledon the greatest number of hours worked by the CPO concerned planning and attending the launch meeting. Most of this work was conducted before the launch of the scheme. The most time-consuming task conducted by the CPO following the launch of the scheme was conducting home security surveys.

In both Acton and Wimbledon the senior officers in the subdivision attended the launch meeting and made no further direct contribution to the scheme. In Acton additional work was performed following the launch of the scheme by the NW police co-ordinator and home beat sergeant. This mainly comprised supplying information to be used at the co- ordinators' meetings or in the newsletter.

The analysis of tasks performed by police officers in establishing and administering the experimental NW schemes revealed that most of the work involved in running the schemes was done by the HBOs. This work typically involved liaison with the local co-ordinators to provide information and to assist in arranging the co-ordinators' meetings. In Acton there was very little contact between the HBO and other residents in the area. In Wimbledon there was greater contact with other residents as a result of the HBO's particular interest in promoting property marking. The work of the CPOs mainly concerned preparing the launch of the scheme and conducting home security surveys. Both CPOs spent some time in arranging the erection of street signs in the area. Senior officers and other officers played only a minor role in administering the scheme, which was mainly concentrated around the launch of the scheme.

The costs of NW to the police

The costs of implementing the two experimental NW schemes and administering them for their first year of operation can be divided into salary costs relating to manhours worked and non-salary costs relating to equipment and other costs.

The salary costs of NW can be defined in terms of additional costs and nominal costs. The additional salary costs of NW to the police result from the employment of additional staff and as a result of paying additional salaries to existing staff for overtime. The nominal salary costs of NW to the police are the costs incurred when an officer is taken from another duty to perform activities relating to NW. It was beyond the remit of the research to investigate additional costs of NW. The additional costs of NW to the Metropolitan Police would have to be calculated by examining employment and recruitment patterns for the force as a whole. It is possible, however, to assess the nominal salary costs of NW by examining the number of hours spent by each officer engaged in NW tasks.

The completed activity sheets provided the basic data on the total number of hours worked by each officer on NW tasks. The total number of hours worked was multiplied by the average hourly salary cost of officers of each rank to produce a total salary cost over the first year of the scheme. The results of the analysis are shown in Table 9.6.

The total nominal salary costs were £1,727 for administering the Acton NW scheme, and £2,118 for administering the Wimbledon scheme during their first year of operation. The great majority of these costs were accounted for in the salaries of police constables. The nominal salary costs of senior officers was small in both areas.

Table 9.6   *Police salary costs of adminstering the experimental NW schemes (pounds sterling)*

	PC	Sgt	CI	Sup't	Total
		Acton experimental area			
Hours worked	103	4	2	0	
Rate per hour	15.61	18.05	23.65	29.75	
Total salary cost	1,608	72	47	0	1,727
		Wimbledon experimental area			
Hours worked	130	0	0	3	
Rate per hour	15.61	18.05	23.65	29.75	
Total salary cost	2,029	0	0	89	2,118

Note:
PC = police constable; Sgt. = sergeant; CI = chief inspector; Sup't = superintendent.
Source:
Rate tables, F2 Branch, Metropolitan (effective from 1 September 1986)

Table 9.7   *Non-salary costs of administering the experimental NW schemes (pounds sterling)*

	Acton experimental area	Wimbledon experimental area
Publicity material	109	118
Street signs	120	120
Hire of hall	12	0
Newsletter	60	15
Telephone calls	7	1
Total	308	254

The non-salary costs for the police in launching and administering the NW schemes include the costs of stationery and equipment. Details of all non-salary costs were collected throughout the year from the key police personnel involved in running the schemes. The costs of publicity material was calculated by obtaining the average unit costs for each publicity item from the Metropolitan Police Publicity Department. The figures obtained did not include development costs. A full breakdown of all non-salary costs incurred is shown in Table 9.7.

The table shows that the bulk of the non-salary costs incurred by the police resulted from the costs of publicity material and from the costs of the production and erection of street signs. Other costs relating to the hire of the hall for the launch meeting (there was no charge for the hire of the hall for the launch meeting in Wimbledon), the production of the newsletter and telephone contacts made by the police to residents in the area (as opposed to being received from residents in the area) were generally low.

The total costs to the Metropolitan Police of implementing and administering the two experimental NW schemes for the first year comprised the addition of salary and non-salary costs. In Acton the total combined cost amounted to £2,035, and in Wimbledon the total combined cost amounted to £2,362. The full costs of the schemes to the police are probably higher than this as officers might not have included all activities carried out in relation to the scheme, and some stationery and equipment costs might have been overlooked. However, it is unlikely that the real costs to the police are greatly in excess of these estimates.

At the time of writing, it was estimated that 10,000 NW schemes had been launched in the Metropolitan Police District since 1983. It is possible to estimate from the figures calculated for the two experimental areas the total cost of all these schemes to the Metropolitan Police during their first year of operation, by taking the mean of the first-year costs of the two experimental schemes. This would result in a total nominal salary costs of £19 million for police work during the first year of all the NW schemes launched so far. The total additional non-salary costs would be approximately £3 million.

10 Interpreting the Results

Introduction

The research results presented in the preceding chapters represent the bare evidence that must be interpreted before a conclusion can be reached. In particular, it must be decided whether the research measured what it was intended to measure; whether the observed relationships between variables can be considered causal relationships; and whether the findings of the research can be generalized to other schemes. The main aim of this chapter is to summarize the evidence generated in the preceding chapters, to assess and interpret the evidence and to arrive at a conclusion about the overall impact of NW.

Summary of main findings

The results of the crime surveys showed that the prevalence (proportion of households victimized at least once) and incidence (total number of offences reported) of household victimizations increased in both the Acton and Wimbledon experimental areas from the pre-test to the post-test period. The prevalence and incidence of personal victimizations either remained stable or increased. These trends were observed using both bivariate and multivariate methods of analysis. There was no evidence that specific subgroups of the samples experienced a significant reduction in victimization rates over the experimental period. All subgroups in the Acton NW area experienced an increase in victimization following the launch of the scheme; and all subgroups in the Wimbledon NW area experienced an increase in victimization, with the exception of non car owners and households containing two children.

There was also no evidence that there were any significant improvements in reporting rates, or in clear-up rates. Reporting rates increased in the Acton area by a small amount, and decreased in the Wimbledon area by a large amount. The clear-up rates of selected offences committed in the subdivision covering the NW schemes either remained stable or decreased from pre-test to post-test period.

The results relating to changes in public attitudes and behaviour were more encouraging, as already described. Overall, there were significant improvements in regard to the fear of household crime, area satisfaction and a sense of social cohesion in Acton, and significant improvements in area satisfaction and home protection behaviour in Wimbledon. In addition, there were some improvements recorded in public attitudes or behaviour among specific subgroups. In Wimbledon there were significant reductions in the fear of personal crime and household crime among females; among respondents who were separated, widowed or divorced; among low-income households and single adult households. In Acton there were significant reductions in perceived probability of personal victimization among unemployed respondents.

In neither area was there an overall significant reduction in fear of personal crime, in the perceived probability of household or personal victimization or in public evaluation of the police. In Acton there was no overall significant reduction in home protection behaviour, and in Wimbledon there was no overall reduction in fear of household crime or in a sense of social cohesion. In both areas there was an overall significant decrease in police contact as measured by the last time that a police officer was seen in the area.

The analysis of telephone calls from the public to the police showed that the total number of station messages decreased from pre-test to post-test periods in both Acton and Wimbledon; and the total number of emergency calls increased in Acton and decreased in Wimbledon. Overall, the total number of telephone contacts between residents and the police decreased following the launch of the NW schemes. The total number of telephone contacts concerning reports of suspicious behaviour also decreased in both areas.

Validity

The statistical analysis has shown that there are some significant changes in levels of crime from the pre-test to the post-test surveys which are in an opposite direction to that hypothesized by proponents of NW. In addition, the statistical analysis has shown that there are some significant changes in public attitudes and behaviour which are in the hypothesized direction. What grounds are there for presuming that either the positive or the negative findings presented represent changes that can be attributed to the implementation of NW?

The extent to which statistical associations can be extrapolated to causal inferences depends, in part, on research validity. The concept of research validity is defined by Cook and Campbell as 'the best available approximation to the truth or falsity of propositions' including propositions about cause (1979, p.37). There are a number of reasons why research results might not accurately reflect the truth of the propositions being investigated. Campbell and Stanley (1966), and Campbell (1969), refer to two principal types of validity: 'internal validity' (i.e. the approximate validity with which statements can be made about whether there is a causal relationship from one variable to another) and 'external validity' (i.e. the approximate validity with which conclusions can be drawn about the generalizability of a causal relationship principal types). Cook and Campbell (1979), and Judd and Kenny (1981), add two further subcategories to these two principal types 'statistical conclusion validity' (a subcategory of 'internal validity', concerning the validity with which statements can be made about the covariation of two variables) and 'construct validity', (a subcategory of 'external validity', concerning the validity with which statements can be made about the association between operational variables and higher-order constructs).

In order to interpret the research findings and arrive at a research conclusion, it is necessary to consider research validity. Therefore, it is appropriate before applying these validity tests to the current research findings, to elaborate the four main types of validity in more detail.

Statistical conclusion validity
Statistical conclusion validity is the extent to which the research design and method of analysis are sufficiently sensitive and powerful to detect covariance between the presumed cause and effect. The main problem concerning statistical conclusion validity is guarding against a conclusion that there is a treatment effect when there is not (Type I error), or a conclusion that there is no treatment effect when there is (Type II error). The primary research design and analysis elements that effect the probability of these two statistical conclusion errors are the size of the sample used (the likelihood of making a Type II error is higher when sample sizes are small) and the extent to which the assumptions underlying the statistical tests used have been violated (the likelihood of making a Type I error is higher if the assumption of independence of observations is violated).

Internal validity
Internal validity concerns the extent to which an association between two variables can be considered causal (in this case the existence of NW and the observed changes in public attitudes and behaviour). There are a variety of threats to internal validity which are outlined in detail in Cook and Campbell (1979) and Judd and Kenny (1981).

The outcome variable might change in the direction hypothesized following the introduction of the treatment variable as a result of some other event which took place between pre-test and post-test periods ('history'). Judd and Kenny (1981) provide an example of the confounding effect of an unexpected rise in the price of alcohol during an evaluation of a programme relating to alcohol consumption.

The outcome variable might change during the course of the experiment as a result of the respondents changing in a way relating to natural growth and maturation such as growing older, wiser, stronger or more experienced ('maturation'). Some subjects attending programmes designed to reduce drug use might terminate their use of drugs not as a result of the programme, but as a result of 'maturing out'. A similar problem exists in evaluating educational programmes among children whose educational ability changes over time independently of the treatment programme.

Respondents can become familiar with the test procedure which can influence the results obtained ('testing'). Judd and Kenny (*ibid.*) cite an example of a study which showed that even one repetition of a test might influence the results obtained. Subjects who had previously been interviewed about cancer were subsequently more concerned about cancer than respondents who had not previously been interviewed about this subject.

Difference between pre-test and post-test outcome measures might result from a change in the measuring instrument ('instrumentation'). Cook and Campbell (1979) note that a change in outcome can occur as a result of a change in the number or type of response categories. Judd and Kenny (1981 also point out the problem of changes in the phrasing of questions from the pre-test to post-test which might result in measuring different constructs.

Uncontrolled variables might artificially or untypically depress or inflate the pre-test score ('statistical regression'). Cook and Campbell (1979) give an example of a student who is unable to sleep prior to a college examination and obtains a low score as a result. The next time the student takes a similar test (assuming that he or she is able to sleep beforehand), it would be expected that the score would be higher. The improvement in score resulted from a natural regression to the student's mean score rather than from any event that occurred between the tests.

The use of different subjects in the treatment and comparison groups and in the pre-test and post-test surveys increases the probability that there will be differences in outcome scores ('selection'). Selection bias is always a problem when subjects are not randomly allocated to treatment and control or pre-test and post-test groups. This problem is particularly acute in quasi-experimental designs where subjects are, to some extent, self-selecting.

Construct validity

Judd and Kenny define construct validity as 'the extent to which the specific outcome measures, treatments, samples and settings employed in the research represent the theoretical construct of interest' (1981, p.21}. They provide an example of an evaluation of a mental health programme on schizophrenia in which it was presumed that the subjects assigned to the treatment and comparison groups were in fact suffering from schizophrenia. Subsequent diagnosis revealed that some of the subjects were not suffering from schizophrenia, but manic depression. A re-analysis of the data revealed that the removal of manic depressives from the sample reversed the results from a treatment to a non-treatment effect. The 'Hawthorne effect' is another example of a problem of construct validity: there was some doubt in the Hawthorne study about whether the experimental intervention (the planned treatment) was the result of changes in levels of illumination or administrative concern over working conditions as demonstrated by the implementation of the experiment.

External validity

Cook and Campbell (1979) define external validity as the validity with which the research findings can be generalized to particular persons, settings and times – and across particular persons, settings and times. The former concerns the extent to which the research findings can be generalized to the target population, and the latter the extent to which the research findings can be generalized to other populations or subpopulations.

Cook and Campbell (1979) list some of the threats to external validity which affect the extent to which research results can be generalized across populations or subpopulations, settings and times. Generalization across subpopulations depends on the interaction between sample group composition and treatment. It cannot be assumed that a treatment effect shown for the population as a whole will be shown for all subpopulations. It might not be possible therefore to generalize the results obtained for the sample as a whole to specific subgroups of the sample (e.g. specific racial or social subgroups). Generalizations across settings depends on the extent to which there is an interaction between setting and treatment effect. Cook and Campbell (1979) query, for example, whether a relationship obtained in a factory setting can be obtained in a bureaucracy, in a military camp or on a university campus. Generalizations across time depend on the extent to which there is an interaction between the period of the research and the effect of the treatment. Research conducted during a period when something unusual happened (e.g. a major incident or event reported widely by the news media) might generate different findings to identical research conducted when nothing unusual happened.

Judd and Kenny (1981) include in their definition of external validity not only the extent to which findings can be generalized across populations, but also the extent to which findings can be generalized from the construct measured (e.g. the experimental programme) to other constructs (e.g. other versions of the programme). They explain the distinction by using as an example the widely reported evaluation of the television programme *Sesame Street* (Ball and Bogatz, 1970). The research aimed to test the effect of viewing the programme on the cognitive development of disadvantaged pre-school children. The external validity of the *Sesame Street* evaluation findings, they argue, is dependent on: (1) the extent to which the findings can be generalized to other populations not included in the research (e.g. advantaged pre-school children); and (2) the extent to which they can be generalized from the construct tested (e.g. reading ability) to other constructs not included in the research (e.g. style of play).

Explaining the results
In order to arrive at a conclusion about the likely impact of the NW programmes, it is necessary to examine the threats to internal validity. In order to arrive at a conclusion about the implications of the findings for other NW programmes in other areas, it is necessary to examine threats to external

validity. The following discussion considers each type of conclusion with respect to: (1) the crime survey results; and (2) the public attitudes and behaviour survey results.

The crime survey results

The results of the crime surveys showed that the prevalence and incidence of household victimizations increased in both NW areas from the pre-test to the post-test period. To that extent can these findings be attributed to the experimental programmes, and to what extent can they be generalized across populations, settings and times?

There are three main competing explanations of the observed findings: (1) the increase in victimization rates was caused by the existence of the NW programme; (2) the increase in victimization was a spurious result of the research (the increase did not happen in reality); or (3) the increase in victimization rates was caused by factors unrelated to the programme (the increase would have occurred anyway). Explanations (2) and (3) concern issues relating to research validity.

The first explanation is based on the assumption that the existence of the NW scheme, in some way, caused an increase in victimization rates. It is an assumption that would be made after all the various threats to internal validity had been considered and rejected. In what way could the existence of a NW programme result in an increase in victimization rates?

In order to explain the increase as a consequence of the existence of the NW scheme, it would have to be argued that the programme altered the decision-making of potential offenders. They would have to perceive the area as a more desirable place in which to commit crime after the programme was implemented than before. One possible explanation is that offenders who seek to steal goods (e.g. burglars and car thieves) are attracted to NW areas because the existence of the scheme suggests to them that there is something in the area worth taking. It could be argued, for example, that the installation of burglar alarms and the fitting of additional security locks might serve to attract offenders because of a possible presumption that there is something in the dwelling worth stealing. The extent to which such cues attract criminals is uncertain. The results of research based on interviews with burglars suggest that alarms and security devices attract only a very small percentage of offenders and the remainder either ignore their existence or are deterred by them (Bennett and Wright, 1984). Another possible explanation is that residents in NW areas become complacent and assume that others are looking after crime prevention and no longer make an individual effort to protect their property. It is also possible that reports from the police or from the area co-ordinator that crime rates are falling (whether or not they are accurate) might encourage a relaxed attitude to crime prevention among residents in the belief that the problem is now solved.

Both explanations are based on the assumption that offenders will be aware of the relaxation in crime prevention behaviour among residents and decide that the area is now a suitable place in which to commit crimes.

The research evidence which is available on the perceptions and decision-making of offenders does not lend much support to the idea that criminals will be attracted to NW areas or that their decision-making will be affected substantially by residents' security behaviour (Bennett and Wright, 1984; Jenkins and Latimer,1987). There is also little evidence from the research that crime prevention initiatives result in complacency and a worsening of crime prevention efforts. The dominant finding is that individual or community-oriented crime prevention programmes either improve or have no effect on crime prevention behaviour (Clarke and Hope, 1984; Rosenbaum, 1986). It is difficult therefore to find support in the available research literature for the proposition that the increase in victimization was a direct result of the implementation of the NW programmes.

The second explanation is based on the assumption that the increase in victimization was spurious and a product of research error. The main problem with statistical conclusion validity is guarding against a conclusion that there is a treatment effect when there is not (Type I error) and a conclusion that there is no treatment effect when there is (Type II error). The observed increase in victimization could be considered an example of a Type I error as there is a possibility of concluding that there is a programme effect (albeit in the reverse direction to that hypothesized) when in fact there was no effect.

What evidence is there to believe that the research finding was spurious and a result of a Type I error? The major threats to statistical conclusion validity concern the power of the statistical test used (in guarding against Type I and Type II errors) and the extent to which assumptions underlying the test have been violated. In order to minimize these threats, two different statistical tests were used. The two tests produced identical results and identified the same comparisons as significant. It would seem unlikely therefore that the observed significant differences were the result of Type I error.

The third explanation is based on the the view that the increase in victimization rate was a result of factors unrelated to the existence of the NW programme. This explanation concerns threats to internal validity.

One threat to internal validity which might affect the research conclusion here is differences in the history of the areas. It could be argued that the increase in household victimizations was the result of an event (or number of events) unrelated to the existence of the scheme which affected the two experimental areas here, but did not affect the comparison areas. Efforts were made during the design stage of the research to ensure (as far as possible) that no avoidable changes occurred the areas which might affect crime rates. This included attempts to ensure that no new police initiatives were launched in the areas during the research period, the home beat officers remained in the areas for the entire twelve-month period, the boundaries of the NW areas were not altered during the experiment and no other NW schemes were grafted on to the experimental programmes. There is no evidence of changes in any of these important parameters during the course of the experiment.

Efforts were also made to monitor the history of each area in order to observe any other important changes that might have occurred which could influence crime rates. One of the areas, for example, had a problem with commuter parking and, for some years, the local council had tackled this problem by blocking street entrances with gates. There is no evidence that any changes were made to traffic or pedestrian access or to on-street parking facilities during the course of the research. Efforts were also made to monitor the arrest patterns of local offenders. It could be argued that crime rates in a small area are particularly susceptible to the activities of a small number of prolific offenders. There were no reports from the police working in the experimental areas that any prolific offenders had been arrested or released from custody during the year of the research.

A more elusive historical event which might explain differences in crime patterns in the NW areas is changes in the decision-making and behaviour patterns of local criminals (apart from whether or not they are arrested or released). It is possible that (for whatever reasons) one or more local criminals might switch their criminal activity from one area to another (e.g. to the NW site). It is also possible that one or more local criminals might increase their rate of offending during the research period and commit more offences in a number of areas including the experimental area. Finally, it is possible, as a result of a change in the wider geographical area (e.g. changes in access routes or the location of leisure centres), that offender mobility patterns might change in a way which brings them into closer contact with the NW site. These changes could not be investigated as part of the research and their effect on crime rates in the area must remain unknown.

A second threat to internal validity which might affect the research conclusion is the effect of statistical regression. Statistical regression might explain the increase in crime rates if the crime level was unusually low in the pre-test period and returned to a more typical level in the post-test period. Were the crime rates untypically low in the pre-test period in the experimental areas? As only one pre-test survey was conducted, it was not possible to compare pre-test rates with earlier rates to determine their typicality. It was possible, however, to estimate longer-term movements in crime by examining the police-recorded crime data (see Chapter 7). In Wimbledon there was little evidence that crime rates were unusually low during the pre-test period. In Acton, however, there is some indication that crime rates in the pre-test period were unusually low. The untypical depression in the number of crimes recorded in the pre-test period could explain, at least, part of the increase in crime in the Acton NW area during the post-test period.

A third threat to internal validity relevant to the research conclusion is the problem of selection. The use of different subjects in the treatment and comparison groups and (in the case of untreated control group design with separate pre-test and post-test samples) in the pre-test and post-test samples increases the probability that there will be differences in outcome scores independent of exposure to the treatment programme. Variations among samples can be controlled to some extent by using multivariate analysis. Nevertheless, it is only possible to control for differences which can be measured in the survey (e.g. the standard demographic variables such as gender, race and class). Inevitably, there will be additional differences between the subjects which cannot be controlled (e.g. personality factors, design features of the respondent's dwelling and geographical position within the experimental area).

Respondent selection might explain the overall increase in crime rates in the experimental areas if the post-test sample comprised a greater proportion of victim-prone respondents than the pre-test sample. The analysis of sample difference (Chapter 5) showed that the only significant differences between the pre-test and post-test samples were a greater proportion of single respondents in the post-test period in Acton and a greater proportion of higher-income homeowners and non-manual workers in the post-test period in Wimbledon. Single respondents have been shown to be less victim-prone than married or separated, widowed or divorced respondents (Chapter 7). High-income homeowners and non- manual workers, however, were shown to be more victim-prone than their counterparts. It is unlikely that the increase in reported household victimization was a result of these differences alone as each of these variables was controlled in the multivariate analysis. Nevertheless, it is possible that there were differences between the samples in terms of unmeasured characteristics related to these demographic variables (e.g. characteristics of the respondents' homes and situation and layout of the dwelling).

Which of the three competing explanations most convincingly account for the research finding that the victimization rate increased significantly following the introduction of the NW programme in the experimental areas? It has been argued that the first explanation that crime rates increased as a direct result of the programme was not considered very convincing as some of the most likely processes by which this might happen were not well supported in the research literature. The second explanation that the victimization was a spurious product of the statistical method used was also considered unconvincing. The third explanation that the increase was the result of factors unrelated to the existence of the scheme was considered the most convincing. The research could not discount the possibility that the increase in crime could be explained in terms of differences in history of the areas investigated or in terms of statistical regression to the mean crime rate or in terms of selection and unmeasured differences between the pre-test and post-test samples.

The most important general conclusion is that the NW programme had no measured impact (either favourable or unfavourable) on the crime rate in either of the two NW areas. To what extent can these results be generalized across populations, settings and times?

Is it possible to generalize the findings for the population as a whole across subpopulations? In the Acton experimental area all subgroups registered an increase in the rate of reported household victimization from the pre-test to the post-test period. In the Wimbledon experimental area all subgroups with the exception of non car owners (who showed no change in mean offence rate) and respondents living in households which included two children (who showed a small reduction in mean offence rate) registered an increase in household victimizations. There is little evidence from these results that there were any significant variations in programme effect among subgroups. Therefore, it is reasonable to assume that the findings for the sample as a whole can be generalized to the sample subgroups.

Is it possible to generalize the findings for the population as a whole to other populations? In order to generalize the results to other populations, some effort would have to be made in designing the research to ensure that the area chosen was representative. In fact the experimental areas were chosen on the basis that the police and the local residents might implement schemes which were better than average. The results of the evaluation cannot be generalized to other populations as those populations selected were not representative of any wider population of people (e.g. all people in London or all people in Britain).

Is it possible to generalize the findings relating to the specific NW schemes investigated (the evaluated NW construct) to other NW schemes (other versions of the NW construct)? This problem differs from the last, in that it concerns the extent to which the findings can be generalized from the version of NW operationalized in the current research to another version of NW operationalized elsewhere. The answer to the question depends on the nature of the theoretical formulation of NW and the range of variations possible in methods of operationalizing the theoretical formulation. There are few references in the published literature to the theoretical process by which NW is supposed to reduce crime or to the efficacy of different methods of operationalizing the theoretical process. It is not possible to arrive at a conclusion therefore about the extent to which the results from the current programme can be generalized to different kinds of programme.

Is it possible to generalize the findings to other times? The answer to this question depends on the way in which the method of operationalizing the concept of NW varies over time and the effectiveness of these different versions of NW. It has been argued by some of the police officers involved in the research that the schemes evaluated represent the first stage in the development of NW in London, and as time passes and lessons are learned the schemes will improve. It would seem likely that during this developmental period the method of operationalizing NW will vary. Consequently, results relating to a type of scheme implemented at one point in time might have little relevance to the type of scheme implemented at another point in time.

It summary, it has been argued that the extent to which the main research findings can be generalized is limited. There is some support for the conclusion that the findings can be generalized to specific subgroups within the population. But there is little support for the conclusion that the results can be generalized to other populations, across settings or across times.

The public attitudes and behaviour results
The results of the public attitudes and behaviour surveys showed that there were significant improvements in the fear of household crime, area satisfaction and sense of social cohesion in Acton and significant improvements in area satisfaction and home protection behaviour in Wimbledon. To what extent can these findings be attributed to the experimental programme, and to what extent can they be generalized across populations, setting and times?

There are three main competing explanations of the observed findings: (1) the improvements in attitudes and behaviour were caused by the existence of the NW programme; (2) the improvements in attitudes and behaviour was a spurious result of the research (the increase did not happen in reality); or (3) the improvements in attitudes and behaviour were caused by factors unrelated to the programme (the increase would have occurred anyway).

The first explanation is that the existence of the NW scheme in some way caused the beneficial changes in fear of crime, area satisfaction, sense of social cohesion and home protection behaviour. In what way could the existence of the NW programme have caused these changes?

It has been argued that fear of crime is related to actual crime rates, to perceived crime rates and to individual differences which predispose some people to be more fearful than others (Maxfield, 1987; Lavrakas, 1980, 1981).

One explanation of the link between the existence of the NW programme and a reduction in fear of crime might be a reduction in actual crime rates. The obvious problem with this explanation is that there was no actual reduction in crime rates in either area.

A second explanation is that the link between the existence of the NW scheme and a reduction in fear of crime is not actual crime rates, but perceived crime rates. It is conceivable that residents in the NW areas believed (perhaps as a result of the mere existence of the scheme or as a result of encouraging reports in the NW newsletter) that crime rates were falling. In order to support this hypothesis, it would have to be shown that residents in Acton (where there was a significant reduction in fear of crime) were more likely than those in Wimbledon (where there was no significant reduction in fear of crime) to perceive crime rates as falling. The results of the pre-test and post-test surveys support this conclusion as they show a reduction (albeit non-significant) in the mean level of perceived probability of victimization in Acton and no corresponding reduction in perceived probability of victimization in Wimbledon. In addition, a greater proportion of residents reported that they believed the number of burglaries in the area had decreased over the experimental year in Acton (41 per cent) than in Wimbledon (23 per cent).

A third explanation is that the reduction in fear of crime was a result of increased social cohesion. The existence of the NW schemes might help integrate fearful people more fully into the community which might lead to a reduction in their fear of crime. There is some support for this conclusion, to the extent that perceived social cohesion increased significantly over the experimental period in Acton, with a corresponding reduction in fear of crime, but not in Wimbledon, where there was no corresponding reduction.

The remaining beneficial changes in area satisfaction, sense of social cohesion and home protection behaviour are less difficult to explain in terms of a programme effect because they represent an essential part of the programme design. Residents in the NW areas were encouraged to co-operate with other residents and with the police in the prevention of crime and are asked to look after each other's homes and to report anything suspicious to the police.

The evidence from the research is not wholly supportive of this conclusion as the level of involvement of residents in the NW schemes was not great: less than half of the residents said that they looked out for anything suspicious during the first year of the scheme; one-fifth of residents in Wimbledon knew their street co-ordinator; and less than half of residents in Wimbledon said that they had received a newsletter. Nevertheless, it could be argued that the level of involvement was sufficiently great in each area to instigate the mechanisms necessary to bring about the recorded improvements. This might explain why the area in which the level of involvement was higher (Acton) recorded a greater number of attitudinal and behavioural improvements than the area in which the level of involvement was lower (Wimbledon).

The second explanation is that the improvements in attitudes and behaviour were spurious and a product of the research design and method of analysis. The issue of statistical conclusion validity has been discussed in the preceding sections and the same arguments apply here. In order to minimize these threats, two different statistical tests were used. Apart from one minor difference in outcome (changes in satisfaction with the area over the period of the experiment was just significant when using ANOVA and just non-significant when using GLIM), the results of the tests were identical.

The third explanation is that the measured improvements in attitudes and behaviour were caused by factors unrelated to the programme. The major threats to internal validity which might support this conclusion are local history, statistical regression and selection.

Local history might explain the improvements recorded if something happened in the area over the experimental period (apart from the NW programme) which independently affected public attitudes and behaviour.

One possible change which might affect attitudes and behaviour is variations in the styles of policing over the experimental period. In practice, it is difficult to identify changes in policing style which were independent of the NW programme as there are no clear guidelines on what does, and what does not, constitute NW policing. The NW areas were monitored closely during the experiment in order to detect any changes that might influence the research findings. There were no noticeable changes in policing style in the experimental areas which could be identified as independent of the NW programme. In fact the results of the surveys showed that the police were less visible in the experimental areas following the launch of the scheme than in the preceding year.

A second explanation is that the changes in attitudes and behaviour resulted from an event (or events) which occurred outside the experimental areas (e.g. a national or a London-based event). Another national crime prevention programme, for example, launched at the same time as the local NW schemes, might have an impact on the attitudes and behaviour of residents in the NW areas, as well as residents in non-NW areas. This explanation could be more easily assessed, had the full experimental–control group design been used. The absence of a comparison group makes interpretation difficult as it is not known to what extent the observed changes are limited to the scheme area. In order to support this explanation, however, it would have to be argued that similar improvements were occurring across London, or across the country as a whole, during the experimental period. It is difficult to believe that such a widespread change could have occurred across London or the country without it being noticed and reported in published research or in the news media.

Statistical regression might explain the improvements in public attitude and behaviour if these attitudes and behaviours were unfavourable at the time of the pre-test surveys . No surveys were conducted prior to the pre-test surveys, and no other data sources were available which could indicate the typicality of pre-test attitudes and behaviours of residents in the experimental areas. It is also not easy to speculate on what might have been the case. It could be argued that fear of crime, satisfaction with the area, sense of cohesion and home protection behaviour (the significant changes) were likely to be in a unfavourable state at the time when residents decided that something needed to be done about the area and sought to establish an NW scheme. However, it is more difficult to argue, without drawing on supporting data, that public attitudes and behaviour were untypically unfavourable at that time.

The problem of selection bias has been discussed in the preceding section, and the same arguments apply here. There might have been differences in the pre-test and post-test samples which independently explained the changes in attitudes and behaviour reported. In Acton there was a greater proportion of single respondents in the post-test than in the pre-test period, and in Wimbledon there was a greater proportion of higher-income, non-manual workers and home owners in the post-test period than in the pre-test (see Chapter 5). It has been shown that single respondents were less fearful than other respondents and also less likely to report satisfaction with the area and a sense of social cohesion. It has also been shown that higher-income respondents and non-manual workers were more likely than low-income respondents and manual workers to report satisfaction with the area and involvement in home protection behaviour. The results do not show any uniform relationship between the direction of the sample bias and the direction of changes in attitudes and behaviour. It is unlikely that the recorded changes were the result of these differences between the samples because each of the variables was controlled in the multivariate analysis.

Which of the three explanations is the most convincing? The first explanation, that the changes in attitudes and behaviours were the result of the NW programme, found some support in the data. The greatest reduction in the fear of crime occurred in the area where residents were most convinced that there had been a reduction in crime and in the area where residents felt that social cohesion had improved. It was argued that both changes could be linked theoretically to a reduction in fear. The second explanation that the improvements recorded were a spurious result of the research method was considered unconvincing because the results were replicated using different methods of analysis. The third explanation, that the improvements were the result of factors unrelated to the existence of the scheme, was also given little support on the ground that no evidence was available which showed that the other events in the history of the experimental areas accounted for the change. There was insufficient data available to determine whether statistical regression could account for the improvements. The possibility that the differences between the survey results could be explained by selection bias was also considered unconvincing on the ground that the main differences between the samples was not in a direction which would generate the differences and that the major sampling variations were controlled using multivariate analysis.

The most convincing general conclusion is that the measured improvements in specific public attitudes and behaviours were the result of the existence of the NW programme. To what extent can this conclusion be generalized across populations, settings and times?

The analysis of changes in the fear of crime, in a sense of social cohesion, satisfaction with the area and home protection behaviour (see Chapter 8) revealed that the changes measured for the population as a whole were not necessarily recorded for all subgroups. In Acton improvements in fear of household crime were recorded for white, (but not non-white) respondents, and improvements in satisfaction with the area were recorded for manual (but not non-manual) workers.

Improvements in a sense of social cohesion were recorded for all subgroups. In Wimbledon favourable changes in satisfaction with the area were observed among older (but not younger) respondents, whereas favourable changes in home protection behaviour were measured for all subgroups. Therefore, there is some evidence of variation among subgroups in their responsiveness to the programme.

The extent to which the results can be obtained across other populations depends on the representativeness of the scheme area. It has been argued in the previous section that the experimental areas were not chosen to be representative of NW programme areas in London as a whole, and it cannot be assumed therefore that the results can be generalized across other populations.

The extent to which the results can be generalized to other versions of NW programmes is unknown because of an absence of knowledge about the theoretical process by which NW achieves its aims, and an absence of knowledge about the extent of variation in the character of schemes in the Metropolitan Police District. Therefore, it cannot be presumed that these findings can be generalized to other versions of NW.

In summary, the extent to which the main research findings can be generalized across populations, settings and times is limited. In order to arrive at a more substantial conclusion about the efficacy of NW in generating improvements in public attitudes or behaviour, it is necessary to replicate the study and to assess the combined results obtained.

Discussion

The most encouraging results of the research are that there were significant improvements in relation to levels of fear of household crime, satisfaction with the area and a sense of social cohesion in Acton, and satisfaction with the area and home protection behaviour in Wimbledon. It has been argued that the most convincing explanation of these changes is that they represent a programme effect. Less encouraging findings are that the NW programmes had no measured impact on the crime rate in either experimental area; there were no improvements in reporting rates; there were no improvements in clear-up rates; there were no improvements in the quantity or quality of telephone contacts from the public to the police; there were no improvements in fear of personal victimization, perceived probability of victimization or public evaluation of the police in either area; and there were no improvements in home protection behaviour. In Wimbledon, there were no improvements in fear of household crime or a sense of social cohesion .

The way in which the balance of favourable and unfavourable results is finally assessed is, to some extent, subjective. Some observers might be encouraged by the small number of favourable findings and perceive these as sufficient evidence of an NW success. Other observers might be discouraged by the absence of a more substantial overall impact and perceive the results as representing less than might have been expected. In my view, the dominant question which arises from these results is: why did the programmes fail to achieve a reduction in victimization and more substantial changes in attitudes and behaviour among residents in the programme areas?

There are a number of reasons why an evaluation fails to observe the effects hypothesized. Rosenbaum (1986) groups these reasons into three broad categories: (1) measurement failure, (2) theory failure and (3) programme failure. The issue of measurement failure has already been discussed at length in respect to statistical conclusion validity and need not be repeated here. The issues of theory failure and programme failure should be discussed.

Theory failure
The limited success of the experimental programmes might be explained in terms of a defect in the theory of NW and the hypothesized process by which it is supposed to bring about reductions in crime and fear of crime.

Some of the elements of the theory of NW have already been discussed in Chapters 2 and 3: NW in London has been described as a network of public-spirited members of the community who become the 'eyes and ears' of the police. The process by which NW is supposed to reduce crime is through opportunity reduction as a result of neighbours looking out for and reporting anything suspicious to the police. Other versions of the NW theory are found in the US literature, which includes opportunity reduction through the creation of signs of occupancy.

The issue of theory failure concerns whether the processes described above can be expected to bring about the claimed beneficial effects. It would be premature to conclude that the limited success of the schemes investigated was a product of theory failure in the absence of a broader research base concerning the effectiveness of opportunity reducing and informal social control enhancing strategies.

There are some problems associated with NW theory, however, which can be identified from what is already known. The effectiveness of public surveillance in small communities is probably limited. Many households in typical suburban areas are unoccupied for a large part of the day while the inhabitants are at work or involved in other activities which take them out of the home. Many dwellings are poorly situated to facilitate effective surveillance. Many areas experience a high turnover of residents, and it may take some time before new residents are sufficiently familiar with the area to know what is, and what is not, evidence of suspiciousness. Many communities are regularly populated by outsiders who enter the area for legitimate purposes, which makes it difficult for residents to identify suspicious behaviour in terms of who should and should not be within the area, or within a certain part of that area.

A further problem with NW theory described above, is that it is unknown to what extent offenders are deterred from offending by the knowledge that residents look out for suspicious activities and report them to the police. There is some evidence from research based on interviews with known offenders that the visible presence of occupants or neighbours, and even signs of their presence, might be sufficient to deter some would-be offenders (Bennett and Wright, 1984). There is no evidence to suggest that the mere knowledge that unseen occupants or neighbours might report suspicious behaviour to the police will deter. It is also unknown to what extent reports of suspicious behaviour lead either to improved arrest rates or to reductions in crime. The research shows that the police strongly rely on information from the victims or witnesses as a means of identifying and arresting suspects (Zander, 1979). The research does not show that an increase in the number of calls from the public about suspicious behaviour leads to higher clear-up rates.

Programme failure

The limited success of the schemes could also be explained in terms of programme failure. Programme failure, or implementation failure, can occur when the scheme fails to operationalize the theoretical construct that is tested. This might occur as a result of implementing a weak version of the right type of programme, or of implementing the wrong type of programme.

The first problem arises when the programme is insufficiently robust to instigate the processes defined in the theoretical formulation. Rosenbaum (1986) equates this problem with medical treatment, whereby the patient is given the right medicine but the wrong dosage. He points out that in order to be effective, the programme must comprise at least the 'minimum dosage' of the treatment.

To what extent can the limited effects of the two programmes investigated be explained in terms of a weak or inadequate programme? There is little evidence available on what might constitute the minimum dosage of NW. Recommendations have been made on the minimum percentage of participants in a scheme area (Turner and Barker, 1983); on the minimum level of support in a community for property marking to be effective (Heller et al ., 1975); and the minimum number of co-ordinators' meetings. These proposals, however, are not based on the evidence of experimental research (e.g. research which attempts to equate measures of involvement with measures of outcomes).

One approach is to argue that the 'minimum dosage' has been achieved when there is evidence of some attempt – no matter how small – to implement the key elements of NW. It would have to be shown, for example, that there was evidence of at least some window stickers and street signs to mark the boundary of the programme area; evidence that residents at least occasionally looked out for suspicious incidents and reported them to the police; evidence that residents at least occasionally met and discussed the running of the schemes and evidence that some efforts had been made to mark property and conduct home security surveys. Applying these criteria to the two experimental programmes would lead to the conclusion that there was some evidence of each of these elements, and to this minimum extent that the schemes had been implemented.

Another approach is to look more closely at the extent to which each of these elements are implemented and to decide (using a combination of research evidence and common sense) whether the levels are adequate. It would appear that the level of demarcation of the NW areas was adequate. Street signs were erected on lamp-posts on every road entering the sites and a high proportion of residents displayed NW window stickers. It would be estimated that only the most unobservant offenders would have been unaware that they were entering an NW area.

It is less certain whether the number and nature of the formal meetings between residents represented an adequate level of implementation. Unlike the organization of many US schemes, residents in the area (apart from area and street co-ordinators) were not expected to attend any formal meetings; and apart from the initial launch meeting, the majority of residents took no further part in the organization of the scheme. The major contribution made by the bulk of the residents in the area was limited to displaying a window sticker and looking out for anything suspicious.

The extent to which the other elements of the schemes represented adequate levels of implementation is open to debate. Just under half of residents in each NW area said that they looked out for something suspicious during the experimental period. This level is not particularly high – although it is probably high enough to instigate the proposed processes. Less than a quarter of residents in Wimbledon, and less than one-tenth of resident in Acton, reported that they had marked their property or had received a home security survey. This level of involvement is almost certainly inadequate to claim that these elements of the programme had been implemented.

The final question for consideration is whether the schemes were examples of NW or some other kind of programme. The precise nature of NW is not specified in the literature. There is little evidence to suggest, however, that the theory and practice of NW in London is fundamentally different to the theory and practice of NW programmes elsewhere.

Conclusion

The most convincing explanation of the limited success of the schemes investigated is programme failure. It has been noted that programme failure can arise from the operationalization of a weak version of NW, or from the operationalisation of a completely different kind of programme. The discussion above leads most easily to the conclusion that the programmes implemented were, in some ways, weak versions of NW, which failed to instigate fully the mechanisms implicit in the theoretical formulation.

The issue of programme failure due to weak or inadequate design is double-edged. On the one hand, it could be argued that the specific programmes investigated were not good examples of NW in the Metropolitan Police District. In this case, it would be expected that other schemes designed more precisely in accordance with the Metropolitan Police guidelines would be more successful. On the other hand, it could be argued that the design of NW in the Metropolitan Police District (as outlined in the official guidelines or as implemented, in practice, on a routine basis) is not a good example of NW. In this case, it would not be expected that other schemes following similar guidelines or practices would be any more successful; the weight of the evidence tends to favour the latter explanation.

It is hard to believe that the schemes investigated were not good or, at least, average examples of NW in the Metropolitan Police District. The co-ordinators of the scheme in Acton, for example, met regularly with the local police, held monthly co-ordinators' meetings which included presentations by outside speakers, contributed actively to the creation of an NW newsletter and, at the end of the year, held an anniversary street party to celebrate the scheme. The local police were also enthusiastic about the scheme and worked hard to make it a success.

It is less hard to believe that the principles and practices of NW in London fell short of the ideal. There are a number of limitations and weakness in the way in which NW is designed and implemented.

One important problem is the lack of detailed guidance in the design and implementation of NW programmes. The *Force Instructions* and the official guidelines do no more than define the main elements and broad parameters of NW. Little information was distributed to divisional commanders, at least during the early history of NW in the Metropolitan Police District, which could give them much insight into what NW schemes looked like in practice. At the time of the force-wide launch, there was little research evidence available on the effectiveness of NW and no bulk of research evidence which could be used to determine which kinds of schemes were more effective. Therefore, it is not surprising that the 'minimum dosage' of NW was defined in official policy in terms of the broad parameters of the schemes rather than their detailed workings.

The choice of limited guidance and a flexible approach has resulted not in imaginative design, tailored to the needs of individual communities, but in minimalism. A commonly held view among police officers of all ranks in the Metropolitan Police is that the reward structure favours quantity (number of schemes implemented per division) rather than quality (how well they operate and how long they last for). As a result, the officers involved in implementing the schemes are under pressure to launch as many schemes as possible and as quickly as possible and there is little time or incentive to do more than the minimum specified in the official guidelines. A consequence of this is that there are now many schemes within the Metropolitan Police District which lack substance.

Apart from this problem of the police achieving no more than what is required of them, there is evidence that they are in fact finding it difficult to achieve what *is* required of them. In many ways, the police have found it difficult to provide the resources necessary to manage the schemes, and in many areas they have found it difficult to deliver the goods. In the experimental areas, for example, it was shown that few residents had marked their property or had home security surveys. Many crime prevention officers are unable to do more than encourage residents to buy a marker pen and mark their own property. The problem of finding sufficient time to conduct home security surveys is an intractable one and many crime prevention officers have had to concede that they cannot fulfil this part of the bargain. It was also shown in the current study that few residents had recently seen their local home beat officer. It is known that home beat or permanent beat officers are often called upon to carry out other duties which take them off their beats (Brown and Iles, 1985). This results in beat officers finding difficulty in fulfilling their obligations not only as NW liaison officers, but also as community constables.

The design of NW in London might also fall short of the theoretical formulation to the extent that it focuses narrowly on the public becoming the 'eyes and ears' of the police as a primary mechanism in reducing crime. In the USA, NW schemes have not focused solely on public reporting to the police of suspicious behaviour. The Seattle programme, for example, included the creation of signs of occupancy and more effective surveillance of one another's properties (Cirel *et al.*, 1977). It is surprising (considering that NW in the Metropolitan Police District is based on the Seattle programme) that the creation of signs of occupancy was not incorporated in the design, and further that signs of occupancy have been consistently cited in the research literature as a situational factor capable of deterring offenders and preventing household crime (Bennett and Wright, 1984; Reppetto, 1974; Walsh, 1980).

PART IV

PROPOSALS

11   Conclusion: Programme Design and Evaluation

Implementing NW

It was concluded in Chapter 10 that there were a number of problems both in relation to the theory and practice of NW, as summarised below.

Theoretical problems

The theoretical problems lie in the general perspectives on the causes of crime underlying NW programmes, and in the specific assumptions about the way in which the component parts of NW are supposed to operate. The theoretical formulation of NW derives in part from the 'victimization' or 'situational' perspective, and in part in from the 'social control' or 'social disorganization' perspective. The publicity material and policy documents prepared by the police and others responsible for launching NW schemes indicate that the theoretical formulation of NW is dominantly conceived as 'opportunity reduction' (i.e. derivative of the 'victimization perspective'). Other writers have stressed the importance of NW in terms of developing or strengthening informal social control (i.e. a derivative of the social control perspective'). The combination of perspectives has resulted in a number of problems which have served to confuse the theory and practice of NW.

The combination of elements of the two perspectives makes it unclear exactly how NW is supposed to work. The dominant conceptualization is that NW reduces opportunities for crime by residents watching out for anything suspicious and reporting what they see to the police. Such acts do not in themselves constitute evidence of informal social control (i.e. residents taking direct actions to control behaviour). It could be argued that watching and intervening in cases of suspicious or unacceptable behaviour is evidence of informal social control as members of the community take direct action to control the behaviour. However, it is more difficult to argue that watching and reporting is evidence of informal social control since residents have not taken direct actions. Watching cannot be considered as informal social control, when behaviour is not controlled by it, nor can reporting what is seen to the police, when behaviour is controlled by a formal agency. One solution of this dilemma would be to conceive watching and reporting – the major elements of NW – as providing a link between informal and formal social control systems.

There are further problems which concern the extent to which holding formal meetings constitutes or strengthens informal social control. It has been argued that research evidence on group dynamics does not support the view that such meetings will lead to greater informal social control

(Rosenbaum, 1986). Rosenbaum argues that the idea that social interaction at NW meetings provides citizens with social support and reassurance that something can be done both collectively and individually to affect the local crime problem is probably unsound. His study found that such meetings can heighten anxiety and reduce feelings of efficacy and social cohesion (Rosenbaum, 1987).

The theoretical formulation of NW is also problematic in terms of the specific assumptions underlying the mechanisms by which it is supposed to achieve its ends. Most of these assumptions concern the way in which the broader aim of opportunity reduction is conceptualized. It has been argued that the principal way in which NW programmes aim to reduce opportunities for crime is as a result of residents watching out for suspicious incidents and reporting them to the police. This process is based on specific underlying assumptions about the way in which watching and reporting affect crime. These assumptions are as yet unproven and can only be speculated upon. Watching and reporting might reduce crime as a result of the message that these actions transmit to potential offenders. Watching and reporting might also increase the number of arrests and convictions, which might reduce the total pool of local offenders and reduce the number of crimes committed. The extent to which either of these effects will occur as a result of increased surveillance among residents is largely unknown.

In order to make progress in the design of future NW schemes, it is important that the theoretical formulation on which they are based is sound and clear. It cannot be expected that police and other organizers of NW programmes will effectively operationalize the theoretical formulation in their programme designs if they do not know what this formulation is in the first place.

It is not the aim of this summary to write the next theoretical basis for community crime prevention programmes. It might not be too immodest, however, to propose that some attempt is made to clarify more precisely the relationship between the theoretical formulation of NW and the two main theoretical perspectives on community crime prevention. If it is decided that NW is dominantly a situational approach to crime, then the opportunity reducing element of the programme should be emphasized. If it is decided that NW is dominantly a social control approach to crime, then activities which strengthen informal social control should be emphasized. Without this clarification, there is a danger that programme designers will promote weak or incompatible versions of both these perspectives.

The second proposal concerns the development of a stronger version of NW based on the situational approach. NW schemes are based on the principle of reducing opportunities for crime in small communities by the collective efforts of residents. This is typically interpreted in a narrow sense of encouraging residents to look out for suspicious behaviour and to report this to the police. It is difficult to understand why the most common theoretical formulation of NW should be defined so narrowly. There are many other actions which neighbours can take which represent collective attempts to reduce opportunities for crime. Some schemes, for example, have adopted a broader theoretical formulation and have included in the programme attempts to create signs of occupancy (Cirel *et al.*, 1977).

Design problems

The analysis of the design and implementation of the NW programme in London suggested that there were weaknesses in both. The Metropolitan Police District adopted a narrowly defined version of NW. Residents were encouraged to do no more than become the 'eyes and the ears' of the police. It has also been noted that the decision not to include signs of occupancy in the programme design is surprising, considering that the programme was based on the Seattle project which included this element and the research literature suggests that this may have been one of the most effective components of NW in reducing crime.

Another design issue concerns the role of meetings. It was originally envisaged that there would be regular meetings among residents (referred to as 'formal meetings') and co-ordinators ('informal meetings'). The available evidence suggests that few NW schemes in the Metropolitan Police District hold regular meetings for residents in the scheme area, apart from the original launch meeting. The only meetings that are held tend to be meetings of street and area co-ordinators and the police. Meetings among co-ordinators and the police (i.e. informal meetings) were originally conceived by the Metropolitan Police as fulfilling a training function and as providing an opportunity to instruct new street co-ordinators in their role. Instead they have developed into opportunities for education and information dissemination among the small proportion of residents who administer the scheme.

The mechanism by which such limited meetings might reduce crime is not immediately obvious. It is possible that they might lead to feelings of support and control over their area, as argued earlier in relation to the development of informal social control. An alternative argument is that these small group discussions do not play a direct role in the prevention of crime (i.e. they do not strengthen informal social control), but they do play a role in supporting the watching and reporting activities of residents (i.e. they help in the attempt to reduce opportunities for crime in the area). This interpretation is perhaps the more realistic as the dominant role of co-ordinators, in practice, has been limited to encouraging scheme membership, promoting the display of window stickers, encouraging watching and reporting and delivering the scheme newsletter.

Another important problem concerned the method and level of implementation of the programme. The lack of detailed guidance given to divisional commanders on the design and implementation of NW meant that they had little idea about what NW schemes looked like in practice. There were also few other sources of information available at the time on the design features or on the effectiveness of NW. This resulted in the implementation of fairly basic schemes which did little more than fulfil the requirements of the *Force Instructions*. This problem was exacerbated by the fact that the Metropolitan Police perceived themselves to be under pressure from the public to launch as many schemes as possible.

The final problem, mentioned earlier, concerned the difficulties of supporting and administering existing schemes. The original aim of the Metropolitan Police was to launch a comprehensive package comprising NW, property marking, home security surveys and initiatives to promote environmental awareness. There is no evidence available which suggests that environmental awareness has been actively promoted by the police as a separate NW element in London. Crime prevention officers have found that they are unable to promote property marking at a campaign level and have tended to do little more than inform residents of where they can buy marker pens. They are also limited in the number of home security surveys that they can conduct. It is unlikely that more than a small percentage of homes in a neighbourhood will receive a home security survey in any one year. The combination of these shortcomings means that, in practice, the NW programme in London has effectively been a single-element programme.

In order to make proposals about the design and implementation of NW schemes, it is necessary to consider the kind of theoretical formulation that should be operationalized. A scheme which aimed predominantly to reduce opportunities for crime would require a programme which operationalized opportunity-reducing initiatives; a scheme aiming predominantly at an increased informal social control would require a programme which operationalized informal control-strengthening elements.

The most common NW design focuses on opportunity-reducing tactics in the form of encouraging residents to watch out for suspicious behaviour and reporting them to the police. Improvements could be made in the method of operationalizing opportunity reduction within NW by attempting to implement a greater number of tactics.

One proposal is to encourage the creation of signs of occupancy and to build this into the programme design. The methods adopted in the Seattle programme included residents mowing the lawn of neighbours who were away, removing newspapers and filling trash cans. These principles might be applied to British designs. While it might not be appropriate to fill trash cans, it might be possible for neighbours to rotate each other's house lights, to check the home periodically and create signs of occupancy by opening and closing curtains at the appropriate times of day. It is also quite possible for residents to create signs of occupancy in their own homes when they are away such as leaving a car in the drive or immediately outside and installing an electrical device to rotate house lighting. There might also be advantages in the occupant creating signs of occupancy even when they are home, for would-be offenders are unlikely to know that the resident is at home unless there are cues which inform them of their presence. This might serve to protect not only the occupants' home, but also neighbouring homes when unoccupied.

Schemes which aim at increasing informal social control might be more effectively operationalized by expanding the role played by the meetings of residents. In order to promote informal social control, the meetings would need to include all (or a large proportion of) residents living in the area. Research on informal social control mechanisms suggests that the nature of the association of residents and the kinds of activities that they engage in is important in determining group effectiveness. Community crime prevention meetings are more likely to be constructive and long-lasting if the group meets to pursue a number of objectives rather than just the one objective of crime prevention (Murphy and Muir, 1985; Rosenbaum, 1987). The more robust meetings comprise residents who are already involved in efforts to improve the quality of life in their area.

The structure and contents of these meeting would have to be carefully controlled to avoid unnecessarily morbid discussions on crime and crime prevention which might lead to an increase in fear of crime. The use of crime information as a means of encouraging motivation or developing tactics would have to be avoided or kept to a minimum.

There might be advantages in ensuring that schemes based on both the situational and social control perspectives are small in size. Schemes in London have covered as many as 3,000 households. Schemes in the USA tend to comprise no more that 20–30 households. The main benefits of smaller schemes are that they are easier to manage and they can involve all members in the area. Meetings can be held in the homes of one of the residents rather than in a hired hall, and each member can make a contribution. It is unlikely that the size of the scheme will directly alter its effectiveness in terms of reducing opportunities for crime. There may be indirect advantages, however, in terms of the proportions of participants to non-participants in an area and the level of activity of participants. There may also be benefits associated with smaller schemes in terms of generating informal social control. Scheme members may interact more frequently and may take an active part in attempting to improve the quality of life in the area.

Any proposals for more effective implementation of NW need to consider whether the scheme should be incorporated into a comprehensive crime prevention package or stand alone as a single-element programme. An important argument against incorporating NW into a comprehensive programme, at this stage in its development, is that it is difficult to evaluate. Apart from the methodological problems associated with determining whether the programme package or some other factor caused the outcomes observed, there is an additional problem of determining which elements, or elements of the programme package, caused the effect. Implementing a comprehensive programme has the advantage that it increases the chances of success. Unless the effect of the individual elements is known, however, the programme is in danger of carrying redundant elements which make it inefficient in terms of police resources and misleading to residents.

Evaluating NW

The review of evaluations of NW (Chapter 4) showed that much of the literature suffered from serious methodological weaknesses which served to undermine the value of the findings. Many studies relied on police-recorded crimes as their primary data source. Police-recorded crimes are difficult to interpret because they are affected by changes in public reporting and police recording practices. This is a particularly important problem in relation to NW evaluations as the treatment evaluated aims to increase information flow from the public to the police.

Many of the evaluations comprise solely 'before'/'after' comparisons with no adequate control area comparison. It is difficult to determine from these studies whether a measured reduction in crime is a result of the programme or a result of broader changes in the crime levels. Many of the evaluations comprise post-test-only, 'treatment'/'non-treatment' comparisons. It is difficult to determine from these studies whether differences in crime rates between participants and non-participants are the result of pre-existing differences between them.

Few evaluations pay any attention to the problem of the nature of the programme implemented and the extent to which it matches the theoretical formulation of NW. Studies often fail to provide an adequate description of the kind of programme being evaluated. Few studies deal effectively with the problem of determining to what extent any changes in crime can be justifiably attributed to the NW programme. Evaluations seldom include statements about the extent to which the findings can be generalized to other programmes or other areas.

Victim survey vs crime analysis

The main advantage of the victims survey method is that the results are not affected by variations in reporting practices or in changes in police recording practices. In fact victim surveys can be used to measure changes in reporting practices from one period to another. The survey can include questions on 'nuisance' offences and incivilities in the area which might not be included in police crime reports. The victim survey can also include questions on public attitudes and behaviour which are often relevant to evaluations of community crime prevention programmes.

The main disadvantage of victim surveys is that they are based on the response of a proportion of the population being studied. The main problem that this produces is that there may be unmeasured differences between the comparison samples. Changes in the outcome measures can only be interpreted if it can be assumed that differences between pre-test/post-test or treatment/ control samples can be adequately controlled. In practice, it is never wholly possible to achieve this as the research instrument can only measure a limited number of sample characteristics.

Another disadvantage of victim survey methods is that it is not wholly obvious what they are recording. The results of victim surveys show that victimizations not reported to the police are often non-serious offences which might not have been classified by the police as crimes, even if they had been reported. It is also uncertain whether all of the events reported are in fact the results of crime. The unwillingness of respondents to report an event to the police might be a reflection of their own uncertainty about its criminal nature (e.g. whether damage to the property was the result of criminal damage or accidental damage).

There is also a problem associated with respondent recall. This might affect whether the respondent remembers or forgets a single victimization at the time of the interview, or it might affect whether the respondent remembers or forgets the total number of offences involved in multiple victimizations. Another problem of recall is whether or not the respondent engages in 'telescoping' (i.e. reporting that a victimization fell within the survey period when it did not or reporting that a victimization did not fall within the survey period when it did) (for a more detailed discussion on the problems of recall see Sparks, Genn and Dodd,1977 ; Sparks, 1981). It has also been shown that reports of household victimizations might vary depending on which household member is interviewed (Bottoms, Mawby and Walker, 1987).

The main advantages of police-recorded crime analysis is that the data is normally easier and cheaper to obtain than victim survey data. There is no need to employ market research companies or to train fieldworkers to collect the data.

There are also few problems with police-recorded crime data in terms of sample comparisons. Crimes recorded will relate to an entire area rather than a sample of households in the area. A repeat survey can be arranged to cover the same area of roughly the same household. Sample changes between surveys will be limited to normal changes in residential composition (e.g. people moving home).

Police-recorded crimes are the product of a process of assessment, guided by the requirements of Home Office counting rules, which aims to ensure that the events recorded constitute breaches of the criminal law. They exclude, for example, offences reported by the public which are later 'no crimed' because it is found that there was no evidence of criminal actions.

The main disadvantages of using police-recorded crimes as a data source concern possible variations over time in public reporting and police recording practices (Hough and Mayhew, 1983). It is possible that residents in a NW area might report a greater number or fewer victimizations to the police following the implementation of the programme. It is also possible that the police might record a greater number or fewer offences as crimes following the programme launch. Changes in police-recording practices can be influential at the initial reporting stage (McCabe and Sutcliffe, 1978) and at the final assessment stage (Bottomley and Coleman, 1981).

Another disadvantage of using police-recorded crimes as the main data source in an evaluation of NW is that it provides data solely on recordable crimes. The data cannot be used to determine changes in minor offences, changes in 'nuisance' offences, changes in reporting rates or changes in public attitudes.

Recommended research designs

There is an urgent need for more evaluations of NW and other crime prevention initiatives in order to determine not only whether they are effective, but under what conditions they are effective. It might be helpful to include in this final section some comments on possible evaluative research design. It is not intended to provide detailed instructions or to enter into a detailed discussion on evaluative methodology as these can be found elsewhere (Cook and Campbell, 1979; Judd and Kenney, 1981; Rossi and Freeman, 1985).

Victim survey design   The use of victim surveys allows a full experimental or quasi-experimental research design. The best method to use is an experimental design; it is unlikely, however, that this can be adopted in relation to evaluations of NW schemes as it depends on the researcher being able to decide (either by random assignment or by matching) on the location of the treatment (e.g. NW areas) and non-treatment areas (e.g. non-NW areas). It is rarely possible for the evaluator alone to be able to make these decisions.

The next best method is the quasi-experimental design, which does not depend on random assignment. There are many quasi-experimental designs to choose from: the best of these is probably the 'untreated control group design with pre-test and post-test' (Cook and Campbell, 1979). The design comprises the selection of treatment and control areas which are measured before and after treatment (i.e. a first survey before an NW scheme has been launched and second survey after the scheme has been in operation for a period of time). The treatment and non-treatment areas should be matched as carefully as possible, depending on the abilities of the evaluator to determine the location of programmes and non-programmes sites (it might be just as dIfficult to control the location of the non-treatment area as the treatment area).

If the area is chosen as the unit of analysis, it would be necessary to include a large number of schemes in the evaluation. One advantage of including a large number of schemes in the evaluations is that natural variations in extraneous factors which might increase or decrease levels of crime during the experimental period will tend to cancel each other out. It would also be necessary to include a large number of control areas as this would also guard against extraneous variations which might affect the results. The number of interviews necessary to complete the survey need not be any larger using a large number of schemes than if a small number of schemes were selected.

There are, of course, practical problems in evaluating a large number of schemes. The NW schemes should be launched in all of the programme areas at about the same time in order to produce a common time period for the surveys. It would also be necessary to ensure that no NW scheme or similar initiative was launched during the experimental period in any of the control areas. These kinds of practical problem are more difficult to overcome when the NW scheme covers a large number of households.

If it is impossible to evaluate a large number of schemes with the area as the research unit, an acceptable alternative is to evaluate a small number of schemes and define the resident as the research unit. If a panel–sampling method were adopted, it would be possible to build into the research design a comparison of the differential effect of the scheme on participants and non-participants.

It is easier to control for variations among the samples between the pre-test and post-test surveys if the same individuals are interviewed in both rounds of surveys. There are a number of advantages in the panel-survey design (interviewing the same residents in both surveys), compared with the cross-sectional survey design (interviewing a random survey of residents in both surveys). The most important advantage is that it is unnecessary to control for sample differences between the pre-test and post-test surveys. There are also a number of advantages in using the cross-sectional design. The most important advantage is that the results obtained will be more representative of changes in the population area. The best solution is to use an embedded panel design, which combines both methods of sampling. In practice, this involves randomly selecting households from an area to be used as the household sample for both the first- and second-round surveys (i.e. there is no re-sampling in the second round). The second-round interviews will include some first-round respondents (which will form the panel sample) and a combination of first-round respondents and first-round non-respondents (which will form the cross-sectional sample).

It is essential that the analysis of the data includes some form of multivariate analysis. Quasi-experimental design is based on non-equivalent comparison groups. It is necessary to control for differences between treatment and non-treatment samples (and pre-test and post-test samples in the case of cross-sectional designs). This can be done at a bivariate level of analysis by comparing specific subpopulations in terms of the outcome variable. This method is not wholly effective, however, as it cannot deal with interactions between the variables. The most effective method is to control for a number of demographic variables simultaneously, and this can best be done using multivariate methods of analysis.

Another reason why it is important to use multivariate techniques it that the effect of the programme on the outcome measure (e.g. victimization rate) must be assessed by comparing the interaction between pre-test and post-test surveys and treatment and non-treatment area. This can be done most effectively by constructing a pooled data set of all pre-test/post-test and treatment/non-treatment area data and creating two dummy variables to identify whether the period is in fact pre-test or post-test and whether that area was treatment of non- treatment. The effectiveness of the programme can then be determined by the significance of the interaction between these two variables.

The results obtained comprise the bare evidence of the evaluation which must then be interpreted. The researcher would have to consider the various threats to internal validity and consider alternative explanations. This would involve monitoring the progress and implementation of the scheme and the history of the area during the course of the evaluation.

Police-recorded crime analysis design   Victim survey designs are expensive and complicated to administer. Useful results can be obtained by using police-recorded crimes as the data source. The most serious weakness of existing evaluations based on recorded crime analysis is not the data source (which is problematic, yet not hopelessly so), but the general research design. It is possible to get more out of recorded crime analysis by improving the methods of evaluation. The best evaluative design using police recorded crime as a data source would include measures for both pre-test/post-test periods and treatment/non-treatment areas.

The principles of the evaluation need not be any different from those described above in relation to victim-survey methods. It would be possible to use a full experimental design if random assignment or some other controlled assignment of treatment (NW) and non-treatment (non-NW) areas could be achieved. If this were not possible, the evaluation could be based on non-equivalent treatment/non-treatment groups. The evaluation would be stronger if it could be based on a composite treatment area, constructed from a large number of treatment areas, and a composite control area, constructed from a large number of control areas.

The evaluation would require collecting crime data for all treatment and non-treatment areas for a period preceding the launch of the programmes and for an equivalent period following the launch of the programme. Attention would have to be paid to the problem of the non-treatment areas receiving treatment (i.e. a NW scheme or some other crime prevention measure) during the course of the evaluation. Attention would also have to be paid to the effective matching of experimental and control areas.

As the crime data relates to crimes committed in areas rather than victimization among groups of individuals, it would not be necessary to attempt to control for pre-test/post-test differences. It might be helpful, however, if the evaluator monitored the programmes and developments in the areas to determine whether there were any important changes over the experimental period.

The data could be analysed using simple bivariate methods of analysis. It is important, however, that the data is presented in a way which reveals details of the interaction between areas and time. This would involve assessing difference in the rate of change of crime between experimental and control areas. Evidence supportive of a programme effect might be forthcoming, for example, when crime in the experimental areas decreased at a faster rate than crime in the control areas, or when crime in the experimental areas increased at a slower rate than crime in the control areas.

The results of the analysis do not in themselves confirm that the programme was successful or unsuccessful. It is necessary for the evaluator to consider the various threats to validity and to consider alternative explanations of the results obtained. An additional problem that researchers using police-recorded crime data would have to face is whether the changes in recorded crime were the result of changes in public reporting or police recording practices. The latter problem might be approached by careful analysis of police recording practices over the course of the experimental period; and the latter problem might be assessed by drawing on the evidence of previous research on changes in reporting practices conducted in similar areas, or an attempt might be made to assess the direction and magnitude of any error that might be produced by such changes and the implications that this might have for the conclusions drawn.

APPENDIX

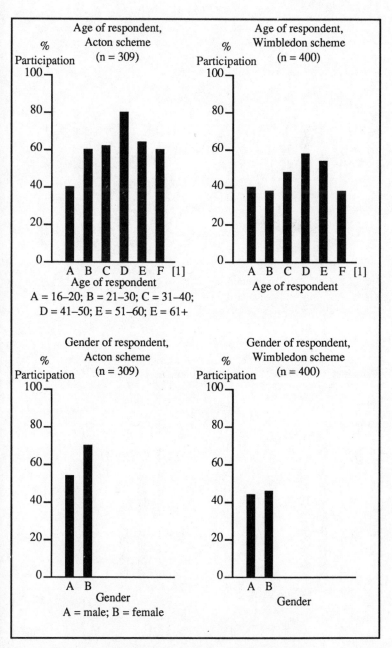

Figure A.1   Percentage participation (self-defined) in the Neighbourhood Watch schemes by selected subgroups

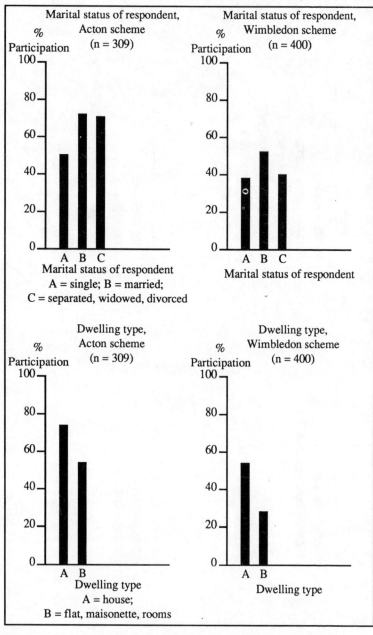

Figure A.1   (continued) Percentage participation (self-defined) in the Neighbourhood Watch schemes by selected subgroups

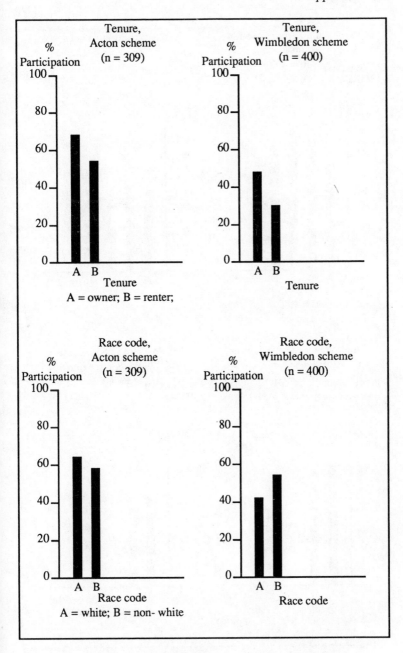

Figure A.1 (continued) Percentage participation (self-defined) in the Neighbourhood Watch schemes by selected subgroups

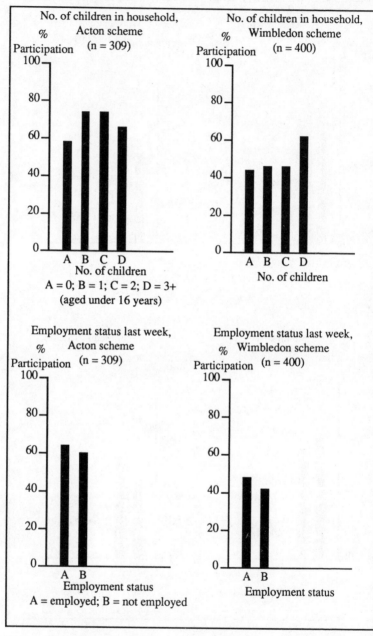

Figure A.1   (continued) Percentage participation (self-defined) in the
Neighbourhood Watch schemes by selected subgroups

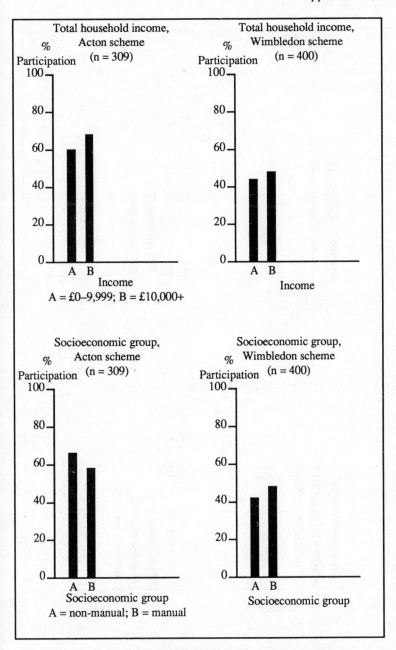

Figure A.1   *(continued) Percentage participation (self-defined) in the Neighbourhood Watch schemes by selected subgroups*

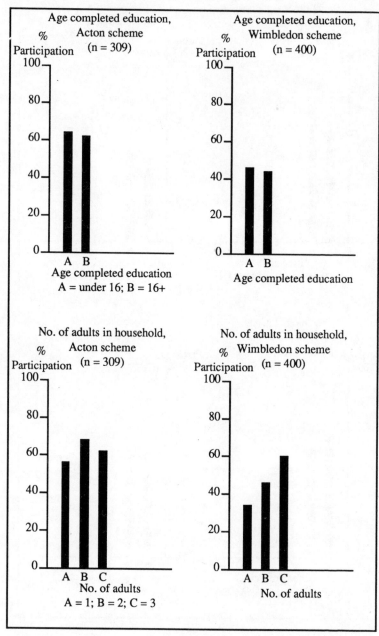

Figure A.1   *(continued) Percentage participation (self-defined) in the Neighbourhood Watch schemes by selected subgroups*

Table A.1   Characteristics of the samples (percentages)

	Acton experimental area		Wimbledon experimental area		Wimbledon displacement area		Redbridge control area	
	Pre	Post	Pre	Post	Pre	Post	Pre	Post
n =	306	309	353	400	323	332	306	330
Age of respondent								
16–50	61	67	63	64	73	69	60	64
51+	39	33	37	36	27	31	40	36
total %	100	100	100	100	100	100	100	100
Gender								
male	47	48	42	49	47	49	46	50
female	53	52	58	51	53	51	54	50
total %	100	100	100	100	100	100	100	100
Race								
white	88	84	80	77	82	80	76	76
non-white	12	16	20	23	18	20	24	24
total %	100	100	100	100	100	100	100	100
Marital status								
single	33	43	32	31	37	33	21	24
married	46	41	45	48	45	48	59	60
single/widowed/ divorced	21	16	23	21	18	19	20	16
total %	100	100	100	100	100	100	100	100
Income								
under £10,000	57	48	54	41	55	53	60	49
£10,000 +	43	62	46	59	45	47	40	51
total %	100	100	100	100	100	100	100	100
Socioeconomic group								
non-manual	55	57	40	48	41	39	45	49
manual	45	43	60	52	59	61	55	51
total %	100	100	100	100	100	100	100	100
Employment status								
in work	62	64	58	63	65	61	55	59
not in work	38	36	42	37	35	39	45	41
total %	100	100	100	100	100	100	100	100

Table A.2 (a)   Mean scale score for fear of personal and household victimisation by selected subgroups

	Fear personal victimization				Fear household victimization			
	Acton experimental area		Wimbledon experimental area		Acton experimental area		Wimbledon experimental area	
	Pre	Post	Pre	Post	Pre	Post	Pre	Post
n =	306	309	353	400	306	309	353	400
Age of respondent								
16–20	2.57	2.47	2.44	2.79	2.14	2.27	2.37	2.41
21–30	2.76	2.76	2.71	2.72	2.30	2.51	2.29	2.33
31–40	2.79	2.84	2.76	2.69	2.32	2.72	2.35	2.32
41–50	2.77	2.77	2.57	2.80	2.66	2.47	2.37	2.56
51–60	2.52	2.61	2.41	2.42	2.27	2.33	2.42	2.06
61+	2.43	2.56	2.28	2.50	2.32	2.57	2.15	2.50
Gender								
male	3.01	3.12	2.95	2.86	2.50	2.71	2.48	2.44
female	2.34	2.31	2.25	2.42	2.22	2.39	2.16	2.28
Race								
white	2.66	2.70	2.55	2.66	2.36	2.60	2.32	2.44
non-white	2.64	2.69	2.52	2.57	2.28	2.23	2.21	2.07
Marital status								
single	2.81	2.79	2.69	2.74	2.43	2.64	2.35	2.31
married	2.57	2.72	2.51	2.62	2.31	2.47	2.28	2.32
single/widowed/ divorced	2.59	2.42	2.43	2.54	2.33	2.45	2.25	2.52
Income								
under £10,000	2.55	2.59	2.44	2.55	2.33	2.47	2.23	2.43
£10,000 +	2.88	2.90	2.76	2.68	2.41	2.67	2.43	2.32
Socioeconomic group								
non-manual	2.78	2.74	2.69	2.64	2.43	2.59	2.34	2.33
manual	2.47	2.64	2.46	2.64	2.23	2.46	2.27	2.38
Employment status								
in work	2.81	2.81	2.70	2.75	2.42	2.49	2.40	2.35
not in work	2.39	2.50	2.34	2.44	2.25	2.63	2.16	2.37
No. of adults								
1	2.56	2.59	2.48	2.64	2.42	2.51	2.23	2.54
2	2.73	2.80	2.57	2.65	2.36	2.55	2.26	2.30
3 +	2.65	2.68	2.58	2.62	2.25	2.57	2.47	2.26

(b) *Mean scale score for perceived probability of personal and household victimization, by selected subgroups*

	Probability personal victimization				Probability household victimization			
	Acton experimental area		Wimbledon experimental area		Acton experimental area		Wimbledon experimental area	
	Pre	Post	Pre	Post	Pre	Post	Pre	Post
n =	306	309	353	400	306	309	353	400
Age of respondent								
16–20	4.29	4.00	4.26	4.10	3.86	3.67	3.89	4.00
21–30	3.96	4.00	4.10	4.09	3.75	3.76	3.80	3.75
31–40	4.10	4.10	4.03	3.88	3.83	3.83	3.80	3.64
41–50	3.91	3.90	3.60	3.98	3.68	3.83	3.63	3.68
51–60	3.85	3.67	3.83	3.68	3.56	3.89	3.61	3.38
61+	3.72	3.85	3.61	3.74	3.65	3.87	3.57	3.67
Gender								
male	4.10	4.03	4.05	4.03	3.82	3.87	3.79	3.77
female	3.78	3.86	3.78	3.74	3.61	3.70	3.66	3.57
Race								
white	3.93	3.96	3.87	3.91	3.72	3.83	3.72	3.70
non-white	3.86	3.88	3.99	3.78	3.61	3.50	3.68	3.57
Marital status								
single	4.11	3.97	4.08	3.94	3.91	3.83	3.85	3.74
married	3.74	3.95	3.83	3.87	3.54	3.74	3.69	3.64
single/widowed/ divorced	4.03	3.86	3.78	3.85	3.76	3.76	3.57	3.62
Income								
under £10,000	3.83	3.88	3.81	3.88	3.66	3.76	3.67	3.68
£10,000 +	4.13	4.05	4.07	3.89	3.82	3.81	3.70	3.66
Socioeconomic group								
non-manual	4.04	4.05	4.02	3.94	3.80	3.81	3.79	3.64
manual	3.73	3.80	3.83	3.84	3.56	3.74	3.67	3.69
Employment status								
in work	4.01	3.89	3.96	3.96	3.70	3.69	3.73	3.65
not in work	3.79	4.04	3.81	3.75	3.74	3.90	3.69	3.69
No. of adults								
1	3.99	3.90	3.83	3.85	3.81	3.80	3.66	3.64
2	3.88	4.01	3.85	3.89	3.67	3.73	3.68	3.64
3 +	3.89	3.90	4.10	3.91	3.63	3.83	3.86	3.75

(c)   Mean scale score for satisfaction with area and social cohesion, by selected subgroups

n =	Satisfaction with area				Social cohesion			
	Acton experimental area		Wimbledon experimental area		Acton experimental area		Wimbledon experimental area	
	Pre 306	Post 309	Pre 353	Post 400	Pre 306	Post 309	Pre 353	Post 400
Age of respondent								
16–20	3.00	3.20	3.11	3.03	1.86	2.07	2.19	2.00
21–30	3.03	3.20	2.87	2.99	1.85	1.95	2.02	2.11
31–40	3.18	3.29	2.93	3.02	1.90	2.11	2.17	2.24
41–50	3.16	3.23	3.03	3.02	2.20	2.27	2.23	2.20
51–60	3.04	3.23	2.93	2.98	2.17	2.49	2.24	2.32
61+	3.29	3.28	3.20	3.33	2.23	2.28	2.33	2.42
Gender								
male	3.13	3.30	2.95	3.09	2.13	2.16	2.20	2.22
female	3.16	3.19	3.05	3.06	1.98	2.12	2.18	2.26
Race								
white	3.15	3.22	2.99	3.03	2.00	2.11	2.16	2.19
non-white	3.11	3.38	3.07	3.22	2.39	2.45	2.32	2.41
Marital status								
single	3.12	3.23	2.99	2.98	1.96	2.01	2.13	2.09
married	3.15	3.26	2.95	3.09	2.12	2.28	2.19	2.33
single/widowed/ divorced	3.16	3.25	3.15	3.18	2.03	2.27	2.27	2.24
Income								
under £10,000	3.13	3.26	3.06	3.23	2.11	2.22	2.26	2.27
£10,000 +	3.18	3.23	2.91	3.00	1.90	2.06	2.06	2.22
Socioeconomic group								
non-manual	3.21	3.18	2.90	3.01	1.96	2.07	2.09	2.14
manual	3.04	3.33	3.07	3.13	2.20	2.29	2.25	2.33
Employment status								
in work	3.13	3.23	2.93	3.03	1.98	2.14	2.11	2.22
not in work	3.17	3.27	3.12	3.15	2.15	2.20	2.30	2.27
No. of adults								
1	3.16	3.24	3.06	3.09	2.04	2.10	2.14	2.24
2	3.11	3.25	2.94	3.05	2.06	2.13	2.14	2.22
3 +	3.18	3.26	3.11	3.11	2.04	2.30	2.21	2.27

(d)   Mean scale score for involvement with others in home protection by selected subgroups

	Home protection			
	Acton experimental area		Wimbledon experimental area	
	Pre 306	Post 309	Pre 353	Post 400
Age of respondent				
16–20	2.00	1.73	1.67	1.72
21–30	1.72	1.66	1.78	1.83
31–40	1.82	1.77	1.83	1.86
41–50	1.77	1.80	1.83	1.98
51–60	1.81	1.95	1.83	1.94
61+	1.75	1.74	1.79	1.87
Gender				
male	1.75	1.74	1.79	1.87
female	1.83	1.80	1.83	1.91
Race				
white	1.80	1.79	1.86	1.90
non-white	1.72	1.69	1.65	1.89
Marital status				
single	1.74	1.67	1.75	1.80
married	1.85	1.87	1.89	1.94
single/widowed/ divorced	1.76	1.78	1.81	1.92
Income				
under £10,000	1.78	1.76	1.82	1.91
£10,000 +	1.85	1.79	1.81	1.89
Socioeconomic group				
non-manual	1.78	1.78	1.75	1.87
manual	1.84	1.76	1.85	1.92
Employment status				
in work	1.78	1.78	1.81	1.87
not in work	1.81	1.75	1.82	1.93
No. of adults				
1	1.69	1.72	1.78	1.85
2	1.85	1.80	1.87	1.91
3 +	1.86	1.79	1.74	1.90

*(e)   Mean scale score for police evaluation and police contact by
selected subgroups*

	Police evaluation				Police contact			
	Acton experimental area		Wimbledon experimental area		Wimbledon displacement area		Redbridge control area	
	Pre 306	Post 309	Pre 353	Post 400	Pre 323	Post 332	Pre 306	Post 330
Age of respondent								
16–20	3.57	3.47	3.00	3.24	2.71	3.62	2.58	1.96
21–30	3.72	3.73	3.46	3.58	3.68	3.06	2.58	2.20
31–40	3.69	3.73	3.76	3.56	3.70	2.98	3.00	2.67
41–50	3.77	3.97	4.11	3.71	4.11	3.79	2.85	2.05
51–60	3.92	3.74	3.63	3.47	3.15	3.02	2.17	1.94
61+	3.90	4.07	3.63	3.79	3.28	2.98	1.99	2.21
Gender								
male	3.66	3.65	3.58	3.46	3.64	3.22	2.64	2.18
female	3.91	3.96	3.65	3.72	3.49	3.01	2.39	2.12
Race								
white	3.81	3.83	3.68	3.62	3.55	3.08	2.54	2.18
non-white	3.58	3.69	3.37	3.51	3.60	3.29	2.26	2.04
Marital status								
single	3.71	3.64	3.49	3.46	3.60	3.03	2.59	1.96
married	3.81	3.89	3.62	3.61	3.61	3.16	2.62	2.26
single/widowed/ divorced	3.86	4.04	3.79	3.77	3.90	3.20	2.12	2.17
Income								
under £10,000	3.75	3.78	3.54	3.68	3.52	3.20	2.32	2.11
£10,000 +	3.87	3.87	3.77	3.55	3.65	2.96	2.88	2.17
Socioeconomic group								
non-manual	3.77	3.85	3.64	3.64	3.58	3.11	2.45	1.90
manual	3.81	3.75	3.61	3.55	3.53	3.11	2.52	2.36
Employment status								
in work	3.70	3.75	3.66	3.59	3.58	3.09	2.75	2.03
not in work	3.92	3.91	3.55	3.60	3.53	3.16	2.15	2.34
No. of adults								
1	3.69	3.76	3.84	3.65	3.58	3.09	2.19	2.09
2	3.74	3.82	3.54	3.60	3.49	2.97	2.62	2.18
3 +	4.00	3.86	3.50	3.51	3.66	3.39	2.60	2.16

References

Alderson, J. (1978), *Communal Policing*, Exeter: Devon and Cornwall Constabulary.

Alderson, J. (1979), *Policing Freedom*, Plymouth: Macdonald and Evans.

Alderson, J. (1981), *Submission to Scarman*, Exeter: Devon and Cornwall Constabulary.

Allatt, P. (1984a), 'Residential security: containment and displacement of burglary', *Howard Journal*, **23** (2), 99–116.

Allatt, P. (1984b), 'Fear of crime: the effect of improved residential security on a difficult-to-let estate', *Howard Journal*, **24** (3), 170–82.

Anderton, K.J. (1985), *The Effectiveness of Home Watch Schemes in Cheshire*, Chester: Cheshire Constabulary.

Assistant Commissioner 'A' Department (1983), *Force Instructions: Neighbourhood Watch*, London: Metropolitan Police.

Ball, S. and Bogatz, G.A. (1970), *The First Year of Sesame Street: An Evaluation*, Princeton, NJ: Educational Testing Service.

Baltimore Police Department (1985), *Neighbourhood Watch*, Baltimore, Md: Baltimore Police Department.

Bennett, T.H. (1987), *An Evaluation of Two Neighbourhood Watch Schemes in London*, Report to the Home Office, Cambridge: Institute of Criminology.

Bennett, T.H. (1989), *Contact Patrols in Birmingham and London, An Evaluation of a Fear Reducing Strategy*, Report to the Home Office Research and Planning Unit, Cambridge: Institute of Criminology.

Bennett, T.H. and Wright, R. (1984), *Burglars on Burglary: Prevention and the Offender*, Aldershot: Gower.

Bennion, C., Dawe, A., Hesse, B.H., Joshua, L., McGloin, P., Munn, G. and Tester, S, (1985), *Neighbourhood Watch: The Eyes and Ears of Urban Policing*, Occasional Papers in Sociology and Social Policy No. 6, Department of Sociology, University of Surrey.

Biderman, A.D., Johnston, L., McIntyre, J. and Weir, A (1967), *Report on a Pilot Study in the District of Columbia on Victimisation and Attitudes to Law and Enforcement. US President's Commission on Victimisation and Administration of Justice, Field Surveys 1*, US Department of Justice, Washington, DC: Government Printing Office.

Bloch, P.B. and Specht, D. (1973), *Neighbourhood Team Policing*, US Department of Justice, Washington, DC: Government Printing Office.

Blue Ash Police Department (n.d.), *Blue Ash Neighbourhood Watch: Training Manual*, Blue Ash, Ohio: Blue Ash Police Department.

Boston, G.D. (1977), *Community Crime Prevention: A Selected Bibliography*, National Institute of Law Enforcement and Criminal Justice, US Department of Justice, Washington, DC: Government Printing Office.

Bottomley, K. and Colement, C. (1981), *Understanding Crime Rates*, Farnborough: Gower.

Bottoms, A.E., Mawby, R.I. and Walker, M.A. (1987), 'A Localised Crime Survey in Contrasting Areas of a City', *British Journal of Criminology*, **27** (2), 125–54.

Bowden, M. (1982), *Community Watch*, *Bridgend*: South Wales Constabulary.

Brown, D. and Iles, S. (1985), *Community Constables: A Study of a Policing Initiative*, Home Office Research and Planning Unit Paper No. 30, London: HMSO.

Brown, L.P. and Wycoff, M.A. (1987), 'Policing Houston: Reducing Fear and Improving Service', *Crime and Delinquency*, **33**, 1, pp. 6–30.

Butler, A.J.P. and Tharme, K. (1983), *Chelmsley Wood Policing Experiment*. Management Services Department. West Midlands Police, unpublished.

Campbell, D.T. (1969), 'Reforms as experiments', *American Psychologist*, **24** (24), 409–29.

Campbell, D.T. and Stanley, J.C. (1966), *Experimental and Quasi-Experimental Designs for Research*, Chicago: Rand McNally.

Cheshire Constabulary (1985), *Crime and the Community, Proceedings of a Conference at the Force Training Centre, Crewe, 17 October*, Chester: Cheshire Constabulary.

Cirel, P., Evans, P., McGillis, D. and Whitcomb, D. (1977), *Community Crime Prevention, Seattle, Washington: An Exemplary Project*, US Department of Justice, Washington, DC: Government Printing Office.

Clarke, A.H. and Lewis, M.J. (1982), 'Fear of crime among the elderly', *British Journal of Criminology*, **22** (1), 49–62.

Clarke, R.V.G. (1980), 'Situational crime prevention: theory and practice', *British Journal of Criminology*, **20**, 136–47.

Clarke, R.V.G. and Hope, T. (eds) (1984), *Coping with Burglary*, Boston, Mass.: Kluwer-Nijhoff.

Conklin, J.E. (1975), *The Impact of Crime*, London: Macmillan.

Cook, T.D. and Campbell, D.T. (1979), *Quasi-Experimentation: Design and Analysis Issues for Field Settings*, Chicago: Rand McNally.

Critchley, T.A. (1978), *A History of Police in England and Wales*, London: Constable.

Crowe, T.D. (1985), *Directed Patrol Manual: Juvenile Problems*, Office of Juvenile Justice and Delinquency Prevention, US Department of Justice, Washington, DC: Government Printing Office.

Daily Telegraph (1986), 'Vandalised estate brands youth "yobbo of month"', *Daily Telegraph*, 28 July.

Decampli, T.R. (1977), *Wilmington Neighbourhood Security Project: A Project Evaluation*, Wilmington, Delamere: Wilmington Bureau of Police.

DeJong, W. and Goolkasian, G.A. (1982), *Neighbourhood Fight against Crime: The Midwood Kings Highway Development Corporation*, National Institute of Law Enforcement and Criminal Justice, US Department of Justice, Washington, DC: Government Printing Office.

Delaney, M. (1983), *The Kingsdown Beat Experiment: the Way Forward*, Police Staff College Ninth Junior Command Course, Bristol: Avon and Somerset Constabulary.

Devon and Cornwall Constabulary (1981), *Neighbourhood against Burglary Campaign*, Exeter: Devon and Cornwall Constabulary.

Donnison, H., Scola, J. and Thomas, P. (1986), *Neighbourhood Watch: Policing the People*, London: Libertarian Research and Education Trust.

DuBow, F. and Emmons, D. (1981), 'The community hypothesis', in D. Lewis (ed.), *Reactions to Crime*, London: Sage, pp. 167–82.

DuBow, F. and Podolefsky, A. (1982), 'Citizen participation in community crime prevention', *Human Organization*, **41** (4), 307–14.

Duncan, J.T.S. (1980), *Citizen Crime Prevention Tactics: A Literature Review and Selected Bibliography*, National Institute of Law Enforcement and Criminal Justice, US Department of Justice, Washington, DC: Government Printing Office.

Eck, J.E. and Spelman, W. (1987), 'Who ya gonna call?: the police as problem-busters', *Crime and Delinquency*, **33** (1), 31–52.

Ekblom, P. (1986), Community policing: obstacles and issues, in P. Willmott (ed.), *The Debate about Community*, London: Policy Studies Institute, pp. 16–30.

Ennis, P.H. (1967), *Criminal Victimisation in the United States: A Report of a National Survey. US President's Commission on Victimisation and Administration of Justice. Field Surveys 11*, US Department of Justice, Washington, DC: Government Printing Office.

Farrington, D.P. and Dowds, E.A. (1985), 'Disentangling criminal behaviour and police reaction', in D.P. Farrington and J. Gunn (eds), *Reactions to Crime: The Public, the Police, Courts and Prisons*, Chichester: Wiley, pp. 41-72.

Finn, P. (1986), *Block Watches Help Crime Victims in Philadelphia*, National Institute Justice, Rockville Washington: National Criminal Justice Reference Service.

Garafola, J. (1979), 'Victimization and fear of crime', *Journal of Research in Crime and Delinquency*, **16** (1), 80–97.

Giles-Sims, J. (1984), 'A multivariate analysis of perceived likelihood of victimization and degree of worry about crime among older people', *Victimology*, **9** (2), 222–33.

Goldstein, H. (1987), 'Towards community-oriented policing: potential, basic requirements, and threshold questions', *Crime and Delinquency*, **33** (1), 6–30.

Greenberg, S.W., Rohe, W.M. and Williams, J.R. (1985), *Informal Citizen Action and Crime Prevention at the Neighbourhood Level*, NIJ, US Department of Justice, Washington, DC: Government Printing Office.

Hampshire Constabulary (1978), *A Study of the Crime of Housebreaking in Hampshire*, Winchester: Hampshire Constabulary.

Harris Research Centre (1987), *Crime in Newham: Report of a Survey of Crime and Racial Harassment in Newham*, London: London Borough of Newham.

Hedges, A., Blaber, A. and Mostyn, B. (1980), *Community Planning Project: Cunningham Road Improvement Scheme: Final Report*, London: Social and Community Planning Research.

Heller, N.B., Stenzel, W.W., Gill, A.D., Kolde, R.A. and Schimerman, S.R. (1975), *Operation Identification Projects: Assessment of Effectiveness. National Evaluation Program. Phase I, Summary Report*, Washington, DC: National Institute of Law Enforcement and Criminal Justice.

Henig, J. (1984), *Citizens Against Crime: An Assessment of the Neighbourhood Watch Program in Washington, DC*, Washington, DC: George Washington University.

Home Office (1982), *Unrecorded Offences of Burglary and Theft in a Dwelling in England and Wales: Estimates from the General Household Survey*, Home Office Statistical Bulletin 11/82, London: Home Office.

Hough, M. and Mayhew, P. (1983), *The British Crime Survey*, Home Office Research Study No. 76, London: HMSO.

Hough, M. and Mayhew, P. (1985), *Taking Account of Crime: Key Findings from the 1984 British Crime Survey*, Home Office Research Study No. 85, London: HMSO.

Jenkins, A.D. and Latimer, I. (1987), *Evaluation of Merseyside Home Watch*, Liverpool: Merseyside Police.

Jones, T., MacLean, B. and Young, J. (1986), *The Islington Crime Survey: Crime, Victimization and Policing in Inner-City London*, Aldershot: Gower.

Jones, T., MacLean, B. and Young, J. (1986), *The Islington Crime Survey:* Aldershot: Gower.

Judd, C.M. and Kenny, D.A. (1981), *Estimating the Effects of Social Interventions*, Cambridge: Cambridge University Press.

Kelling, G.L., Pate, T., Dieckman, D. and Brown, C.E. (1974), *The Kansas City Preventive Patrol Experiment: A Technical Report*, Washington, DC: Police Foundation.

Kinsey, R. (1984), *The Merseyside Crime Survey: First Report*, Liverpool: Merseyside Metropolitan Council.

Lavrakas, P.J. (1980), *Factors Related to Citizen Involvement in Personal, Household, and Neighbourhood Anti-Crime Measures: An Executive Summary*, NIJ, US Department of Justice, Washinton, DC: Government Printing Office.

√ Lavrakas, P.J. and Hertz, E.J. (1982), 'Citizen participation in neighbourhood crime prevention', *Criminology*, **20**, (3), 479–98.

Lea, J., Jones, T. and Young, J. (1986), *Broadwater Farm: A Strategy for Survival*, Middlesex: Middlesex Polytechnic.

Lewis, D.A., Grant, J.A. and Rosenbaum, D.P. (1985), *The Social Construction of Reform: Crime Prevention and Community Organizations*, Evanston, Ill.: Northwestern University Press.

Lewis, D.A. and Salem, G. (1981), 'Community crime prevention: an analysis of a developing strategy', *Crime and Delinquency*, **27**, July, 405–21.

Lindquist, J.H. and Duke, J.M. (1982), 'The elderly victim at risk: explaining the fear–victimization paradox', *Criminology*, **20** (1), 115–26.

McCabe, S. and Sutcliffe, F. (1978), *Defining Crime*, Oxford University Centre for Criminological Research. Occasional Paper No. 9, Oxford: Basil Blackwell.

Maclean, B.D., Jones, T. and Young, J. (1986), *Preliminary Report of the Islington Crime Survey*. Middlesex: Centre for Criminology and Police Studies, Middlesex Polytechnic.

Maguire, M. and Bennett, T.H. (1983), *Burglary in a Dwelling*, London: Heinemann.

Manning, P.K. (1984), 'Community policing', *American Journal of Police*, **3** (2), 205–27.

Marx, G.T. and Archer, D. (1971), 'Citizen involvement in the law enforcement process: the case of community police patrols', *American Behavioural Scientist*, **15** (1), 52–71.

Maxfield, M. (1987), *Explaining Fear of Crime: evidence from the 1984 British Crime Survey*, Home Office Research and Planning Paper No. 43, London: Home Office.

Metropolitan Police (1983), *Crime Prevention – Neighbourhood Watch and Property Marking Schemes*, Police Order 24, London: Metropolitan Police.

Murphy, C. and Muir, G. (1985), *Community Based Policing: A Review of the Critical Issues*, Ottawa, Canada: Solicitor General.

Newman, K. (1984), *Report of the Commissioner of Police of the Metropolis for the Year 1983*, London: HMSO.

NOP Market Research Limited. (1985), *Community Watch: Evaluation Report*, Northampton: Northampton Police.

Northamptonshire Police (1985), *Community Watch: Evaluation Report*, Northampton: Northampton Police.

O'Leary, J.M. and Wood, G. (1984), *A Review of the Experimental 'Neighbourhood Watch Scheme' Holmcroft/Tillington*, Stafford: Staffordshire Constabulary.

Ortega, S.T. and Myles, J.L. (1987), 'Race and gender effects on fear of crime: an interactive model with age', *Criminology*, **25** (1), 133–52.

Park, R.E., Burgess, E.W. and McKenzie (1925), *The City*, Chicago: University of Chicago Press.

Pate, A.M. (1986), 'Experimenting with foot patrol: the Newark experience', in D.P. Rosenbaum (ed.), *Community Crime Prevention: Does it Work?*, London: Sage, pp. 137–56.

Pate, A.M., Wycoff, M.A. Skogan, W.G. and Sherman, L.W. (1986), *Reducing Fear of Crime in Houston and Newark*, Washington, DC: Police Foundation.

Pilotta, J.J. (n.d.), *Community Networking Strategy for Crime Prevention*, National Institute of Justice, Rockville, Washington: National Criminal Justice Reference Service.

Reiss, A.J. (1967), *Studies in Crime and Law Enforcement in Major Metropolitan Areas. US President's Commission on Victimisation and Administration of Justice, Field Surveys 111*, US Department of Justice, Washington, DC: Government Printing Office.

Reppetto, T. 1974, *Residential Crime*, Cambridge: Ballinger.

Riger, S., Gordon, M.T. and Bailly, R. (1978), 'Women's fear of crime: from blaming to restricting the victim', *Victimology*, **3** (3), 274–84.

Rosenbaum, D.P. (ed.) (1986), *Community Crime Prevention: Does it Work?*, London: Sage.

Rosenbaum, D.P. (1987), 'The theory and research behind Neighbourhood Watch: is it a sound fear and crime reduction strategy?', *Crime and Delinquency*, **33** (1), 103–34.

Rosenbaum, D.P., Lewis, D.A. and Grant, J.A. (1985), *The Impact of Community Crime Prevention Programs in Chicago: Can Neighbourhood Organization Make a Difference? Final Report, vol. 1*, Evanston, Ill.: Northwestern University Center for Urban Affairs and Policy Research.

Rossi, P.H. and Freeman, H.E. (1985), *Evaluation: A Systematic Approach*, London: Sage.

Russell, J. (n.d.), *A Guide to Neighbourhood Watch Schemes*, 'A' Department, London: Metropolitan Police.

Schwartz, A.L. and Clarren, S.N. (1977), *The Cincinnati Team Policing Experiment: A Summary Report*, Washington, DC: Police Foundation.

Shaw, C.R. and McKay (1942), *Juvenile Delinquency and Urban Areas*, Chicago: University of Chicago Press.

Short, C. (1983), 'Community policing: beyond slogans', in: T.H. Bennett (ed.), *The Future of Policing*, Cambridge: Institute of Criminology.

Skogan, W.G. and Maxfield (1981), *Coping with crime*, London: Sage.

Skogan, W.G. and Wycoff, M.A. (1986), 'Storefront police officers: the Houston field test', in: D.P. Rosenbaum (ed.), *Community Crime Prevention: Does it Work?*, London: Sage, pp. 179-99.

Skogan, W.G., Lewis, D.A., Podolefsky, A., DuBow, F., Gordon, M.T., Hunter, A., Maxfield, M.G. and Salem, G. (1982), *Reactions to Crime Project: Executive Summary*, US Department of Justice, Washington, DC: Government Printing Office.

Skolnick, J.H. and Bayley, D. (1986), *The New Blue Line*, London: Collier Macmillan.

Smith, D. (1983) *Police and People in London: A Survey of Londoners* Vol 1. London: Police Studies Institute.

Smith, L.J.F. (1984), *Neighbourhood Watch: A Note on Implementation*, London: Home Office Crime Prevention Unit.

Sparks, R.F. (1981), 'Surveys of victimisation: an opportunistic assessment', in M. Tonry and N. Morris (eds), *Crime and Justice: An Annual Review of Research No. 3*, Chicago: University of Chicago Press, pp. 1-60.

Sparks, R.F., Genn, H. and Dodd, D.J. (1977), *Surveying Victims*, London: Wiley.

Spelman, W. and Eck, J. (1987), *Problem Oriented Policing*, US Department of Justice, Washington, DC: Government Printing Office.

SPSS Inc. (1986), *SPSSX User's Guide*, Chicago: SPSS Inc.

The Times (1982), 'The very model chief of the omnicompetent constable', *The Times*, 2 October.

Titus, R., (1984), 'Residential burglary and the community response', in R.V.G. Clarke and T. Hope (eds), *Coping with Burglary*, Boston, Mass.: Kluwer-Nijhoff, pp. 97-130.

Trojanowicz, R.C. (1986), 'Evaluating a neighbourhood foot patrol program', in D.P. Rosenbaum (ed.), *Community Crime Prevention: Does it Work?*, London: Sage, pp. 157-78.

Trotman, M., Russell, J., George, D. and Jenner, R. (1984), *Review of Neighbourhood Watch on No. 1 Area*, London: Metropolitan Police.

Turner, B.W.M. and Barker, P.J. (1983), *Study Tour of the United States of America: 7th March 1983 to 21st March 1983*, London: Metropolitan Police, Vols 1 and 2.

Veater, P. (1984), *Evaluation of Kingsdown Neighbourhood Watch Project, Bristol, Bristol*: Avon and Somerset Constabulary.

Walsh, D. (1980), *Break-ins: Burglary from Private Houses*, London Constable.

Washnis, G.J. (1976), *Citizen Involvement in Crime Prevention*, London: Lexington Books.

Weatheritt, M. (1983), 'Community policing: does it work and how do we know?', in T.H. Bennett (ed.), *The Future of Policing*, Cropwood Conference Series No. 15, Cambridge: Institute of Criminology, pp. 127-42.

Weatheritt, M. (1987), 'Community policing now', in P. Willmott (ed.), *Policing and the Community*, London: Policy Studies Institute, pp. 7-20.

Wood, D.S.(1983), *British Crime Survey: Technical Report*, London: Social and Community Planning Research.

Wycoff, M, A. and Skogan, W.G. (1985), *Citizen Contact Patrol: The Houston Field Test*, Technical Report, Washington, DC: Police Foundation.

Yin, R.K., Vogel, M.E., Chaiken, J.M. and Both, D.R. (1977), *Citizen Patrol Projects*, US Department of Justice, Washington, DC: Government Printing Office.

Zander, M. (1979), 'The investigation of crime: a study of cases tried at the Old Bailey', *Criminal Law Review*, April, 203–219.

Index